Magical Dogs

Love and Lessons from our Canine Companions

Patti Kerr

Along the Way Press
Flemington, New Jersey

MAGICAL DOGS: Love and Lessons from Our Canine Companions

Front Cover Photos (from top left): Brooke on her maiden voyage in Cape Cod, Quincy (courtesy of Jenna Perfetta Photography), Frankie (photo by Legacy Studios), Ava (courtesy of Photography by Sharyn), and Spirit Le Fleur (courtesy of Joan Clark and David Bartholemew).

Back Cover Photos (top to bottom): Mattie (courtesy of Dot Barad and Harry Bowers), Sativa and Shakespeare, aka "Shakespeare in Love" (courtesy of Bonnie and Ryan Alley), and Brooke at the lake.

Cover Design: James Lebbad (Lebbad Design)
Editor: Raquel Pidal
Text Design: Sans Serif, Inc.

ISBN: 978-0-9845989-0-8
Library of Congress Control Number: 2015920304

Disclaimer:
This book and any associated products (including websites, blogs, e-books, promotional products, and other products) are provided for entertainment and informational purposes. The author is not a veterinarian or dog care professional and does not advocate any particular product, item, technique, or position contained herein. Nothing herein should be interpreted as a substitute for professional medical care by a qualified veterinarian or professional. Check with your veterinarian if you have any concerns about your pet or before embarking on or pursuing any treatment protocol. Every effort was made to ensure that all links or contact information provided were correct at the time of writing. The publisher and author cannot be held responsible for any inconvenience or damage caused by any subsequent changes or for the use (or misuse) of information contained or implied herein.

To Brooke and Ava,
for the love, magic, and inspiration;
and to Robb, for bringing the magic,
and the dogs, into my life.

Contents

Acknowledgements

Writing this book has been a journey made possible, and infinitely more wonderful and magical, because of an abundance of kind, loving, wonderful souls.

First, I would like to acknowledge the magical group of dogs and humans (in alphabetical order): Bonnie Alley, Heesun Andes, Donna Arold, Dot Barad, Chrissy Bistis, Nora Brindle, Shirley Weiss Burd, Becky Ciurczak, Joan Clark, Sarah DeRemer, Shari Grant, Corinne Humphrey, Meg Hutchinson, Trish Ortiz Kent, Zach Kerzner, Matthew J. Kiener, Tracy Leaver, Rachel Lehner, Jean Loobner, Anna Newmark, Michele and Dan Reilly, Mary Siracuse, Mary-Antoinette Smith, Barbara Techel, Connie Vasquez, Jillene Zander. Thank you all from the bottom of my heart for trusting me with your stories. I am both honored and humbled.

Next, my gratitude to the organizations and experts who stepped forth to add their expertise, experience, and knowledge to this book: Laura Ortiz (Great Dawg Rescue), Becky Causey (Causey Labradors & Training), Leslie Grinnell (Eddie's Wheels), Linda Stowe (Dodgerslist), Dr. Deborah Custance, Cydney Cross (Out of the Pits), CattleDog Publishing and Dr. Sophia Yin, Marta Williams, Kathleen Prasad, Dr. Michael Dym, Dr. Demian Dressler, Rhonda Hovan (Golden Retriever Club of America), Kathy Klotz (Intermountain Therapy Animals), Diabetes Alert Dog Alliance, Stephanie Colman, Behavioral Health of the Palm Beaches, Jennifer Wright (Labs4Rescue), Rich Errico (Home for Good Dog Rescue), Christina Dorchak (Grey2K USA Worldwide), and Morris Animal Foundation.

I was blessed to work with a Creative Dream Team: James Lebbad of Lebbad Design who put together another ahhh-mazing book cover; Sharyn Hankins of Photography by Sharyn who took many of the incredible photographs of dogs both on the cover and in these pages; Susie Kenyon of Sans Serif for the beautiful interior layout of this book; and my editor, Raquel Pidal, whose brilliance and guidance helped make this book all it could be.

I would like to acknowledge and thank the following: my friend Bob Fouse for his ongoing and never-ending support and early-morning Facebook pep talks, which helped get me to the finish line with this book; my friend and Sister Debbie Freund for the hours spent floating in your magical pool chatting and brainstorming for this book; and my Goddess Prayer Circle who surrounded this book and me with their love and prayers. You *are* the light in the world.

And my never-ending love and gratitude to my family whose love, understanding, encouragement, and support allow me to continue to follow my dreams and do what I love. I love you more than you will ever know—forever and always.

Prologue: Magical Dogs

One morning, while having coffee with my father, out of the blue he said, "I think you should start your book with the story from Wisconsin." So here, with gratitude to my father and his infinite wisdom, is:

THE STORY FROM WISCONSIN

While on tour in Wisconsin with my first book, *I Love You, Who Are You?: Loving and Caring for a Parent with Alzheimer's,* I visited a friend's mother who was living in an assisted living community outside of Green Bay.

Since we had never met before, I asked an aide in the memory care unit to introduce us. Walking into the community room, the aide pointed across the room at a woman sitting alone in a wheelchair. Unlike the others, she had her back to the television—and the other residents—and was hunched over, staring solemnly at the ground.

"Mrs. Y?" the aide said. "This is a friend of your daughter's. She's come all the way from New Jersey to visit you." Mrs. Y's gaze lifted slightly as I sat down across from her and smiled. I sat and quietly talked with her, and in time she began to tell me stories of her family and life. I knew, from my friendship with her daughter, that some of the stories were based in reality; others were based on the reality now being written by Alzheimer's disease.

More than once, Mrs. Y mentioned a dog, so I asked, "What was your dog's name?"

Without hesitation, she said, "Killarney."

A nearby aide, overhearing our conversation, smiled and said, "She talks about that dog all the time."

I suddenly had an idea and, promising to come right back, I walked out of the building and called my friend. She picked up and asked, "How's it going?"

"Great! She's a delight! She keeps telling me about a dog named Killarney."

My friend laughed and said, "Killarney was the love of my mother's life."

"What kind of dog was he?"

"A yellow Lab," she said. "He died fifteen years ago but I wish he was still here because my mom would be so happy."

I thanked her, hung up, and drove to a nearby department store where I found a soft, cuddly stuffed yellow Lab. I bought it, along with several other stuffed dogs and cats, and returned to the assisted living.

Walking back into the community room, Mrs. Y saw me and smiled. I held up the stuffed yellow Lab for her to see and immediately her eyes lit up as she held out her hands to take hold of it. Staring into the stuffed dog's eyes, she brought it to her face, kissed it, and then placed it in her lap. Slowly petting it she said, over and over, "Killarney."

I allowed the staff to distribute the rest of the stuffed animals and spent another hour with Mrs. Y. Then, since I was to speak at a hospice conference that evening, it was time for me to get back on the road. As I said goodbye to Mrs. Y, she smiled and reached out to hug me. Before leaving, I glanced back. Mrs. Y was smiling and contentedly petting Killarney.

After returning home from the book tour, I received emails from several staff members thanking me for my visit. They explained that afternoons had always been a difficult time for Mrs. Y. She would get agitated or angry and the staff had struggled to find ways to keep her calm and content. Now, they said, placing Killarney in her lap calmed her down and she would sit, quietly petting him, for hours. Every night, she slept peacefully, curled up with Killarney at her side.

The Story From Wisconsin is a beautiful example of the incredibly intense, far-reaching, and never-ending connection that often exists between a person and their dog. Despite all the precious moments and memories Alzheimer's had already stolen from this loving woman, wife, mother, and grandmother, what still remained was her strong emotional connection, attachment, and love for her dog Killarney.

That connection, attachment, and love is something anyone who has been blessed with a dog understands. It is a common link among "dog people" and in the pages that follow you're going to meet some of these dog people. A few are some of my oldest and dearest friends; others were total strangers—until this book.

In the journey of writing this book, one person led me to another person and slowly the book began to take on a new direction and depth I never imagined, which I wrote about one afternoon on Facebook:

> "Writing this book is like making a patchwork quilt. I put a piece in place thinking I know what I'm creating but that one piece inevitably leads me off in a new, unforeseen direction. There are so many times in writing this book where it feels like the dogs are the ones writing it ~ and choosing the stories. I am but the seamstress piecing it all together."—Magical Dogs Facebook page[1]

I am honored and humbled to be the person, and seamstress, these dogs and their humans chose to tell their story. They are all incredible people with stories of incredible dogs who were their faithful companion, confidante, mentor, healer, muse, inspiration, or spiritual guide. Many are stories of lives changed and lessons learned because of a dog.

I am excited to introduce you to them, but before we begin, a few housekeeping notes.

Many of the stories have an additional informational article following them. This was driven by my curiosity as well as my desire to make this book both entertaining and educational. You will also see footnotes that refer you to the "Notes" section at the back of this book, which contains additional information, valuable resources on organizations and experts referenced in the book, as well as inspiration.

Next, in the event you skipped over the Disclaimer section at the beginning of the book, I want to repeat it here: This book is provided for entertainment and informational purposes. I am not a veterinarian or dog care professional and don't advocate any particular product, item, technique, or position you may find on these pages. Nothing you read should be interpreted as a substitute for guidance or advice from a qualified and trusted veterinarian or professional. Please check with your veterinarian if you have any concerns about your pet before embarking on or pursuing any treatment protocol.

Now, without further ado: Let the magic begin …

Chapter One
BROOKE

I GOT MY FIRST DOG IN 2001 AT THE AGE OF FORTY-SEVEN. BEFORE that, the only pets I had were a rooster named Chippy that I got on a fifth-grade class trip and goldfish I won every year at the county fair.

My mother didn't want animals in the house and I didn't mind because cats made me sneeze and I was petrified of dogs.

It wasn't until I was in high school that I met a dog who would begin to change my mind about—and my fear of—dogs. After my brother got married, he and his wife adopted a toy poodle they named Pon. Pon was short for Sunfish Pond, which was one of their favorite hiking destinations at the Delaware Water Gap. Pon was a sweet, gentle, and loving dog. She never ran up to me the way other dogs did but instead gave me the chance to approach her at my own pace. Slowly, Pon chipped away at my fear of dogs and I often thought if I ever got a dog I hoped it would be just like Pon.

Pon passed (after being struck by a car) while I was away at college and my brother didn't get another dog until many years later when he bought a small farm for his family. By then, I had a family of my own and loved watching my sons play with their cousins and the dogs on the farm.

Brooke on the day we brought her home
(Photo: Photography by Sharyn)

1

I considered getting a dog from time to time but, as a single mom of twin sons, there never seemed to be an abundance of time, energy, or money to devote to a dog. Still, in 1985 (when my sons were only two years old), I wrote "My Life List" (what many today call a Bucket List). Number seven on the list was: "Own a dog."

In 1999, after reconnecting with and marrying my first love, Robb, we began to seriously discuss getting a dog. Two years later, we found a breed we both liked: the Polish Lowland Sheepdog. As I researched the breed, I learned that in their native Poland they are known as Polski Owczarek Nizinny and are therefore often called "PON" for short.

Having just been accepted into the American Kennel Club the prior year, there had been a flurry of interest in PONs, and every rescue, shelter, or breeder we contacted didn't have any available. Just as we began to give up hope, we made one more call.

Magda, a PON breeder in Washington State, had a litter of puppies. All but one had been adopted, and when we asked about the one remaining she said, "I'm not sure I want to let her go. I may want to keep her. She was only six ounces when she was born and is quite demanding. In fact, we call her The Queen."

I laughed. My annual birthday party is called The Queen's Jubilee, so when Magda referred to the puppy as The Queen, I knew she was our dog. After several more phone calls, Magda agreed and, one week later, we drove to Newark Airport to pick up my first dog and our little queen, Brooke.

The airport personnel brought out the crate and when they opened it, a six-pound ball of white and black fluff walked out of the crate and straight into my arms and my heart. I was in love.

Back home, we played in the backyard before bringing her into the house to show her around. Brooke walked around inside the house as though she had been here before. That night, we put Brooke in her crate and I assumed, having never had a dog before, she would curl up and we would all sleep peacefully through the night. Before long, I heard a whimper and sat up in bed. Robb whispered, "Don't get out of bed. Don't move. She'll stop." As the whimper grew louder, Robb continued to reassure me, saying, "She'll settle down. Just don't get her or even look at her. She'll stop." She didn't. Next, Robb put a blanket over the crate so she couldn't see us but the crying continued. The crying and howling continued for over an hour until, exhausted, we pulled Brooke into bed with us. She smiled, curled up between us, and fell asleep.

We tried again the next night, and the next, until finally on the third night we packed the crate away.

Brooke had taught us her first, and most important, Lesson In Life: Together Is Better.

Unlike crate training, housetraining went extremely well so next we decided to move on to puppy training. I signed us up for puppy classes along with my best friend Sue and her puppy Jigga.

Sue is an exceptional person and friend. We have been through many of life's ups and downs together and, in the best of times and worst of times, Sue always sees the positive side of a situation and can make me laugh. And that's exactly what happened over the next few weeks. Sue, Jigga, Brooke, and I played, talked, laughed, and did everything except listen to the instructor. There was definitely very little training taking place and, knowing we (and our puppies) were about to fail miserably, we skipped graduation.

I immediately signed up for classes at another location without Sue and Jigga to distract us. This time, it was Brooke and I laughing, playing, and having fun. Once again, there was very little training taking place and we skipped graduation, leading me (and Robb) to the conclusion that perhaps the problem had nothing to do with Sue and Jigga.

"I think I'll take over," Robb said. Within a few weeks, Brooke was walking calmly on a leash, knew basic commands, and became a certified therapy dog at fourteen months old. Just as he had housetrained her in the first few weeks, Robb was training her to be a wonderful, loving companion to us and others.

Despite being a frisky little puppy, it was obvious that Brooke was an old soul. She settled into our life and home without issue. She knew things without us ever having to teach or tell her. She accepted our comings and goings without concern or issue, always remaining calm and serene.

Having never had a dog before, I talked to her as I did my own sons and she understood. In our early days together I would kiddingly tell her, "Girls don't walk, they sashay," and I would walk across the room moving my backside from side to side. After a few lessons, Brooke got up and began walking, wiggling her backside from side to side. At my next birthday party, all of my girlfriends—and Brooke— were in attendance. As Brooke walked across the art studio where we had gathered, my girlfriends laughed and said, "Oh my goodness! She's sashaying!"

Since this was my first dog I assumed all of this was all quite normal and natural. I thought this was how all dogs behaved and responded. Oftentimes, it felt like I could sense what Brooke was telling me with her eyes, her old soulful eyes. But, just as quickly, I would discount it, thinking she really couldn't communicate with me. Had I only known then what I know now.

Our early years with Brooke were filled with fun, travel, and adventure. Robb and I loved to travel so we bought a small used camper to continue travelling with Brooke. On our maiden voyage to New England, we set out one afternoon for an off-leash walk near Cape Cod. Brooke took off running towards a massive green field. About twenty feet in, she disappeared with a splash. We ran, yelling, just as her little puppy head popped out of the water and she began paddling confidently towards us. Reaching the water's edge, she climbed out, shook herself off, and smiled. The field actually was a pond filled with green grasses and water plants. After that, we kept her leash on during our adventures and travels.

Brooke became our gypsy dog and loved being on the road, going new places, meeting new people and dogs, and sleeping curled up between us at the end of each day. We spent a week in Lake Placid. We went on a family trip to Disney World to watch my sons, Mike and Sean, compete in a paintball tournament. They were thrilled to at long last have a dog in their lives, and every day she sat by the front door waiting for them to come home from work or a paintball tournament.

But there was one place Brooke loved above every other place on Earth: our cabin in New York State.

We purchased the cabin a year before Brooke came into our lives. We were still in the midst of repairs and renovations but Brooke loved working alongside us, often sitting on the front porch staring out at the lake with the breeze blowing through her hair. She loved our early morning walks and canoe rides, and especially enjoyed winters with the mountains of snow she could plow her head and nose through. No matter what we did, Brooke always made it abundantly clear that, more than anything, she loved the three of us being together.

Then life took a few unexpected turns. My mother was diagnosed as being in the early stages of Alzheimer's disease and, shortly thereafter, with non-Hodgkin's lymphoma. Although the cancer was tamed, the Alzheimer's continued to progress, and eventually I stopped working to help my father care for my mother. And then the other shoe dropped.

Robb was diagnosed with stage 3 colorectal cancer and he chose to follow an alternative, holistic approach devoid of any chemotherapy or radiation. Knowing Robb believed and trusted in the path he had chosen, I supported him, but as traditional doctors continued to tell me he needed to reconsider his approach for his own survival, I grew increasingly concerned and afraid. I was also exhausted from the increasing demands of caring for my mother. In short, I was a mess.

Brooke became the ultimate therapy dog. She provided much-needed love and laughter to my mother, father, and me. She became my support when Robb began the alternative treatments, and when he underwent surgery to have the tumor removed, she was my roommate at the hotel in New York City. Through it all, she provided me with the love, comfort, and distraction I so desperately needed.

She provided the same for Robb as well as the motivation to keep on fighting for a clean bill of health. He often said he wanted—and needed—to get better for Brooke. He didn't want to miss a moment or a memory with her.

Two years later, there was no longer any sign of cancer in Robb but my mother continued to slowly disappear behind the veil of Alzheimer's.

Something else had begun to disappear: our relationship. Robb was spending ever-increasing periods of time with Brooke at our cabin. I knew the solitude and his time with Brooke were important to his mental and physical health, but since the demands of caring for my mother were increasing, it was difficult for me to join them. Our lives had begun to change and a divide had begun to grow between us until, shortly after our tenth anniversary, Robb and I got divorced.

In the eyes of the law, it was a simple legal proceeding asking for the dissolution of our marriage and joint custody of Brooke. Outside of the law, the divorce was devastatingly difficult. Robb and I walked into the courtroom holding hands and when the judge granted our divorce, I sat and quietly cried. We walked out of the courtroom, still holding hands, and asked our attorney if he would like to join us for lunch. He looked at us, shook his head, and said, "I need to tell you that this is the weirdest divorce I have ever done. It's obvious you two love one another."

We did and we do. We knew it was important to take some physical and mental space from one another to process all we had been through but, since we shared custody of Brooke, our paths continued to cross on a regular basis. Ultimately Brooke brought Robb and I back together and, in doing so, she once again got what she loved most in the world: the three of us together.

Brooke had been born the day before Valentine's Day and every year we celebrated our fuzzy little Valentine with a special dinner followed by her favorite part: opening presents. Brooke had always loved playing with and opening boxes. Unassisted she would rip off the wrapping paper and open the box. Unless it was food, what she enjoyed most was the simple act of unwrapping and opening a box.

In February 2014, we celebrated Brooke's twelfth birthday at the cabin. We spent four days laughing, opening presents, hiking through the snow, and just playing with and loving her. She was happy and relaxed.

When we returned, Robb prepared for a six-week trip to Mexico. He invited me to join him but, for the first time, things in my life had aligned where I was going to be able to spend those six weeks uninterrupted with Brooke. I was excited and couldn't wait.

Our six weeks together began early on a Friday morning when we took Robb to the airport. Brooke whimpered as she watched him walk away but we spent the weekend playing, sleeping, and cuddling. On Tuesday we went for her weekly appointment with our longtime and much-beloved friend and groomer Debbie, then spent the rest of the day relaxing together.

Shortly before bedtime, Brooke got her favorite ball and happily played catch for several minutes, looking at me with those big, beautiful brown eyes. She paused to get a drink of water from the kitchen. As I sat on the couch, I heard a thud. "Sweetie, are you okay?"

Another thud. Running into the kitchen, I found Brooke lying on her side on the floor having a seizure. My son Sean drove me to the emergency animal hospital while my other son Mike called ahead to alert them to our arrival. They took blood, did tests, and told us the results would be ready on Thursday. Until then they told me to keep an eye on her and bring her back if necessary.

While we waited for Robb to return from Mexico, I researched seizures and found an article that discussed a technique that had been tested on fifty-one epileptic dogs. It involved firmly holding a bag of ice to the small of the dog's back, and in every case, it had either stopped the seizure or shortened its duration.[1] Whenever there was evidence of a possible seizure, I held the ice pack on Brooke's back and every single time, it fended off another seizure. She was also eating and drinking normally again.

My friend Sharyn stopped over to do energy work on Brooke. My father, brother, and sons all visited Brooke. Then, in the wee hours of Friday morning, Robb walked into the house. Brooke woke up and ran around the living room, excited and happy, like she always did whenever he returned home. Bending down to hold and kiss her, he said, "I was so afraid she wasn't going to make it until I got home." The next morning when we all woke up it was as if nothing had happened. Brooke was our little puppy again—full of life and energy. For the next few days, we went for walks, played, ate, and slept together. It was as if the seizure had simply been a freak occurrence and I told Robb, "I feel guilty for making you come home." However, in the coming days we would learn that she had a tumor on her liver, another on her pancreas, and a suspected brain tumor.

When Brooke was a puppy, Robb had built a bridge across a small creek in his backyard for her. We named it The Brooke-Lynn Bridge. On Tuesday afternoon, the three of us laid in the sunshine on The Brooke-Lynn Bridge reminiscing and thanking Brooke for everything. Later that day, exactly one week after her seizure, Brooke passed at home in our arms with us telling her how much we would always love her.

Brooke had never given any indication, until the seizure, that anything was wrong. That was one of many gifts she bestowed on us in that final week, for it allowed Robb to leave so she could gift me with a few

Brooke, The Lady of the Lake

sacred, special days alone with her.

Brooke knew it was time for her to make her transition. Robb was healed, the renovations on our cabin were complete, my sons were on their own and happy, and I had evolved from being a caregiver to an author, speaker, and Alzheimer's educator. She knew we were all fine. She had seen us through so much over the years and her job here was over. She knew it and accepted it was the next natural step on her journey. She was ready but one thing stood in her way: she needed to get Robb home.

Her seizure brought Robb home so that the three of us could spend a few precious, joyful, magical days with her. In the end, she left with a heart full of what she always loved the most: the three of us together.

Robb and I were shattered and headed to Mexico to begin our healing journey. While there we talked, reminisced, and cried about our twelve years of memories and history with Brooke. Knowing our time with her was something no one else on Earth could fully or completely understand or appreciate, we found ourselves growing closer than we had been in years. We recommitted ourselves to one another and our life together.

Our little queen, the love of our lives, was still with us, reminding us even to this day what she taught us on the first day she walked into our home, lives, and hearts: Together Is Better.

Chapter Two
AVA

DURING OUR TIME IN MEXICO, ROBB TOLD ME TWO THINGS THAT surprised me. First he said, "If we ever get another puppy, it has to be a Polish Lowland Sheepdog, a girl, and she has to be the tiniest one of the litter. Just like Brooke." Then he told me he had emailed several PON breeders while we were still home but that none of them had a tiny female puppy. Hearing his words gave me a small sliver of hope that maybe one day we would be blessed with another dog. But not yet. Not now. We both knew it was too soon.

I returned home to spend Easter with my family and, while home, I found myself at the computer looking at PON breeders. Like Robb, I wasn't looking seriously; I was just passing time. One breeder's name kept sticking out above the others: Snowhill PONs. I sent them an email and told them about Brooke. I explained that while we weren't ready for another dog, if in the future they ever got a small female puppy to please keep us in mind. Shutting off my computer, I went to bed, put it out of my mind, and fell asleep.

Three nights later, the phone rang. "I'm Kristine from Snowhill PONs. If you have a few minutes, I'd love to talk with you."

We talked for over an hour and, as the conversation drew to a close, Kristine said, "I have a little girl I'd like to talk to you about.

Ava on the day we brought her home
(Photo: Photography by Sharyn)

9

She was born on March 1 and was only four ounces." I explained we weren't ready and that I was heading back to Mexico. She said, "It's fine. There's no pressure. Just think about it while you're away."

Over the next few days, as I packed to return to Mexico, Kristine sent me photos and information on the puppy. Before talking to Robb, I needed to first settle this in own my mind, heart, and soul. I prayed, night after night, for clarity and to know, somehow, how Brooke felt about the puppy.

As I finished packing, a business card someone had given me several months prior fluttered to the ground. It was for an animal communicator, and it seemed to be a sign.

The next day, I connected with the communicator, and told her I had one question: Was Brooke okay with us getting another dog?

Brooke's answers (via the communicator) came fast and furious. She told us she absolutely was okay with it "*as long as you're okay with it.*" I asked what she meant.

"You're going to have to take the lead with this puppy," she said. I would have to initially love and care for the puppy since Robb, in Brooke's words, "was still too broken." She assured me Robb would come around in time but initially it would all be up to me, again reassuring me she was fine with it as long as I was.

I hung up the phone and looked over at the small ceramic jar labeled "Pixie Dust," which held some of Brooke's ashes, when I heard something fall off my desk. It was a small plaque that read: "All You Need Is Faith, Trust, and a Little Bit of Pixie Dust."[1] I looked back at the ceramic jar and smiled, knowing the words on the jar and the plaque were yet another message from Brooke.

Robb met me at the airport in Puerto Vallarta. Halfway through lunch at one of our favorite little restaurants, I said, "Something happened when I was home . . ." and with that, I pulled out pages of puppy pictures and information. As he looked at the pictures, his face mirrored what I was still feeling. The puppy was cute, but was it too soon? Or was this our next little girl? He looked at me and I said, "I don't know what any of this means, but maybe together, we can figure it out."

We arrived home from Mexico on a Sunday night and Wednesday morning we got in the car to meet the puppy. We were a bundle of nerves on the four-hour car ride and I kept reminding Robb (and myself) that we weren't under any commitment to bring the puppy home. "Kristine has other people who are interested in her. Or she may keep her. After we meet her, we can decide."

We met Kristine in Lynchburg, Virginia, and there, hiding under a table, was the little black and white puppy whose pictures we had been staring at for the last few weeks. Within the hour, we were in our car heading back to New Jersey. In the backseat, on the dog bed Kristine gave us, was our little girl Ava.

On the entire four-hour ride, Ava lay in her dog bed and stared at me with a fierce intensity. Once home, she ran, hopped, and rolled around in my backyard. For the first time, she let me hold and pet her. I took her in the house and, like Brooke, she sniffed around but seemed completely at ease and familiar with everything—as if she'd been here before. When I went outside to tell Robb, he was gone.

I remembered what Brooke had told me: that I would be the one who would have to love and care for the puppy at the start. For the next few days, I continued to play with, bond with, and take care of Ava and gave Robb the mental and physical space I knew he needed to sort out his feelings.

Robb drove us to Ava's first vet appointment. There was concern in his eyes as she got her shots and he held her and talked to her. After the visit, he dropped us off and headed to the cabin alone.

I gave him a week to be alone before Ava and I hopped in the car and drove to the cabin. I knew the three of us being together at the cabin was another important step. We had so many memories at the cabin but, up until that point, they were all with Brooke. It was time to begin making memories with Ava.

Arriving at the cabin, Ava saw Robb and immediately ran to him, excited. He smiled but remained guarded and distant. Sitting on the deck several hours later, he picked Ava up and cuddled with her for the first time.

When it was time for me to head back to New Jersey, Robb said he wanted to keep Ava with him. When I returned the following weekend on Father's Day, it was obvious he and Ava had grown closer.

We spent that spring and summer between New Jersey and the cabin with Ava. Just like Brooke, Ava loved being at the cabin and especially going for canoe rides around the lake. As summer turned into fall, it was obvious that another level of healing had taken place and that the three of us had become a family. And in the coming weeks and months, Ava would let us know, in no uncertain terms, that just like her sister before her, she, too, loved the three of us being together.

On Halloween morning, Ava and I drove Robb to Newark Airport. He was heading back to Mexico for six weeks and, while it was eerily reminiscent of the six weeks I had so eagerly anticipated with Brooke back in March, I tried to focus on the weeks ahead.

From the first day Robb left, Ava began challenging me, physically, emotionally, and mentally. She was difficult and defiant. She pulled and bit at the leash when I tried to walk her. She refused to eat. She was constantly getting into trouble and I had to keep a constant, vigilant eye on her.

Since Robb had trained Brooke, I didn't have any firsthand knowledge (or confidence) in how to train Ava. Two different trainers came to the house but they both used training methods much harsher than I was comfortable with, so I signed us up for puppy class.

At our first class, Karen the trainer gave us basic obedience tasks to work on with our puppies. Ava did great and I walked out of class with a newfound confidence. I had also told the trainer what was happening at home and she encouraged me to stay calm. "Don't let your emotions trickle down the leash to her." That was Wednesday night. By Saturday, it began to unravel and by Sunday night, I sat on the couch crying. Ava stared at me as I said, "I don't know what's wrong with me. It feels like I have PMS." I woke up the next morning and Ava was in heat.

Then things got even more difficult. Taking the trash to the curb would spark an episode of Ava howling, crying, and frantically scratching at the door or digging under the fence in a desperate attempt to be with me. She followed me everywhere and never wanted me out of her sight. In the shower, I would see her little head constantly popping around the shower curtain to make sure I hadn't left her. Our cute little puppy was now an overly anxious and fragile dog that couldn't leave my side for even a second. I was weary to the depth of my soul.

One afternoon, feeling trapped and desperate to get out of my house,

I put Ava in the car and we went for a ride. An hour later, we found ourselves at a pet store and as we walked in I heard someone say, "Oh, good, you're here!" I looked at the grey-haired woman sitting at the folding table in the corner, confused.

"Are you talking to me?" I asked.

"Yes. You're here for a reading, correct?"

I glanced at the sign on the table. She was an animal communicator. I explained we were just there to look around, not for an appointment, and she immediately said, "Your dog has a lot she wants you to know. I have a few minutes before my next client so if you're willing, have a seat."

I sat down in the chair and Ava relaxed under the table as the communicator began talking. "She says that being alone is extremely difficult for her. When she's alone it is an actual physical feeling. It's disorienting and unpleasant for her and she feels like her head is spinning. She wants you to know she feels safe and loved but she also feels anxious. When she was a tiny puppy, she wanted to be close to her mom. Then, when she was around two months old, she started feeling nervous. When she came into your life, being in different places made her feel disoriented and unstable. She wants her paws to be energetically connected to you. She doesn't feel grounded to one place and wants certainty that your home—and you—are her home base.

"You are both so delicate and she feels your fears," the communicator continued, recommending I try meditation to help ground and calm me. "By meditating, you would also demonstrate for her how to remain calm and at peace.

"She's a homebody. She loves being home but says she wants to be truly adopted by you. She wants the sharing between you and someone else to be reversed. She wants to spend more time with you." With that, Ava got up and came over to sit down next to me. The communicator continued. "She feels she has a job here because you need her." With that, Ava leaned against my leg as if for emphasis.

I thought everything would abate when Robb returned but that didn't happen. We talked and decided that now that she had been through one heat, we would get her spayed. We also knew we needed to put a plan in place so I could do normal everyday things, like going grocery shopping or taking out the trash, without Ava anxiously pacing at my side. Little did I know that things would fall magically into place.

We made an appointment at All Pets Vet Hospital for Ava's surgery. The staff was extremely understanding and accommodating about her separation anxiety. They allowed us stay with her until it was time for her surgery and promised to bring us into the room as soon as she was coming out of the anesthesia.

During her surgery, a young woman approached us and introduced herself as Heesun. She explained she was the Head Trainer and Behavior Consultant and asked about Ava. We talked at length and she told us about her background and training and said she ran a playgroup at All Pets, inviting us to visit with Ava when she came to get her stitches out.

Two weeks later, Ava and I met with Heesun and Ava officially became a member of the playgroup. Dropping her off the first day reminded me of my sons' first day of kindergarten: a lot of crying and everyone walking away upset and in tears. But slowly, we began to make a major shift in Ava's attitude and anxiety. She went to playgroup two and then three times a week and before long would get excited as soon as we pulled into the parking lot. In the ensuing weeks and months, Ava began to understand that being away from me meant playtime with her friends. It was fun!

March 1 was Ava's birthday and we awoke to freshly fallen snow and temperatures in the single digits. Since she loves the cold, we headed out for an early morning walk and played in the snow, and at lunchtime we celebrated her birthday with my father. That night, I gave her some new toys and treats and the next day her friends at playgroup celebrated with her and she got a special pumpkin-filled Kong toy.

That night, I was in the kitchen when I heard a noise coming from the living room. Walking back into the living room, I saw Ava relaxing. The television was on but I hadn't turned it on and I knew Ava hadn't either. Confused, I again looked at the screen. It was on a channel I didn't normally watch and a well-known dog trainer was being interviewed. The first words I heard him say were, "Every pet comes into our lives to teach us a lesson."

I shut the television off and looked at the photos of Brooke spread throughout the house. In a few days it would be the one-year anniversary of her passing. I thought about the lessons Brooke brought us in our twelve years together as well as possible lessons Ava had brought into the world for us.

Brooke and Ava have very different energies and personalities. I believe that is because they came here for different reasons and to teach us different lessons.

Brooke was a happy, calm old soul, and as my first dog, her sweet, gentle nature was a beautiful introduction for me into the world of dogs. Through Brooke, I experienced for the first time ever true, unconditional love. I was introduced to the connection and communication that exists between a human and their canine companion.

Ava, thus far, is the quintessential puppy. She is all about playing and having fun and is a constant reminder for me to step away from the computer and stop working so we can go for a walk or a canoe ride. Her spirit and silliness are contagious and she has allowed me to reconnect with the joyful, playful spirit inside me that had been dormant and buried after years of caring for others.

With Brooke, I never truly participated in—or paid attention to—puppy classes or training. Now, as the one responsible for Ava's training, I realize the training is as much for me as it is for her. In learning how my emotions and behavior impact Ava, and especially how my fear and anxiety can trickle down the leash and impact her, she has become my teacher and my emotional mirror.

I found it ironic that much of the advice being given to me for Ava was the same advice I gave to those caring for a loved one with Alzheimer's: staying in the present moment; remaining calm and understanding how our emotions impact them; and the importance of laughter and joy. Every time I spoke to caregivers, it made me a better dog parent; and every time I trained Ava, it made me a better, more understanding, and wiser speaker and educator.

Although Brooke came into our lives in large part because of my Life List, I believe she came here for Robb. Their bond was undeniable and indescribable. And just as I believe Brooke came here for Robb, I believe Ava is here for me.

When I think back to my conversation with the communicator and the things we discussed—love, loyalty, feeling grounded and calm, and

Ava's hope to be with me and know that I am her "home"—I believe Ava is here to help me understand and harness my inherent knowledge and power. She is here to encourage me to be aware of my thoughts and to let go of my fears and anxieties so that both of us can move forward with confidence and courage.

Brooke was happiest when the three of us were together. Ava feels the same but she has taken that up a notch. She doesn't tolerate the separation as well as Brooke. Ava constantly holds a mirror up for us to examine and understand the choices we have made, and continue to make, in our life and decide if they are still right and true for all three of us.

I am sure, in the years to come, Ava will continue to pass on more lessons and we will continue to uncover lessons passed on to us by Brooke. But right now, in this moment I am happy to be writing in our cabin, which has been renamed Brooke's Bungalow. There are photos and memories of Brooke everywhere in this cabin, and Robb and I are now able to honor Brooke and all that she was, and still is, in our life.

Looking out at the lake, I can see the final renovations to Ava's Lakeside Cottage coming together. Soon both of our girls will have their own cabins here at the lake. I can hear Robb's laughter filter up the hill and can picture him and Ava down there working side by side—just as he and Brooke worked side by side on this cabin.

Here at the lake, I can see and feel how much healing has taken place. It is real and palpable. And perhaps the biggest lesson our girls have taught us is that, through it all, we are a family and that, above all, Together Is Better.

Ava, Patti, and Robb: Together is Better
(Photo: Photography by Sharyn)

Chapter Three
HEESUN

Heesun is the Head Trainer and Behavior Consultant where Ava goes to a puppy playgroup. Through Heesun, I began to learn about animal behavior, puppy socialization, positive training techniques, and, most importantly, about Ava—and myself. Heesun is a remarkable, beautiful, and brilliant young woman and a blessing to many dogs and their owners. Curious about how she began working with dogs, we sat down over a cup of tea and she told me a fascinating story of family, travel, and a dog named Trinity.

I WAS BORN IN KOREA AND RAISED IN NEW YORK CITY. My father's side of the family owned a farm in Gyeongsangbuk-do Province, Korea. My grandfather had dedicated the farm to boarding and caring for horses and dogs as well as cultivating ginseng for holistic medicine.

Heesun and Trinity

Before I was born, my dad took over the farm and utilized it as a sanctuary for unwanted dogs. Many of the dogs were rescued from the meat markets. After my dad completed his years of military service, he volunteered for the Korean Coast Guard and local search and rescue associations, training canines for wilderness air-scent tracking.

Since both of my parents were big dog rescuers, I grew up in an environment where there was always a new dog being added to the pack. We always had twenty-five to thirty dogs on the farm, and they were all part of our family. In Korea, the weather is beautiful, especially in the spring and fall, so the majority of the year the dogs lived outside off-leash and would be rotated to stay in the main house for socialization. In the winter and summer, the dogs used the indoor equestrian run for shelter. They were all well cared for and loved.

When I was a young girl, my family rescued a Korean Jindo dog. The Jindo is a double-coated spitz-type dog much like the Dingo in Australia and is the feral dog of a particular island in Korea. The Jindo we rescued bit my father so severely that he had to get stitches to close the wound. Being a child, I was distraught over seeing my father hurt but I will never forget what he said to me. With blood streaming down his hand, he said, "I'm okay. It wasn't the dog's fault. It was my fault, sweetheart." I stopped crying as my father continued to reassure me and explain. "I pushed him too soon. I should have given him more time before trying to get so close to him." That was my introduction to the world of dog behavior and dog psychology. I learned at a young age that dogs react to what humans do, and many times environmental factors determine their reaction and behavior.

When I was seven, our family rescued a Jindo we named Gorguryeo. The first two weeks Gorguryeo was with us, he was isolated from the family in an outdoor run because he would growl, snarl, lunge, or bite at anyone who tried to enter his cage to feed him.

Gorguryeo refused to eat. My father theorized that Gorguryeo was refusing to eat because his prior owner had died and, out of fierce loyalty, Gorguryeo was determined to starve rather than eat from another human's hand. Jindo dogs are widely known to exhibit this type of self-inflicting behavior when under distress. Gorguryeo, who had never been socialized, was clearly depressed from losing the only guardian he had ever known. Occasionally, we would see him dipping his tongue into a tiny puddle of rainwater in the back of his cage. In two weeks time, Gorguryeo went from fifty pounds to mere skin and bones.

The local veterinarian made regular house calls to check on our dogs, and on his next visit, the good doctor left with a bloody hand. Gorguryeo was the culprit. My mother was mortified and began yelling at my father that it was time to get rid of the dog. The veterinarian, search and rescue crew leaders, and law enforcement officials all agreed that Gorguryeo should be put down. They all felt a primitive, untamed, and vicious Jindo dog could never change.

My father decided to try to rehabilitate and train Gorguryeo. He agreed that, if the dog remained unchanged after a period of time, he would heed their advice. Day in and day out, I watched my father visit Gorguryeo's cage and slowly build a relationship of respect and trust. Little by little, Gorguryeo let down his guard and began his transformation. As time passed, the once ferocious Gorguryeo grew to love my father so much that not only would he let my father pet him but he also took food from his hand. Gorguryeo would do anything to please my father, including guarding the chickens from the other dogs (an amazing feat considering that Jindo dogs have an extremely high prey drive). Ultimately, Gorguryeo made a complete transformation. It took a lot of work and patience, but seeing him become one of the best dogs I ever met had a huge impact on me and how I view animals. My father had given Gorguryeo a second chance at life.

My father and Gorguryeo taught me that every dog, no matter how bad the issues, deserves a chance to be rehabilitated and to live a good life. I also learned Gorguryeo's aggression was a symptom of his fear: fear of losing his owner, fear of a change in environment, and fear of humans who, until he met our family, had proven to be untrustworthy.

In the summer, Gorguryeo never left my side. Gorguryeo became my protector, companion, and loyal friend and, as I got older, he accompanied me on hikes. If I ever lost my way in the mountains, he always led me back home. When I cried, he rubbed the top of his tawny head into the crook of my arm and gazed at me with his wise, compassionate eyes. While outside playing, Gorguryeo warned the other dogs to be gentle with me.

Gorguryeo died of old age in my father's arms when he was seventeen. I cried for several weeks. I will never forget my dear friend and companion, Gorguryeo.

When I was twelve, my parents separated and my mom, brother, and I moved to Queens and then to Manhattan. Even though I had grown up working alongside my dad and he had taught me so much about rescue work and dog training, I was no longer interested in becoming a dog trainer. My life now revolved around friends, fashion, and society. Rather than working with animals, I now wanted to work for the New York Historical Society. I stopped summering in Korea and instead spent my summers in the Hamptons with my friends and their families.

After high school graduation, I was accepted to Rutgers University so my mother, brother, and I moved to New Jersey. It was a more rural environment than I was used to and, initially, an enormous culture shock. Over time, I began to appreciate the natural beauty of New Jersey, and its mountains, beaches, and rolling hills reminded me of Korea.

While at Rutgers, I met and began dating a young man named David. We shared many of the same passions, including serving the poor, nature, and a love for animals.

After graduating from Rutgers, I wanted to raise a dog for competition and found an AKC breeder of American Staffordshire Terriers. The breeder said all but one puppy from the new litter had been sold. The one remaining was a female tri-colored and the runt of the litter. Even though she came from a long line of champion dogs, her tri-colored coat was considered a fault for competition, which allowed me to bring her home at a fraction of the price. In commemoration of her tri-coloring, I named her Trinity. Trinity became my faithful shadow and never left my side for more than a few hours. Wherever I went, she was not far behind. She was one of the most well-socialized pups I ever raised, but in 2007, when Trinity was four years old, everything changed.

My father was suddenly and unexpectedly diagnosed with stomach cancer. Since my grandparents had passed, my father had no one to take care of him. I love him and wanted to be there for him so I rushed back to Korea. Unsure exactly how long I would be gone. I left Trinity in the care of David's parents. It broke my heart to be separated from Trinity but I had no choice.

My father went through a series of surgeries and treatments over the next two years before ultimately triumphing over the disease. To this day, he is fine and healthy.

During my time with my father in Korea, I began to reconnect with my original passion for animals and especially animal behavior. Since my dad was still rescuing dogs, it was easy for me to get involved once again. One day, my father and I were working with a few dogs when I said, "I'm not ready to do search and rescue or tracking but I want to be a trainer. How do I do that?"

My father looked at me, questioning my sincerity since my life had become all about fashion and my social life. Finally he said, "If you really want to get into it, the first thing you need to do is get involved in rescue work. Volunteer and immerse yourself. That's how you set a strong foundation. Until you do that, I'm not going to take you seriously."

I worked and learned from my dad for as long as I could, but my job with the church required me to travel and do mission work in other countries. I learned I would be travelling to Greece, Brazil, and Guatemala to work with the children in these countries. I decided, while in those countries, I would also volunteer on my days off with the local animal shelters.

In Greece, I worked with the University of Athens assisting with their spay and neuter program. In Athens, as well as in most of mainland Greece, the dogs live on the streets and roam freely begging for food at restaurants and private homes. The dogs are very sweet, humble, and love tourists. Most of the dogs had no shelter, were not vaccinated, and had not been given proper medical attention. They were malnourished but not overly emaciated. On a scale of one to ten (with one being horrific and ten being excellent), the conditions for homeless dogs in Greece were about a five or six.

What was interesting is the dogs in Greece did not have behavioral issues like so many dogs in the United States. They were so busy trying to survive that they developed natural obedience and manners as a tool to get food from people. Since they were outside meeting strangers on a daily basis, they were also fairly well socialized. They weren't feral, but more like domesticated dogs with no shelter who knew how to be humble and gentle to humans for survival.

After Greece, I went to Bahia, Brazil. The situation there for stray dogs was much worse. The dogs were reproducing at an alarming rate, had horrible mange, and were severely emaciated. On the same scale of one to ten, these dogs were a two or three at best. In Bahia, I assisted local veterinarians with volunteer spaying and neutering.

The streets of Bahia were filled with speeding cars that didn't stop for pedestrians, much less a dog. The result was a multitude of dogs with missing legs, eyes, or other body parts or severe wounds from being struck by a car. From Bahia I went to Palestinia, Guatemala.

The conditions there were, by far, the worst I'd ever seen in my life. It was a completely different way of life for me—we had to use outhouses the entire time and the tap water had visible parasites. Roofs consisted of cardboard, egg cartons, and metal slates. It was freezing at night, and our bedding was infested with fleas and bedbugs. When we complained to our pastor about the bug bites, he told us to imagine what the people who live there go through on a daily basis. We stopped complaining.

Conditions for the dogs were unimaginable. They were so emaciated that they didn't even look like dogs. Their eyes were lifeless and hollow and they looked like the walking dead.

One day, while singing songs with the children during vacation bible school, a dog wandered in. He was going to everyone gently, sweetly begging for food. He was so emaciated I wanted to give him food, but a teacher said even if I fed him, he wouldn't make it. It was heartbreaking.

While it was extremely hard for me to witness the conditions in Palestinia, I knew it was important for me to not judge but to try and understand their culture and their living conditions. The people there were living in extreme poverty. All they ate for an entire day was a small portion of soup and a piece of cornbread. When you understand that people's own survival is at risk, you can begin to understand why they were unable to feed or take care of their animals.

I had now been away from home and my beloved Trinity for three years: two years with my dad and an additional year traveling doing missions and rescue work. While I always thought of Trinity, after witnessing how dogs were treated in other parts of the world, I was grateful she was being well cared for, healthy, and had everything she needed: a home, backyard, food, treats, and toys.

I missed Trinity so much and imagined that when we saw one another again, we would run into each other's arms. I replayed that scene over and over in my mind. However, when I finally came back, she ignored me. She had grown loyal to David's father, and like any grandparent, he had spoiled Trinity. She was overweight and all of her training had gone out the window. While I was thankful they had cared for her so well, it had done a lot of damage to her behaviorally. I initially believed her behavior was simply from being spoiled for three years, but then David told me Trinity often growled at him before he left for work. She had never growled at anyone before so I knew there was something really wrong. David was nonchalant and said it was probably just play growling. His father brushed it off, too, saying, "It's nothing. She is just excited. Don't worry about it. She's a good girl."

Since I had not yet found a place where I could live with Trinity, David's father was still taking care of my dog. Between that and the fact that he is my elder, I had no power in the situation and really couldn't say anything.

I continued moving forward with my pursuit of a career in dog training. Even though I had experience internationally, I needed experience here in the States and began volunteering at St. Hubert's Animal Welfare Center as a foster parent. Eventually, I assisted with behavior modification and training for pet parents and their newly adopted shelter dogs and took every class available. I became certified through the Association of Professional Dog Trainers[1] and then began apprenticing for Dr. Ian Dunbar.[2]

Dr. Dunbar is one of the pioneers of positive dog training and has been running off-leash puppy classes since the 1970s. He was kind and gracious enough to take me under his wing and, since there are different schools of thought on dog training, I am grateful to have learned from Dr. Dunbar and his network because their entire focus is on positive training. It was what I witnessed growing up and what had worked over and over for my father and his dogs.

After David and I were married in 2012, we brought Trinity to live with us. We didn't realize until Trinity became a part of our household how much our separation had impacted her and her behavior. There had been some foreshadowing: she would shake in the morning but we thought she was just overly excited to eat and do things she had never done before.

Then she began to exhibit troubling new behaviors. The first time we walked her in public, I was shocked. She lunged and barked at other dogs and I learned she hadn't been walked the entire time I was gone because they thought she was getting sufficient exercise in the backyard. She had become completely unsocialized.

Literally every behavioral issue under the sun came out in that first year together. Trinity was dog reactive, food reactive, you name it and she had it, including a bad case of separation anxiety.

Through my training, I had learned that actual clinically diagnosed separation anxiety is quite rare. What many people think of as separation anxiety can actually be a lack of basic manners or training. Sometimes it is a case of separation fun: the dog will chew things, get into the garbage, or do other things they aren't permitted to do when their owners are present.

For Trinity, it wasn't a lack of training or basic manners. For her, it was full-blown severe separation anxiety. Every morning, when David came down or she heard his car keys jingle, Trinity would have panic attacks. She shook to the point where she actually fell over. It looked like she was having a seizure. She drooled until she was sitting in a puddle, which was followed by growling, lunging, and snapping at my husband. Trinity was never destructive but it was horrible to see how distraught she became.

Even though I had some training, I didn't have the expertise, extensive knowledge, or years of experience that Dr. Dunbar and his colleagues had, so when Trinity showed signs of separation anxiety I did what I knew at the time: redirection and counter-conditioning. We began by moving her to a different room to remove the trigger. When David came out of the bathroom Trinity growled so I would redirect her to another room. We just kept moving her to different places to try and keep her calm.

We tried praising her during the moments when she was calm. We tried everything under the sun to treat her separation anxiety, including avoiding her, placing her in different rooms, redirecting her, correcting her. We tried positive methods, counter-conditioning—you name it, we tried it. Trinity only got worse.

Everyone started telling us we needed to either drop Trinity off at a shelter or have her put down. My husband had become fearful every morning—even though Trinity never bit him, he was still afraid. I understood but he didn't have the background and passion I had for dogs.

I had Trinity since she was a puppy, and while she was my baby in every sense of the word, it was getting worse and I was getting desperate.

I was also a newlywed trying to adjust to married life while dealing with the problems with Trinity. I was completely overwhelmed—and embarrassed. How could I, as a dog trainer, help people with their dogs when I couldn't help my own dog?

I was desperate and continued searching for more knowledge. I began doing field work and working with other dogs from our local ASPCA, hoping I would find information that would help me and Trinity. My dad advised us to work slowly and progressively and gave us amazing advice on countless occasions.

I called a local dog trainer who trained military dogs and, after explaining the situation, he said, "I'll be there in the morning but first I need you to understand you are letting her do this to you. I need you to understand you need to severely punish her because she is being inappropriate and the punishment needs to fit the crime. She is being aggressive but since there are no consequences she is becoming more aggressive." He explained that through punishment corrections and the use of a prong collar he would help us fix Trinity. I am grateful we never let him come over because if we had added physical punishment on top of everything else Trinity was dealing with, she would have gone off the edge or gotten more aggressive.

Instead, David and I began play therapy with Trinity. Play therapy incorporates the use of toys and play periods to shift negative associations—like us leaving the house each morning—to positive ones. Every morning when David went into the bathroom, I took Trinity outside. When we came back in, David would get her toys and puzzles and play with her and then we would feed her and leave. Over time, Trinity made the connection that our leaving wasn't as bad as she had once thought and her state of mind changed from panic to happy-go-lucky. Trinity is now eight and no longer has panic attacks and is no longer aggressive. It's nice to see her happy.

It took about a year to get Trinity to that point. These things take time and a lot of patience and there is no magic formula. It is a progressive transformation and sometimes is never completely resolved. The earlier you begin working on issues with a puppy, the easier and quicker they can be resolved. Puppies are naturally curious, outgoing, and unafraid. If you have a puppy that is fearful of being touched on the head, oftentimes you can resolve the issue in about a half hour.

However, once a dog reaches adolescence, it can take four to six months to resolve the problem. The older they get, the longer it takes, and sometimes the issue is never resolved. That's why I place so much emphasis on puppy training. Preventing behavioral issues early is easy and so much fun!

When I come across dogs who have been pegged as hopeless, too vicious, or unpredictably aggressive, I think back to what my father did and am forever grateful for his early example and the years he spent guiding and teaching me. No matter how bad the case is, I look at the circumstances and give the dog both the time and opportunity for rehabilitation, because I believe we should at least try before condemning any animal. Dogs need to feel differently about a situation in order for healing to begin. Just like Gorguryeo, every dog should be given an opportunity to be its best self.

I am grateful for the mentorship of Dr. Dunbar, who is one of the best dog behaviorists in the industry. I am honored to be able to carry on his legacy of innovative, fun, and effective dog training with the dogs I now work with. At my current position, I have created an off-leash class and playgroup identical to the model set by Dr. Dunbar. Like my parents, I have also started a small business, Pet Karma NJ[3], which involves pet rescue. It is because of my beloved Trinity that I will devote my life to saving as many unwanted and mistreated dogs from a life of fighting, abuse, and destruction.

But I am mainly grateful to Trinity. The three years Trinity, David, and I were separated were traumatic for all of us—but especially for Trinity. My family and I were all Trinity knew; we were her pack and then, all of a sudden, her pack dispersed and she had to adjust to a new family structure and culture. But when we were finally reunited as a family, we worked together through every issue, always letting God take the lead, to ultimately becoming a happy, balanced, and peaceful family. All our struggles made us stronger and we were truly blessed with the miracle of healing, forgiveness, and, most of all, love. Trinity taught us that no one is perfect and to never give up on those you love. She reminded

us how to love uncondi-
tionally and forgive one
another.

Trinity is the reason I
pursued a career in dog
behavior. She is now a
happy-go-lucky, gentle,
and friendly dog and we
spend our free time training in dock jumping, rally,
obedience, and agility.

Knowing my story with
Trinity could have had a
very different ending, it is
now my mission to help
every pet parent build a
deep and joyful connec-
tion with their dog.

Trinity

THE IMPORTANCE OF PUPPY SOCIALIZATION

Dr. Sophia Yin was a veterinarian, animal behaviorist, author, and international expert on low stress, pet-friendly techniques for animal handling and behavior modification. The following is from Dr. Yin's blog on her website and is adapted from her book, Perfect Puppy in 7 Days: How to Start Your Puppy Off Right.[1] *It appears here with the express permission of CattleDog Publishing.*

FROM ABOUT THREE WEEKS TO ABOUT THREE MONTHS OF AGE, puppies are primed for bonding to other animals and individuals, for learning that objects, people, and environments are safe, and for learning what the body cues and signals of others mean. It is their sensitive period for socialization and it is the most important socialization period in a dog's life. Puppies who do not get adequate socialization during this period tend to be fearful of unfamiliar people or dogs, or sounds, objects, and environments.

By starting early and being consistent, owners will provide the best chance that their pup will grow into a happy, confident dog. Here are some recommendations.

- **Provide Puppies with Positive Experiences with Unfamiliar People of Different Sizes, Genders, and Ethnicities.** Invite guests to come interact with the puppies while providing treats and toys to ensure the puppies are having a positive experience. Interacting with only household humans is not enough.

- **Socialize Puppies to Children.** To puppies and dogs who have never seen kids, children can look like little aliens. As puppies mature, children can also start looking more like toys or things they should chase because they scream and run and flail their arms like injured prey. If the breeder does not have or know children whom the puppies can interact with, the new family should also be told that the puppy is lacking in this experience and that they should make a special effort to provide good interactions with children.

- **Socialize Puppies to Other Species.** Many puppies will live with cats or other animals at some time during their life. It would be best if they could react calmly instead of barking, lunging at, or chasing these other animals.

- **Reward Calm Behavior when Other Animals Are Present.** Not only do we want dogs to feel safe and unafraid around other animals, we also want them to behave calmly. So we should reward calm behavior.

- **Introduce Puppies to Other Man-made Objects and Sounds.** Most people never appreciate the everyday sounds and sights that might be frightening to a pet, but if you have a dog who missed out on key environmental experience when young, it can be overwhelming to deal with all of the objects they fear.

Some additional pointers and advice on socialization include:

- Being mindful of the people, places, and situations you are introducing to your dog. Explain to the person what you are trying to do and ask for their assistance to reinforce good behavior in a positive manner.

- Using treats, play, and praise to reward the behaviors you want repeated. Likewise, ignore or use a verbal signal or time out for behaviors you don't want to reinforce or see repeated.

- Never put your dog in a situation where they might feel threatened.

- Begin socializing them in small groups before introducing them to a large group.

- Be aware of your body language and reaction to a situation. Dogs are very intuitive and sensitive and may pick up on your behavior or reaction to a situation. Make sure you remain positive and upbeat.

In their early weeks, puppies learn essential behaviors from their mother and siblings, including bite inhibition and appropriate play. That is why it is recommended puppies not be separated from their mother and littermates before eight weeks of age.

Socialization does not end after the first three months. A responsible pet parent will continue to reinforce and encourage appropriate behavior and responses throughout their dog's life.

Chapter Four
TRISH

Trish and I worked together back in the '90s. On my first day of work, Trish said, "If you need help with anything, let me know," and she meant it. Over the years, she was kind, considerate, helpful, and even-tempered. Several years later, Trish moved to Florida but we kept in touch. During Brooke's final days (and the weeks and months that followed), Trish was one of the people I leaned on for her insight, wisdom, and compassion. All of those traits and qualities that blessed my life have blessed the lives of many dogs over the years, and I am honored to share that part of her story with you.

WHEN WE WERE YOUNG, OUR FAMILY LIVED IN FLORIDA AND our father worked at the Space Center. One day, he came home and told us a coworker had a litter of Gordon Setter puppies. We adopted a female, the runt of the litter, and named her Gypsy. In the years to follow, we realized just how appropriate her name was because our family moved with her several times: Florida, Long Island, and Mexico. She was a wonderful, sweet dog.

Bear

In 1980, my father got a job working at the World Trade Center in New York and we began to pack for our move to New Jersey. Learning our landlord didn't allow dogs, my father's parents agreed to take Gypsy to live with them in Miami.

Since they were family and had a yard, it seemed a perfect solution for everyone, but I think the heat in South Florida was tough for Gypsy. Over the years, she grew more and more sickly and was on all kinds of medication.

One morning, my grandmother let Gypsy out and she never came back. They asked everyone and looked everywhere but there was never any sign of Gypsy. It's like she just disappeared. Even though we knew Gypsy had a good life, it was tough on us because we never had a chance to say goodbye to her.

I met and married my husband, Brian, in New Jersey, and in 1991 we moved into a community that permitted cats but no dogs. Since Brian always had a dog we promised one another that if we ever got a house we would get a dog.

Seven years later, we moved to Florida and bought a house and, within the month, Brian's parents (who lived in New Jersey) told us about a two-and-a-half-year-old Chesapeake Bay retriever that had broken its back right leg. The dog's owners, who had trained him to compete in field trials, felt the dog was of no further use to them and had simply returned it to the breeder and gotten themselves a new puppy.

No one was ever able to determine exactly what happened to the dog. She had a pin and four screws in her leg and our vet said someone may have accidentally stepped on her leg since it would have taken that kind of pressure and weight for such a severe injury.

A few months later, Brian's parents drove from New Jersey to Florida and brought the dog to us. Her name was Kelly, although for the first six months I rarely called her anything other than "that damn dog." Kelly and I despised one another. Anything that had my scent on it was open season for her and I cannot tell you how many pairs of leather shoes I went through in those early months!

Finally, Kelly and I came to a mutual understanding. It was quite clear that we both loved Brian. It was equally clear that neither of us was leaving so we had to find a way to coexist. I put away my leather shoes and we both softened in order to keep the peace and live in harmony. Our home was no longer a battlefield as it had been and we had a wonderful twelve-and-a-half years together. She really was a great dog and absolutely loved the beach and the water.

When Kelly was ten, we rescued a four-and-a-half-year-old chocolate Lab. We had seen his pictures online and called the shelter who told us the dog had been found on the streets of Miami. We decided to adopt the dog, sight unseen, and two hours later, we picked up our new dog in the parking lot of a Cracker Barrel restaurant in Fort Pierce, Florida.

His name was Bear and he was our junkyard dog. Kelly took one look at him, rolled her eyes, and gave us a look that clearly said, "What are you doing to me? He's a madman!"

Having learned how to live on the mean streets of Miami, Bear was a tough nut to crack. Brian and I tried every method of home training we knew in the hopes he would eventually soften and we would get to his juicy center. We thought we had made some headway with basic commands like sit, stay, and heel but it was short-lived. He eventually became destructive and began to pull anything and everything from our kitchen counters: appliances, flour, coffee and tea containers, vinegar. He also learned how to open and spin the two lazy Susans in our corner cabinets.

No matter how he was reprimanded, the destruction continued. Brian finally cleaned his hands of the situation and told me I needed to find Bear another home. I was heartbroken and began instead to exhaust all resources so he could be "fixed."

I spoke with several animal behaviorists in our area and finally one, Barry, agreed to come to the house and meet Bear. Barry could not have been a kinder, gentler soul and was soft-spoken. He explained that it was not only Bear that needed to change his behavior but us as well. It was quite humbling to know we had been approaching the situation all wrong.

Barry began coming to our house for an hour every Friday afternoon for the next eight weeks and, in between visits, we all had homework. Barry didn't mince words and, without ever raising his voice to Bear (or us, for that matter), got his point across.

Our junkyard dog turned out to be the sweetest, most loyal dog we could have wished for. The wild child had been tamed but his spirit was never broken.

When Kelly was nine, she was diagnosed with degenerative myopathy (DM), which is fairly common in certain breeds such as boxers, corgis, German shepherds, and Chesapeake Bay retrievers. With DM, the dog loses the nerves in their hind quarters and begins dragging their back legs when they walk. Eventually they lose all motor function in their back legs and the disease begins to move up their body, eventually impacting their kidneys and other organs.

DM did not become a problem for Kelly until she was almost twelve years old. We began using a harness to take Kelly outside to do her business and eventually she was in diapers. We did all we could for her over the next six months to keep her comfortable. Brian kept telling me it was time to put her down but I couldn't do it. Even though I knew it was a progressive disease and there was no cure, I just couldn't bring myself to say goodbye to her.

Finally, seeing how difficult and painful it was for Kelly, we had her put down. It was devastating. Although Brian had suffered the loss of many pets over the years, this was my first and I was not prepared.

After Kelly passed, Brian wanted to get another dog for Bear and told me, "Bear needs a companion." I understood what he was saying but Kelly was the first dog I had lost and I needed time to heal.

Two months later, I came home from work on a Friday night and Brian asked if I wanted to go for a ride the next day.

"Sure, where?"

"I just want you to see something," he said.

That night, as I sat looking through the newspaper, I spotted a classified ad for an eleven-month-old Chesapeake Bay retriever. "Brian, look!" I said and proceeded to read the ad to him. "It says he's not quite a year old and needs a good home. His current owners are an older couple and the dog is too active so he needs a home where he can run and play."

Brian looked at me. "What do you think? Should we go meet him?"

"I told you it's too soon."

The next morning, Brian, Bear, and I climbed into the car for our mystery ride but, before long, I realized where we were going. "We're going to meet that dog, aren't we?" I asked Brian.

"Yes," Brian confessed. "I saw the ad yesterday and talked with the owners. He sounds like a good dog and I thought we should just meet him."

The owners came out with the Chessie and immediately Bear and the other dog started playing. They ran and played for hours. Bear had been mourning the loss of his sister and was lonely. It was wonderful to see him so happy again.

The owners were wonderful people. The husband explained that the retriever had simply gotten too big for him to exercise in the way the dog needed or wanted. When they went for rides, the dog stayed in a crate in the back of the truck. The dog had also been in a crate on the porch and wasn't allowed in the house because, the owner explained. "He's like a bull in a china shop."

We stayed for a couple of hours and, when we got up, the owner said, "If you want to think about it and let us know . . ."

We knew this was a two-way street. It was his dog and we wanted him to feel comfortable with us so we immediately said, "They get along great, but if you want to think about it and let us know . . ."

The gentleman immediately said, "If you don't take him now, I won't be able to do this." As soon as we put our leash on the dog to take him, the owner began to cry and walked into the house.

We walked towards our truck and opened the door. The dog had no idea what to do because he had never ridden inside a truck before. When we got home, he stopped at the back door because he had been trained that he wasn't supposed to go into the house. It took us weeks before he came in the house without stopping at the back door.

Duke and Bear had their moments adjusting to one another. Over the course of the next year, Duke established himself as the alpha and Bear succumbed with dignity. There was a new sheriff in the Kent home now.

Then, shortly after Bear turned twelve, he got leukemia and passed. Bear was our first rescue from a shelter. He had taught us so much in our early days together and had opened our hearts and minds even further to providing a home for these dogs.

In June 2009, my sister, called us and told us she was desperate. "I have a dog, a little chocolate Lab puppy named Brady. She's going to be picked up at the end of the weekend so I just need you to watch her for one or two nights. Can you check with Brian?"

Brian immediately agreed but, once again, I was the one to resist. I fi-

Duke

nally relented only because I knew my sister needed help.

At first it seemed odd to bring a strange dog in with our close-knit clan but when she arrived the boys were curious and receptive. I was the one with reservations, but, within hours they were all playing together and the weekend sleepover was a hit!

When my sister picked up Brady, I looked at Brian and said, "We can do this. We can foster dogs." That was our initiation into fostering rescue dogs and we haven't stopped.

When Benny came into our lives, he had several strikes against him. He was a chocolate Lab-hound mix and between eleven and twelve years old. His owner, an elderly gentleman, had passed and the family didn't know what to do with him. They were going to turn him into the shelter but, thankfully, called a Lab rescue instead.

On examination, the vet found a tumor on Benny's heart that was fairly large and inoperable. He also had a pendulous fatty tissue tumor on his belly that, while benign, made it difficult for him to relieve himself due to its location.

The vet told us Benny was very sick and had maybe two or three weeks to live. Laura asked us if we would keep Benny until his time came. Brian and I talked and didn't see any other option. We didn't want Benny to spend his final days in a shelter and, since we didn't have a foster at the time, we decided to bring him home and make him comfortable until he passed.

I fabricated a harness with Velcro that we wrapped around his midsection. It held the tumor up against his belly, making it easier for Benny to walk. His appetite improved and the longer Benny was with us the better he seemed to be feeling.

After six weeks, we took him back to the vet. He told us Benny had put on weight and reminded us that, while Benny would never get better, he was clearly in a good environment and seemed to be doing fine.

Benny had become a part of our lives and our neighborhood. He would lay out in the driveway and all day long, as the neighbors walked by, they would call out to him. "Good morning, Benny!" "Hi, Benny!"

From the minute Benny came home he knew he was in a place where he would be well cared for and you could tell he was grateful. He would come up and lay next to you and tell you with his eyes, "I'm having fun. This is a good place. Thank you." He knew he was with people who loved him. He didn't care that he was sick or wearing a girdle. He was just happy.

Benny's eyes always said it all. You could tell he knew his time was near but you could also tell he was happy to have another chance. Every time we took him for a walk, he would look at us with those eyes that said thank you. He was just a sweet dog and he loved every extra minute he had.

Benny was with us through that fall and Christmas but then he started to get sicker. The vet explained that because of his large chest cavity, we had been unable to see just how much the tumor around his heart had grown. The weight of it was putting pressure on his heart and lungs. His breathing was impaired and we were no longer able to take him for long walks. At night, when we brought him into our room to sleep, every breath was labored.

Brian kept gently telling me it was time but, over and over, I insisted, "Not yet, not yet."

On a Wednesday morning in March, my sister called and said, "I talked to Brian. It's time."

Brian, my sister, and even Benny knew it was time but I was heartbroken. I just kept crying and telling Benny how sorry I was. He kept looking at me with those soulful eyes and then finally put his head on me and stared at me with a look that said, "It really is okay."

With Benny, as with all of our dogs, when the time comes we take all of our dogs with us to the vet. At first, they get anxious because they can't figure out why we're all together in the room. They also can't figure out why one of the dogs is up on the table even though they instinctively know the dog is ill. After the vet gives the dog the first shot and it calms down, the other dogs start sniffing him or her. This gives them a chance to see, and be a part of, the process of the other dog getting put down and passing. It is cathartic and healing for them. They get to say their good-byes.

So all the dogs went with us and got to say their goodbyes to Benny.

Benny had become our dog in every sense of the word so we paid the medical bills, we paid for his cremation, and his ashes are in our living room along with the ashes of all of our other dogs.

People always ask me how I can do this—not necessarily the foster-ing but giving them up when they are adopted. I always say it's the hard-est thing I have ever done but I can't imagine not doing it. It is wonder-ful to see a dog come out of their shell. You get a dog who has been abused and is absolutely petrified who cowers in the corner every time you pick up a broom to sweep the floor. Then you get to see that same dog regain trust in humans and it is indescribable.

We had one dog that wouldn't come out from under the coffee table. It was his safe place. It was like he felt if no one could see him, he couldn't be hurt. He hid under the table for the first few months. Eventually, he went to the edge of the table, and then under a chair and slowly we were able to pet him.

He was adopted by our neighbors. Initially, we didn't make any con-tact because you don't want the dog thinking he's coming back to your home. You want the dog to bond with their new family. After about six months, I called our neighbors to see how he was doing. They told us, "Why don't you come over and see for yourself?"

He was a completely different dog. He had come out of his shell and was happy and gregarious. The couple was retired and they all went for walks several times a day. He used to run and hide anytime the doorbell rang but now he was friends with all the neighbors—including the mail-man. When you get to witness that, it's the biggest blessing you can imag-ine—for the dog and for us.

Rescue dogs are just so grateful. They know it could be worse. They have been in shelters. Shelters can be scary for humans so I can't imag-ine what it is like to be on the other side of that cage. It can smell bad and people might be loud or yelling at them.

When you bring them out of there as a foster they understand. They understand it may not be permanent but it's a lot better than where they were and that maybe the next place will be better, too.

Our dogs, especially Benny, have taught us that no one—not even the best doctor or veterinarian—can predict the future or an accurate outcome. Despite the doctor's predictions for Benny, he still had a lot of good life in him.

And, most importantly, our dogs have taught us the importance of Enjoying Every Precious Moment Together.

Benny

✦ LAURA AND ✦ GREAT DAWG RESCUE

I asked Trish to tell me more about the foster work she was doing and she immediately introduced me to her sister, Laura. Laura told me about a dog named Romeo and how she was led to rescue work and to starting her own rescue organization, Great Dawg Rescue.[1]

I GOT MY FIRST RESCUE DOG WHILE WORKING IN A MEDICAL office. A patient was checking out and started telling me about an AKC purebred dog he had once bred with his dog. At seven, the breeder could no longer use the dog to breed and therefore no longer wanted the dog.

Without even knowing what kind of dog it was, I immediately said I would take it. It turned out to be a gigantic, healthy yellow Lab named Simba. Simba was absolutely gorgeous, inside and out, and it was hard for me to imagine someone not wanting him.

I changed his name to Romeo and he fit into my life and lifestyle incredibly well. I am very active—I walk, run, work in the garden, ride my bike—and Romeo loved doing all of it with me. I wish I could have kept Romeo for the rest of my life, but after about five years, he developed kidney failure and other maladies we were unable to fix.

Romeo was such a great dog but after he passed, I didn't think I would ever rescue another dog. Then I

Romeo crabhunting in Florida

began to learn about the abundance of Labs who needed a home, including a foster home. I knew, from my experience with Romeo, that they fit beautifully into my lifestyle. I could take them for walks, train them, and love them. That was how I got involved in fostering animals. Over time, realizing I could do a much better job for the dogs by creating my own local rescue, I started Great Dawg Rescue.

Great Dawg Rescue, located in the Volusia/Flagler area of Florida, is a volunteer-driven dog rescue dedicated to retriever and senior sporting breed dogs. We specialize in Labrador retrievers since they are dogs often overlooked at shelters here in Florida. Many people in our area live in condos and want a smaller dog. Labs are physically big, but they also have big hearts.

At Great Dawg, we typically have ten to fifteen dogs at all times and every dog is different. For that reason, we don't just place dogs, we "fit" them, making us a unique type of rescue. We have a wonderful group of volunteers, from foster parents to veterinarians, and do intense interviews with potential owners before they ever meet one of our dogs. Our comprehensive system has earned us a wonderful reputation as well as wonderful outcomes for our dogs. We will take as long as a dog needs to find its forever home because we don't want to set them up for failure. We want them to feel safe.

It is natural, when you rescue a dog, to wonder "What's their story?" Most times, you can surmise based on their physical appearance what may have happened but you don't know the whole story. What I have learned is that a dog's spirit is so strong that no matter what happened they don't want to be pitied. They don't have time for that. If you have a ball in your hand, they just want you to throw it. They are incredibly forgiving and want to move on. In that way, and many others, dogs are incredibly superior to a lot of human beings I know.

We got a dog yesterday who looks like a rat mole. He has no hair and is itchy and scratchy. We took him to the vet and the first thing he did was crawl right into the vet's arms. Despite what may have happened to him before that moment, he was completely open to trusting someone all over again. I, and many people I know, would be angry but dogs don't get stuck.

The local police called the day before Christmas to tell me they had just raided a house where a bunch of meth addicts had been camped out. Everybody was taken to jail but the lady next door told the police she believed there was a dog in the house. The police went in to investigate and, sure enough, there was a dog they believed to be a Labrador, so they immediately called and begged me to take him. He was one the saddest, most beat-up dogs I had ever seen. His teeth had rotted out, he had no fur, and he had open wounds all over his body. He was so physically scarred I couldn't imagine what had happened to him. I also couldn't imagine him staying there or being alone for Christmas.

After the vet bathed him, he told us the dog had likely been impacted by the smoke in the house since his corneas were permanently scarred and he had huge patches of hair that would never grow back. Besides being neglected, they suspected the people in the house may have come after him and that the dog probably had to fight for his own safety.

I took him home and named him Sammy. I gave him time to feel comfortable and at home and, after about three months, he finally laid his head in my lap.

Many people assume that if they no longer want their dog they can drop it off at a shelter and it will find a better place for the dog to live. But a lot of times that doesn't happen.

Shelters can't say no to anyone and therefore take in hundreds of dogs every month. Where we live, if a dog is surrendered by its owner, it is euthanized immediately. Dogs that come in as a stray typically get five to seven days and, at the end of that time, if there are no adoption papers for the dog, it is euthanized. Most of the shelters within a three-to-five-hour radius of where we live are high-kill shelters.

That is why independent rescues, like ours, are so important. Even if a shelter says it's a no-kill shelter, if they get overloaded they have to make a decision. We go to the shelters and tell them to please call us. Some shelters do, some don't.

I always encourage people, if they can no longer keep an animal, to contact a rescue group first. The majority of rescue groups won't euthanize an animal unless they are terminally ill. Every breed has a breed-specific rescue somewhere in the United States and they are always your best bet. If you can't find a breed-specific rescue, or if there isn't one in your area, search out a general rescue. As a last resort, if you are forced to take them to a shelter, always ask if they are a no-kill shelter.

We recently launched an Almost Home program at Great Dawg Rescue for dogs who, because of age or illness, won't be with us much longer and are not adoptable. These dogs deserve to have a home and have someone love and be kind to them during this last part of their journey so we're actually creating a hospice-type environment for them. The funding we receive for this program allows us to take care of food, supplements, medical visits, and other needs and we are fortunate to have people open their hearts and homes to these dogs.

People ask me why I do what I do and, honestly, I don't know. Part of it, I suppose, is because it's the right thing to do but it's more than that. A lot of us in rescue don't like to talk about what we do because it's difficult to explain and is either a part of who you are or it's not.

Every morning when I wake up and see those eyes and faces staring up at me, I always tell them, "How lucky am I?" and I mean it. I can't believe how lucky I am.

For so many years, the one thing I heard over and over was, "He's a great dog but . . ." The "but" could be anything from health issues to a new baby or home. I have known people who gave a dog up simply because the dog didn't match their furniture.

Through my work with rescue dogs, I have come to understand that *all* dogs are great. I have also learned there are great families and volunteers and veterinarians who believe as much as I do that with a little time, love, and work we can turn around the future for every one of these Great Dawgs.

BEFORE YOU FOSTER

FOSTERING A DOG CAN BE A PRECIOUS AND GENEROUS GIFT TO AN animal, shelter, or rescue and yourself. For many dogs, fostering is a gift of life. Since it is often impossible for a rescue organization or shelter to house every pet that comes to them, in some instances opening your home to one of these animals can save them from being euthanized simply due to a lack of space.

As a foster parent, you will be responsible for housing, feeding, and caring for your foster dog. However, your responsibilities go far beyond that and it is important you understand exactly how this new dog may impact you, your home, and your family. Fostering a dog with your eyes wide open and with sufficient knowledge will ensure the foster experience is effective, successful, and as stress free as possible—for you, the rescue, the future adoptive parents, and, most importantly, the dog.

- **Find a Rescue Organization.** Whether you are interested in a senior dog, a puppy, a dog with special needs, or a specific breed or size of dog, begin by finding a few rescue organizations that may have the type of dog you want to foster. Contact them, visit them, and request an application. Make sure you find a rescue group whose mission seems clear, fits your personal values and goals, and is willing to help you through the entire process. Are you confident in the rescue organization's ability to find a new home for the dog? Talk to others who have worked with the group and learn about their experience. Every rescue and adoption agency has their own individual policies and procedures so make sure you know, and are comfortable with, the ones established by the organization you choose before you foster.

- **Ask Questions, Get Answers.** Review the rescue or shelter's application and policies carefully. If you have questions, ask and get answers! We all know the only dumb question is the one you didn't ask.

- **Understand Your Responsibilities.** Know well in advance exactly what you will be responsible for—including financial responsibilities. Who is responsible to cover the cost of food, supplies (leash, harness, bowls, etc.), grooming, and medication? If the dog needs veterinary care, who is responsible for those bills? What do you do if there is a medical emergency? What happens if you have a family or work situation that takes you out of town during the time you are fostering? Will the rescue organization assist in finding (and paying for) someone to temporarily care for the dog? How long will you be expected to foster the dog? How much are you responsible for finding the dog a new forever home? Will you be responsible to bring the dog to adoption events and, if so, how often and where? Will potential adopters come to your home? If you are expected to keep the dog until a suitable home is found, can they tell you approximately how long that might take? What happens if the dog is deemed unadoptable? Can you adopt the dog if you choose?

- **Know Your Home and Your Family.** It is important to be honest with yourself and the dog as to how well a dog will fit into your home, your family, and your lifestyle. This will save you and the rescue from trying to find a new home if, for some reason, you are unable to keep the dog. Do you have other dogs, pets, or young children, and if so, how will they react to a new pet coming into your home? While the hope is they will all blend and live together in peace and harmony, the truth is your other pets may not welcome the new dog regardless of how temporary the situation may be. Can your family meet the dog prior to committing to fostering? Do you have sufficient space in your home? Do you have a fenced-in yard? Do you have a quiet area where you can take the dog to help him or her adjust to their new home and environment? If the dog needs to be quarantined for a period of time (to ensure it doesn't have kennel cough or other upper respiratory infections) how will that impact your family, the other animals, and your home? Senior dogs, whelping mothers, or dogs with special needs do much better in a quiet home environment. Take an honest look at your home environment and determine what kind of dog would best fit into your home and lifestyle.

- **Know the Dog.** Find out as much as you can about the dog before they come into your home. How did the dog come to the rescue or shelter and how long has it been there? Has it been neutered or spayed? Is it up to date on all vaccinations and examinations? Does the dog have any medical conditions? Does it need to be quarantined? Is the dog good with other dogs, animals, young children, and strangers? Will it be comfortable around your grandmother's walker when she comes to visit? Is the dog potty-trained? Crate trained? If it is a puppy, has it been successfully weaned from the mother and properly socialized? How does the dog do if left alone? Understand that initially the change of environment may be stressful for the dog and may impact if and how much they eat, pee, and poop.

- **Know Yourself.** What kind of behavior problems or health and medical issues are you comfortable handling? Are you comfortable giving injections or medications on a regular basis? Will you be responsible for potty-training the dog? Are you comfortable and confident with training the dog in basic obedience and manners? If it's a puppy and hasn't been socialized, do you have the time and skills to do so successfully? Are you able to keep the dog groomed and sanitary? And, most importantly, do you have the time and energy to devote to this dog?

- **Prepare Your Home.** Do you have a "home" at your home for the dog? It could be a crate or carrier but it's important the dog has a familiar-smelling, quiet refuge. Find out what kind of food the dog eats. Ensure you have a sufficient supply of food as well as access to fresh clean water. Do you have a collar, harness, leash, poop bags, toys, and bowls for food and water? Do you have a dog bed or towels and blankets the dog can lay on? Ensuring your home is ready to welcome the dog will help with a smoother transition for everyone.

- **Begin With the End in Sight.** Remember this is a temporary situation so before you say hello, be prepared to say goodbye. It will be bittersweet when they leave your home but know that you have given your furry friend your time, love, and energy, which will allow it to be a loved and cherished member of its forever family.

- **Expect the Unexpected.** As much as you prepare, expect the unexpected. This isn't just true of fostering a dog—it is true of life. And, as in life, it helps to keep your sense of humor and remember that nothing, including your time as a foster parent, is forever.

Chapter Five
ZACH

The summer of 2008, while vacationing with my sons on Long Beach Island, New Jersey, I went to Acme Surf & Sport to rent bikes. I met the owner, Zach, and his dog Krypto, who worked alongside him at the shop. I never forgot the connection I witnessed between Zach and Krypto and have always held Zach in high esteem because of those early impressions he and Krypto made on me. The summer of 2015, while working on this book, I was back on LBI for a week and was extremely happy when Zach agreed to sit down with me to share his story.

I GREW UP IN A SPRAWLING SUBURBAN TOWN IN NEW JERSEY. IT was the '60s and our childhood was very much like *The Wonder Years*. We walked to school along streets lined with nice, neat little homes and grass everywhere.

In the summer, our family vacationed at the Jersey shore. My brother told my dad we should visit a place called Long Beach Island, and the day my dad and I came across the bridge onto LBI, I promised myself that one day I would live there. I never wanted to go back up north again. Ever.

As kids, we were taught by our parents to love animals and we always had a

Krypto

dog. While every one of those dogs was special, I came to understand that if you take the time to teach a dog, they all have the potential to be special.

My first childhood dog was a mutt named Happy who was born around the same time I was in 1960. Happy loved to wander around town and everyone in town knew her. If she wandered too far from home, people would simply tell her, "Happy, go home," and she would. When Happy and I were both thirteen, she died of old age and I was extremely sad. We had grown up together and it had never dawned on me that one day Happy would die.

After Happy passed, we got a black Lab named Yogi. Yogi was our first Lab and my introduction into the world of Labs. I love Labs because, to me, they are so in-tune with their owners that they are almost like a person shoved in a dog suit.

Yogi and our family spent every summer vacation on Long Beach Island and, by the time Yogi passed in 1986 at the age thirteen, I had realized my dream of becoming a full-time resident of LBI. I had also visited Colorado a few years prior, and between my love of the mountains and being completely captivated by its beauty, I decided to buy a second home there.

My brother Seth, who was living full time in Colorado, got a Lab puppy he named Petro (since he was working in the petroleum business). Petro was an amazing dog, shockingly athletic and brilliant on every level so when Seth eventually mated Petro with a beautiful, sociable Lab named Custer, I told him I wanted one. My brother said I could have the pick of the litter so when the puppies were born, my girlfriend Nina and I flew out to see them and immediately gravitated to the sickly runt of the litter. I picked her up and she immediately curled up in my arms and fell asleep. I knew she was the one for me.

Since the puppies were only four weeks old, Nina and I returned to get her when she was around nine weeks old. Since we were into inline skates at the time, and Kryptonics made my favorite wheels, we named her Krypto.

When I have a dog, it tends to be with me for most of the day, and that's how it was from our first day together. Krypto began her day by running five miles with Nina on the beach and then came to work with me for the rest of the day.

Wherever we went, Krypto was with us and she was fine. We once went to a music festival and it wasn't until we got there that we found out dogs weren't allowed. However, after seeing how well-behaved Krypto was, they let her in. People couldn't resist Krypto and she instinctually knew how to behave in every situation and setting. She never hurt a fly, never chased a rabbit, and simply believed in live and let live. As long as we were having fun, life was good.

Our travels together were amazing. Other than our flight back home when we got her, we never again traveled on an airplane because I didn't want to stress her out. We drive everywhere and even though it takes longer, we're together in the car and we're fine.

Every winter, Krypto and I drove to Colorado. We loved everything about Colorado: the wide open spaces, the snow, and Nordic skiing with Krypto running alongside me as I skied.

We once rented a house in California and one of the first things I did was walk the perimeter of the property to show Krypto the boundaries. She understood and never once wandered off the property. Krypto knew things other dogs wouldn't understand and had unbelievable instincts.

Even a good dog can be a nuisance but, time after time, people told me that Krypto was a pleasure to have around and that she and I were always welcome in their home. People often invited me to visit but if I couldn't bring Krypto, I didn't go since I would be thinking about and missing her the whole time. We were just as happy hanging and working here at the beach.

Not too long after Krypto came to live with Nina and me in New Jersey, we got a kitten, Woody (aka Woodman). Krypto and Woody became best friends and were ridiculously close. They slept together and absolutely loved one another. Thankfully Woody lived a long life because when he died of kidney failure, Krypto was in the last year of her life so Woody's passing didn't seem to impact her that much.

As Krypto got older, she began to lose her vision and had more and more aches and pains, and the vet suspected she'd had a couple of heart attacks. When she began having trouble walking, I built ramps for her to get in and out of the car and bed until, eventually, I had to carry her up and down the stairs. My neighbors in Colorado were kind enough to actually switch homes with us. They moved into our upstairs unit and we moved downstairs so it would be easier for Krypto.

They say you know when it is time to make the right decision for your dog but with Krypto, I wasn't sure I would ever want to make that decision. Then, one morning, I heard her screaming. She was just lying there looking at me, unable to get up. I held her thinking I would give her some time. My hope was that maybe she was just having a bad day but, as the hours passed, it was obvious Krypto was asking for help. When I looked into her eyes, it was as if she was telling me, "I can't do this anymore. I can't go on." I knew I had to do the right thing and that this was going to be our last day together.

We drove to the vet but didn't go in. Instead, we lay outside under the shade of a tree and I told the vet that's where we would be. He said he was busy and wouldn't be able to come out for a while. I assured him that was fine and, whenever he was ready, we would be out there under the tree. I wanted Krypto's last moments to be non-stressful, which isn't always the case inside a vet's office. About an hour later, the vet came out. That was a tough day.

Krypto was one of ten puppies. None of the other puppies survived to their eleventh birthday. Krypto lived to fourteen and a half. I always fed her organic, healthy food and exercised her seven days a week. She was loved and well cared for on every level. I believe you can extend a dog's life by feeding them good food, taking great care of them, and ensuring they have minimal stress and a good life.

Many of her siblings died younger than they should have. I believe this was because in the part of Southern Colorado where they lived, many of the rivers had been used by the mining industry and the water in many of those rivers was filled with poisons and toxins. More than one of my brother's dogs in Colorado died in his arms from cancer.

Thankfully, Krypto's bloodline is still in our family to this day and they have all been amazing dogs. None of them have papers of any kind but they are all a testimony that if you raise a dog properly you get a great outcome.

I think the only way to ever really get over the loss of a dog is to eventually find another dog to love. It's different with people. You can get divorced or lose someone but you don't necessarily need to find someone else to get over them. It's not like that with a dog. Another dog helps you get over the loss.

Krypto died in September 2009 and I decided to take some down time in Florida that winter. I was considering traveling the world by ship or visiting places where I couldn't go with a dog.

My landlord came down to Florida mid-winter with his golden retriever, Mulligan. Mulligan fell in love with me. He laid next to my desk and napped and just generally loved being around me. I was really trying to fight any urge to get a dog but everywhere I turned, Mulligan was there.

I am a slow reader and actually have difficulty reading but that winter I kept finding all these books about dogs: *A Dog's Purpose, Merle's Door, Racing in the Rain*. They were all really good for me but after finishing Dean Koontz's book *Watchers*, I decided, "That's it. I'm getting a dog."

I started searching online and while scrolling through pictures on the Labs4Rescue website, I saw a picture of a little red dog that was not only the spitting image of Krypto but also had been born the same month Krypto died. I knew that little red dog was my dog and felt, on some level, it was Krypto reincarnated. I nervously contacted Jennifer, the woman in charge of the rescue, and told her I had found my dog.

Jennifer called back the next day. After interviewing me, she said since the dog had been abused, was depressed, and avoided interaction with most humans, she didn't think the dog would do well in my bike shop and living situation. In short, she didn't think the dog and I were a good match. I begged Jennifer but her answer was still no.

I began to learn more about the dog and found out it had been living in an abandoned apartment complex just south of New Orleans, Louisiana. The bank had hired a great guy named Rick Attaway to oversee the renovations of the apartment units. The only things living in the apartments were some raccoons—and a dog who was maybe seven or eight months old.

There was one unit with a broken door. When the weather was bad the dog stayed in there, but the rest of the time she moved around the property. Rick found her every morning by looking for the pile of stuffed animals she always kept with her.

Rick quickly put an end to the kids who had been throwing rocks at the dog and also began bringing her plates of food. Initially, the dog wouldn't go near Rick and only approached the food after he left the area. After about four months, the dog approached Rick one morning when he showed up with food. That same day, when Rick hopped in his truck to go home, he looked in his rearview mirror and saw the dog running after him. Stopping his truck, he opened the door and the dog slowly got in. She had finally decided it was safe to trust him.

Since Rick already had four rescue dogs at home, he contacted his friend Jennifer from Lab4Rescue and asked if she would help get the dog adopted. And that is when and how I found her.

After a lot of begging and intervention by Leslie, a local policewoman here on LBI, Jennifer finally agreed that I could adopt the dog. I promised if it didn't work out, I would drive her to the new home Jennifer found her, even if it meant driving the entire East Coast. A few days later, Ruby Red Dog (which is what I named her) was put in a transport truck in Louisiana and, a few days after that, I drove to Bernardsville, New Jersey, to pick her up.

Ruby took one look at me and wanted nothing to do with me. We went for a short walk but it was obvious she wasn't happy. I bought a sandwich from a nearby Starbucks and took out the bacon and rubbed some treats with it. Ruby could resist me but she couldn't resist the bacon, so finally I got her into my truck. Shortly after getting on the road, she ate another bacon-soaked treat, let out a huge sigh, lay down, and slept for the next three hours.

Three weeks passed and Ruby still didn't want anything to do with me. She avoided eye contact with me and was obviously depressed. I was bummed out too. I called Jennifer and told her, "You were right. This isn't a good fit. Find her a home and I'll drive her." Jennifer was going out of town and said when she got back the following week she would take care of it.

It was as if Ruby understood the conversation. The very next day, she started making eye contact and listening to me. All of a sudden, she wanted to be a part of my life. When Jennifer called back, I told her Ruby had turned a corner and to forget our prior conversation.

From that point on, while we had our challenges, Ruby and I were also building a solid relationship. Krypto had been 100 percent Lab; Ruby was a hound-Lab mix. When you add in hound, you get a degree of stubbornness and boundless curiosity. Any time I tried to fence Ruby in, she figured a way out.

Once, when we were out for a run on the beach, she ran down the beach straight into a gull and grabbed the fish out of the gull's mouth. Her feistiness and instincts had probably helped Ruby survive those early months of her life as a street dog.

The first summer Ruby came into my life, we got up at 5:00 every morning and drove up the beach road to a place where there weren't any people so I could let her run and swim in the bay. By the end of the summer, even though she could still be a challenge at times, we had a connection and I loved her dearly. She was starting to trust me, which I believe was one of the hardest challenges of her life.

Now, years later, she has become a remarkable dog. Just like Krypto, she is well trained and can be off-leash when the environment and circumstances allow. For the most part, she just hangs around the bike shop or the house with me all day.

Last winter in Steamboat Springs, we hiked together every morning, and in the afternoons, she hung out with her dog friends. Every time I whistled for her, she always came right back. I would tell her, "Okay, good girl," and off she would go to hang out with her friends again. Once I knew she was okay, I was okay. We have a half acre of land in Colorado so she has a lot of freedom when we are there.

It's different on LBI. This is a crowded island environment, but she's a street-smart dog. Every morning, I bike while Ruby runs alongside me. That is followed by her much-anticipated swim in the bay. She gets a marrow bone while I finish my exercise and then we both hang out in the bike shop all day. Ruby lays in the center of the floor and greets the customers. In October, after the bike shop is closed, Ruby still wakes up every morning anxious to go to work, and sometimes she sits at the corner trying to figure out where everybody went.

We were here on the island for Hurricane Sandy. We actually had a reservation at a hotel in Marlton, New Jersey, but I had injured my back and the pain medication made me groggy. I decided it was safer to wait until morning to head out. By morning the Boulevard was already flooding.

The police came to tell me National Guard trucks would be coming by to get us. Even though the Boulevard was flooding, in all the years I'd lived here water had never come into the house, so I told them Ruby, Alley Cat, and I were going to stay put.

By noon, water started coming up over the deck. Knowing the major surge hadn't yet hit, I called the mayor and said, "I think I screwed up." He told me to get in my truck and head over to the police station.

"I'm bringing my dog," I told him.

"Fine, just get here as quick as you can."

Knowing the trip would be difficult for Alley Cat, I promised her we'd be back the next day to get her, and Ruby and I got in the truck. We arrived at the police station around 1:00 p.m. Three hours later, a National Guard truck arrived to take us over the bridge to the mainland.

I was so crippled from my back injury that the National Guard had to lift Ruby into the truck. The drive to Ship Bottom through four feet of water was eerie but nothing compared to the drive over the bridge. The wind was unbelievably fierce and the rain, coming sideways at the truck, was unrelenting. All I kept thinking was "Wow ... this is how I die."

Once over the bridge, it was fine. My friend Anne picked us up to stay at her house in Manahawkin along with a random group of other refugees from the storm.

The next morning, I was anxious to get back to my home and Alley Cat, but slowly we all began to realize the horror and reality of what had happened. There was mass destruction and fires and the police and National Guard weren't allowing anyone back onto the island.

Two days later, I was able to get a ride onto the island with a contractor friend, and when we got to my house I couldn't believe what I saw. While the two feet of water that had filled my home had receded, what remained was almost a half foot of thick mud everywhere. I saw Alley Cat's muddy paw prints on the kitchen counter but, not seeing her anywhere, began calling for her.

We had arrived at my home around 4:00 p.m. and there was a strict curfew. Everyone had to be off the island by 6:00 p.m. I kept calling for Alley Cat, and shortly before we had to leave, I heard a meow and saw her turning the corner on Beach Avenue. She was muddy from head to toe but when she saw me, she ran. I picked her up, put her in the truck, and we headed back to the mainland.

Ruby and Alley Cat were really good guests at Anne's house, and most nights, Ruby slept with her arm around Alley Cat. Ruby and Alley Cat had always gotten along (just like Krypto and Woody had) but now it was like Ruby understood we were in hurricane mode and gave her little sister some extra love.

Despite how well things were going off-island, on the island everything was a disaster. Having seen the amount of destruction on the island and in my home, and realizing Ruby, Alley Cat, and I would be out of our home for a long time, I bought a home on the mainland for us to live in. Hurricane Sandy happened on October 29, 2012, and we moved into the new house in Manahawkin on November 10. After that, I set to work rebuilding our homes and lives.

Typically in a hurricane or Nor'easter, the water fills up the bay and spills over onto the island. In Hurricane Sandy, the ocean breached and met the bay and in the process churned everything up. The whole area was filled with mud like none of us had ever seen before. Nobody knew where the mud came from or what it consisted of but it was horrible. It was impossible to get rid of and took me weeks of powerwashing my house, including the inside and the hardwood floors, to even begin to get the mud out. Even now, three years later, I still find pockets of mud in my home.

For many people, their home on the island was a second home. I owned three buildings, including one that for a long time had been my home. Every one of them needed massive repairs and renovations.

I began with the building that housed a vegetarian restaurant. It had five feet of water and a ton of damage but, wanting my tenants to be able to reopen their business and get their life back, we started work there.

After that, we started on my bike shop next to that building. Since it had been destroyed from the sewer line up, it had to be completely gutted. The renovations on those two buildings took from November to

April. Then I and my long-time friend Jack began renovations on my home and the bike shop adjacent to it.

As the summer of 2013 approached, even though the renovations were coming together, I wasn't ready to go back to the island yet. We came back to the island for the summer of 2014 but it wasn't until the summer of 2015 that I was mentally and emotionally back to normal. There had never been water like that on the island and recovering from the hurricane was an exhausting, traumatic experience.

Ruby Red Dog
(Photo: Jack Reynolds, The Sandpaper)

Rick, the contractor who had found Ruby in Louisiana, checked on us constantly after the hurricane, wanting to know if we needed anything. I assured Rick we were fine and he kept telling me, "Just follow your dog. She's a survivor. Follow her." And it was true. Ruby handled everything like a pro.

The morning of the storm, Ruby had kept nudging my arm as if to tell me we should leave the island, but I kept assuring her we would be fine. When the water came over the deck and I finally looked at her and said, "We have to go," she looked at me like, "You're kidding me, right? Isn't that what I've been telling you for the last few hours?" I think if she could have, she would have rolled her eyes at me.

At the police station everyone said what a great dog she was. Even in the National Guard truck, amongst a random group of scared individuals, Ruby just stood there calmly. She was perfect, a real trooper, and an inspiration. I think her childhood was so tough that whatever we do together she understands everything will be fine.

And it is. I am absolutely crazy about Ruby. I can't believe that, once again, I found the best dog on Earth. Sometimes I swear that on Krypto's way up to Heaven, she collided with a hound dog and the result was a Labbyhound dog named Ruby Red Dog.

For me, a dog becomes your best friend, companion, and roommate, and they only get better with time. You learn what makes them tick and they learn what makes you tick. It is a friendship that continues to grow until, way too soon, they get old, die, and break your heart.

My dogs point out the important things, the simple things, in life for me. I don't care about most things but I do care about my dogs, and without fail they always help me remember what is most important in life.

Growing up there was a note hanging on my father's office wall that said, "In every man's life, he deserves at least one good dog and one good woman." I'm lucky. I've been more than blessed in both categories.

JENNIFER AND LABS4RESCUE

While working on Zach's story, I contacted Jennifer from Labs4Rescue to clarify something. She was in the middle of a very busy day but when she heard why I was contacting her, she said, "Wait! You're writing about Zach who adopted Ruby?" When I told her I was, she stopped what she was doing to share more pieces of Zach and Ruby's story and to tell me about her friend Rick and Labs4Rescue.[1]

I HAVE BEEN DOING RESCUE WORK FOR TEN YEARS AND HAVE some amazing stories but Zach and Ruby's story is exceptional. It is very special to me in large part because of the man who found Ruby, Rick Attaway. Rick was bigger than life and one of the finest human beings to ever set foot on this Earth. It brings tears to my eyes to even talk about him.

Rick came to us through his daughter who wanted to volunteer with Labs4Rescue. Rick had two Labs but wanted to try fostering a dog. The first dog he fostered was a Lab named Holiday. The day before Holiday was to be transported to her adoptive home, Rick brought her over. I came out and there was this sixty-two-year-old man on my front porch crying. I knew we had

Rick Attaway

done the right thing in sending the dog to the person who had already adopted her, but I couldn't sleep that night. I felt like the cruelest person in the world who had taken this man's most treasured possession and given it away.

Rick said it was fine and asked if he could please try fostering again. So we did. This time he was fostering a black Lab named Decoy. Unlike his first fostering experience, when the day came for Decoy to be transported to his adopter in New England, Rick was composed and stoic as Decoy left. However, his daughter called a few days later and said, "He's a basket case again." We ended up calling the transporter and telling him to bring Decoy back to Rick. Rick called him Big Boy and loved that dog forever and ever.

Rick was never too busy for the dogs and came over at least once a week to see them. If he saw us out walking the dogs, he would stop, get out of his truck, and talk with them. One time we had a dog that needed to get to the vet but were having difficulty getting him into the truck. Rick left work, wrapped the dog in a blanket, and carried him out to the truck for us. No matter what, Rick was always there for us.

One time, I was going to Africa and had a group of dogs all set for transport so Rick agreed to meet the transport and put the dogs on. At the last minute, the transport company had to cancel so Rick took care of all the dogs for two weeks until I came back.

Rick was my closest friend. I loved him dearly and I miss him immensely. He passed away two years ago.

When Rick met Ruby, he was overseeing work at a job site where he found a really frightened feral dog. Rick had been trying to bring food to the dog and called me to find out how to approach her.

I told him he needed to systematically get the dog to come to him by laying the food down without reaching for the dog or making eye contact. The most important thing was to be consistent so the dog would learn Rick was always going to be there.

Rick was extremely patient and eventually the dog came to him. He brought the dog over for me to meet and she was so pitiful. She was a mess, didn't know how to be around people, and was going to the bathroom everywhere. The first thing we did was get her spayed. She tested positive for heartworm so we began treatments for that and nicknamed her Ratta (short for Rick Attaway).

Rick wanted to foster her and ended up nicknaming her Whiney Baby because she constantly whined at his house. He took her for rides in the car and began to teach her how to be around people.

Then one day I got an application from this funny fellow named Zach. Again, I have been doing this a while and typically get the standard application and interview—and then there was Zach's. His was the oddest application and oddest interview I had ever done. Zach lives in both New Jersey and Colorado and his dog is his constant companion, even at work. He is such a free spirit and has a much different lifestyle than most of the people who apply to adopt a dog. But what really stuck out about Zach was that he loved his last dog and he desperately wanted Ruby.

When Zach got Ruby, initially it was a disaster, but I really believed it would work. Thankfully it did.

The first time Zach took Ruby to Colorado, he sent me hundreds of pictures of her. I looked at those pictures and thought about where Ruby had been and the circumstances and environment she had been in when Rick found her. Now this dog was running free on mountaintops with a man who was cross-country skiing. Her life was so amazing now—and that was all because of Rick and Zach.

Even though Rick and Zach never met, they were close. They talked on the phone and by email. Rick had been so determined to rescue and save that dog. Even though he was this big man, whenever he talked about Ruby, he would cry. I think before Zach got Ruby he had begun to see Ruby through Rick's eyes and fell in love with her even more.

I love Zach and I love that he is such a free spirit. While his adoption was a little different than most, it was perfect because he truly loves Ruby. Zach told me he thought Ruby looked like Krypto, and while she does, she is also a very different dog. What really matters is that Ruby is absolutely with the right person now and I couldn't be happier for both of them.

I used to train service dogs and through that work fell in love with Labs. I was brought into rescue work because of Hurricane Katrina.

I have lived in Louisiana for fifty years and have seen a lot of hurricanes. Typically, it's a three-day evacuation. Everybody always brought enough clothes and supplies to last them for three days. A lot of hospital workers bring their animals with them to work. They leave their dog or cat in a crate or tied to the bumper of their car in the parking garage at the hospital and, on their breaks, go out and take care of them. Normally, the whole system works well for everyone because, again, usually it's only for a few days.

Then Katrina happened and, as we all know, there was nothing normal about it. Suddenly there were over forty-five dogs and cat in crates or tied to car bumpers in the hospital garage. I got a call saying there were all these animals that needed help. The mayor was staying at the West Jefferson Hospital (one of the two hospitals that were open in West Jefferson) and he gave me permission to set up a kennel at the hospital. I was given forty crates for dogs and cats that I put in the X-ray room, since it was one of the few spots in the hospital that had air conditioning.

That was my first experience with rescue work. I had always loved Labs and learned that more Labs than pit bulls were being euthanized in Louisiana. Part of this was due to the fact that Labs had bigger litters so there were more Lab puppies. There was also a mentality amongst many owners not to spay or neuter their dogs in order that their kids could see the miracle of birth. The puppies were handed out and they, too, weren't spayed or neutered.

Around here, Labs are also used for hunting. If the dog turns out to not be the greatest hunting dog, at the end of the season some owners simply leave the dog in the woods. When you put all of those pieces together, there is an abundance of Labs in the high-kill shelters. While the shelters are getting better, there are still too many dogs.

Labs4Rescue is a volunteer non-profit organization dedicated to providing a new life for rescued or displaced Labrador retrievers and Lab mixes. All of our dogs undergo an initial veterinary screening, and treatment of any issues is required before they are placed in a loving foster home. Only Labs with socially acceptable behaviors and who can be responsibly placed are offered for adoption. Before being placed for adoption, every dog is vaccinated, sprayed or neutered, placed on heartworm prevention, and treated for any health conditions. Since our goal is to promote and advance responsible pet ownership, we also offer educational materials, brochures, educational events, and articles on our website and Facebook page.

Labs4Rescue has an incredible transport system, which is one of the reasons everything works as well as it does. There are adoption coordinators in Louisiana, Alabama, Tennessee, and Georgia. In the beginning, we used volunteer transports to get the dogs to Connecticut but it took so long to organize that today we use two transport companies: Rescue Road

Jennifer with several Labs4Rescue dogs

Trips and Pets Inc. They are professional transporters with eighteen-wheelers. Just like the Postal Service, nothing stops them. They never cancel for weather, vacations, or for any other reason and are always there for us and the dogs.

Initially I planned on doing this for a couple of years, making an impact and then getting out, but here I am, ten years later, still working with Labs4Rescue. And I couldn't be happier.

Chapter Six
CONNIE

Connie and I crossed paths in 2008 while I was working on my book for Alzheimer's caregivers. Connie's mother had been diagnosed with Alzheimer's disease and, like me, she had cared for her mother for a period of time. Over the years, we discovered we also shared a love for dogs. Connie is an intelligent, vibrant woman with a quick wit and a passion for all animals. We have yet to meet face to face, but it is my hope that this book and our dogs will change that.

WHEN I WAS YOUNG, MY BABYSITTER HAD A BEAGLE. AT THE END of a long, dark hallway in her home was a big pantry. The pantry was bigger than most NYC apartments and had a farm door that opened at the top. When nobody was home, the beagle stayed in the pantry.

Stella and Connie

One day, when I was four years old, I ran down the hallway, threw my arms around the beagle, and was bitten in the face.

I was taken to the hospital for stitches, which was horrible and traumatic since back then they didn't use any anesthesia. For many years I was terrified of dogs and became a cat person.

When my last cat, Gwydion, died, I was depressed. My mother had

63

died the year before from Alzheimer's and I was now grieving Gywdion too. I briefly considered adopting another cat but I wasn't ready.

My therapist knew how profoundly the loss of my mother affected me and that, in many ways, I had stayed alive for Gwydion because I would never leave a pet without a parent. But now Gwydion was gone.

One day, completely out of the blue, my therapist said, "I think you should get a dog."

Looking at him like he had nine heads, I said, "Dogs are fine but I can't picture myself getting up at 6:00 a.m. in the pouring rain to wait for a dog to pee."

At my next appointment, he brought it up again. "I really think you should get a dog."

I rolled my eyes and shook my head. However, when your therapist tells you something, even if you think the idea is crazy, you still mull it over. So when he got more specific at the following session and said, "I think you should get a greyhound," I found myself intently researching them. At the same time, on a visit to the local dog run, I met a man with two magnificent, sleek greyhounds.

When the subject came up for the fourth time, I finally asked my therapist if he had a greyhound.

"Yes," he said, smiling. "I don't get a kickback for greyhound placement but they need to be rescued. Often, if they don't end up being good racers, they are euthanized because it costs more to keep them than they earn at the track."

He continued explaining, "Since you get them when they are between two and four years old, they are already housebroken and walk beautifully on a leash. They are like the cat of dogs—they almost never bark and are really couch potatoes. Greyhounds are very sweet and are great apartment dogs."

He connected me with the National Greyhound Adoption Program (NGAP).[1] I filled out their five-page application, provided them with the required references, and paid the adoption fee (which covered spaying, all shots, teeth cleaning, and microchipping).

For the next few days, I looked at NGAP's online gallery of available dogs and continued to educate myself about greyhounds. After several days, my heart was set on one, but since NGAP hadn't called me, I decided to call them.

Bobbie, NGAP's rescue coordinator, explained the goal was to find the dog best suited for me and my lifestyle. My requirements were few: female and cat-friendly in case I adopted a cat in the future.

I was happy to learn every one of my references (my landlord, my vet, friends, and family) had received calls because it meant the organization truly cared about their dogs and their placement.

Finally, I got The Call. Bobbie had two female dogs she wanted me to meet. She told me about each dog and asked which one I wanted.

"I'm going to let the dogs choose," I said. I rented a little four-door car to drive from Manhattan to the NGAP office near Philadelphia. All the way there I kept thinking: What if neither dog liked me? What if the people at NGAP didn't think I would be a good adoptee?

When I arrived, Bobbie took me into a large room, sat me in a chair with my back to the door, and brought the first dog in. The dog was gorgeous—and terrified.

Fear isn't uncommon for greyhounds right off the track, and because of that, they sometimes have a reputation for being skittish. The truth is they simply haven't been exposed to a lot of things. For instance, they don't know what a window is or how to go up stairs. They really don't even know how to play because they begin training to be a racer when they are still just puppies. At the racetrack, they can spend up to twenty-three hours a day in a two-by-four crate. Oftentimes when you get a greyhound, there is a lot to teach them.

Bobbie and I both agreed the first dog probably wouldn't do well in New York City so she brought in the second. She, too, seemed a little scared but after a few minutes she came over, stuck her nose in, and nuzzled my face. She chose me and I chose her new name: Stella.

Bobbie invited me into her office to fill out some paperwork so the dog could go home with me. I was stunned. "She's going home with me today? Now?"

"Just as soon as we give her a bath," Bobbie said, walking away with Stella.

Looking back, even though I had been thinking about it for weeks, when it happened it was like getting shot out of a cannon. I had no idea

I would be going home with a dog that day. I didn't know what I was getting myself into and was completely unprepared. I had no supplies or food. I didn't even have the right-size car—her crate, still disassembled and in the box, was too big to fit inside. We ended up strapping the crate (still in the box) to the top of my rental car and Stella and I headed to Manhattan.

Stella didn't enjoy the drive and was nervous the entire trip. That was completely understandable since she had probably only been in a truck while being transported to different race tracks. I doubt she had ever been in a car and now she was in one watching the world go by at lightning speed with a woman she had just met.

I was nervous, too—as well as stunned, scared, and excited. I had never had a dog before and was afraid I wouldn't know what to do.

When we arrived at my neighborhood in northern Manhattan, I parked the car and took her for a walk. Stella had never been in a metropolitan area and now she was out going for a walk in Manhattan. Even though it is a relatively bucolic part of the city, it is still Manhattan. She couldn't stop shaking. I thought she was going to have a nervous breakdown, so for her next walk, we chose a quieter street to allow her to get acclimated.

I had taken a week off from work so we could get settled and get to know one other. I also wanted to gradually get her used to being home alone for a few hours. Since greyhounds are bony and like soft surfaces, I put a plush pad in her crate. I also left the door to the crate open so Stella would know she was free to go in and out and that the crate was her place to feel safe. She curled up in a ball, stuck her head out the door, and looked up at me with an expression that said, "Now what?"

While Stella watched, I pulled out the package of paperwork Bobbie had given me. I studied Stella's Bertillon card that listed fifty-six physical identifying points, right down to the color of each of her toenails. Every registered racing greyhound also has its Bertillon number tattooed in its left ear, and the month and year of their birth as well as their litter order is in their right. Stella's right ear read F09F: July 2009, sixth in her litter.

Like so many other greyhounds, Stella had been viewed by her prior owner as an income-generating commodity. She was somebody's property. To determine the value of that property, greyhounds have six maiden races. How they do in those races determines whether or not they become a racer. In many states, if the dog performs poorly it is killed because it costs more to keep them than they earn in prize money.

Stella hadn't done very well in her six maiden races in Daytona, Florida. She fell twice, came in last twice, and went off track twice chasing butterflies or something. I am eternally grateful beyond measure that her prior owner surrendered her to NGAP to become a retired racer rather than having her euthanized. I wrote him a thank-you note so he would know she is loved and has a wonderful life, and also to encourage him to keep giving dogs up for adoption.

Before I brought Stella home, I had read everything there was to read about greyhounds, positive training techniques, rescuing a dog, and possible issues that could arise and how to overcome them. I had also hired a dog trainer and walker, Sherri, who lived a block away. Even though Sherri came highly recommended, I put her through the same vetting process the rescue agency had put me through, checked her references, and interviewed her as if I were sending my child to daycare.

Sherri only used positive training techniques and was wonderful with Stella. By the end of the week, Stella had begun to successfully settle into her new home and her new life.

The first week I went back to work I insisted on regular phone calls from Sherri. In particular, at midday, I asked for a poop report since I was having trouble getting Stella to poop. Sherri continued to assure me that Stella was pooping just fine, so we had a long conversation.

I had never had a dog and no idea that dogs sniffed the ground before they poop, so every time Stella started sniffing, I thought she was just lollygagging and stopped her. I had given Stella a case of what I call Poopus Interruptus.

The first three weeks went really well—and then the elevator in my apartment building broke. It was one of the hottest summers on record with about 98 percent humidity. We lived on the fourth floor and Stella had no idea how to climb stairs. After taking her paws one at a time in an attempt to teach her how to climb stairs, I finally realized that could take us hours so I did the only logical thing: I picked up my sixty-two-pound uncooperative, scared greyhound and carried her up the stairs.

Stella simply didn't know how to do it and I had no other choice. And Stella had no other choice but to trust me.

I'd read that greyhounds don't swim due to their chests and long limbs, so while walking through the park a few weeks later, I decided to see if Stella liked water. Dogs aren't allowed in the water, and I thought she would probably only get her paws wet, but Stella jumped right in.

Greyhounds have necks that are wider than their heads so they wear martingale collars, which are much more difficult to slip out of. However, when martingale collars get wet, they expand and slip right off the dog with little to no effort. So there was Stella, without a collar, looking at first like she was going to drown. Then, a few seconds later, Stella was swimming behind some ducks and heading towards the Hudson River!

Preparing to dive in to get Stella, I spotted a friend from my kayak club paddling towards me. As he got closer, he called out, "Connie, is this your dog?" Stella, it seems, had ditched the ducks in favor of the big green kayak.

She smelled like the Hudson River but was so pleased with herself. I couldn't scold her but instead had to reward her for coming back to me. Stella now wears an unslippable harness.

One day, there was a flyer in our local pet store about a meeting for people interested in becoming a therapy team with their dog. It was being held at our local hospital by a national organization called Pet Partners.[2]

I like helping people and believe whole-heartedly in the role therapy animals play in hospitals for patients as well as for doctors, nurses, and families. They explained that the training requirements for the exam were pretty stringent but I thought it would be a good way for me to deepen my relationship with Stella and also have a structured goal and timeframe.

To pass the certification test, Stella would be expected to sit, stay, and remain calm around wheelchairs and with awkward hugs. Greyhounds don't naturally sit because of their long backs so I called the Pet Partners evaluator. She said Stella had to be able to sit, even if her butt only touched the ground on my command for a moment.

Committed to training her in a way that would honor her physiology, I researched and found information on the internet explaining how to teach a greyhound to sit. [3] Essentially, you find a hill and the pup's behind needs to be on the uphill slope, thereby making it already naturally raised slightly. Then, while facing your pup, you take a treat close to their nose and have them follow the treat until their head rises up towards the sky. The dog's bottom will automatically touch the ground as their nose goes skyward.

We passed the certification test with flying colors and continued to do therapy work through Pet Partners. Pet Partners respects the therapy dogs and is committed to the belief that visits be as rewarding for the dog (and me as her handler) as it is for those she visits.

Stella

Perhaps the most important lesson I learned, and one that stays with me to this day, is that I need to be Stella's advocate. It is important for me to know when Stella is tired, anxious, or just not in the mood to visit and honor that.

Because of the respect I have for all animals and, in particular, my pets, I have never raised my voice to them or hit them and am a firm believer in positive training. Having a greyhound has taught me more about compassion, respect, trust, and responsibility than I ever thought possible.

Stella has a wonderful life but what she has given to me is so much more: love, fun, companionship, serenity, and a new group of human and canine friends. I have established a formal plan with a designated adopter and a small trust fund so that, in the event something ever happens to me, Stella will always be safe, cared for, and loved.

Stella and I would like to thank Grey2K USA Worldwide for the work they do around the world in abolishing greyhound racing. We would also like to thank the team at NGAP for all they do in rescuing greyhounds and ensuring that retired racers are adopted into loving forever homes. I am grateful for the words of wisdom given to me a few years ago and share that same wisdom with you: "I think you should adopt a greyhound."

GREYHOUND RESCUE AND GREY2K USA

To learn more about greyhounds and greyhound rescue, I spoke with Christina Dorchak, Esq., president and general counsel for GREY2K USA. Christina is one of the original founders of the organization, which is working to pass stronger laws to protect greyhounds and to end dog racing around the globe. The following is from our conversation.

IN 2015, GREY2K USA WORLDWIDE[1] RELEASED THE FIRST COMPREhensive report on commercial dog racing in the United States, thanks to a grant provided by the ASPCA. Titled *High Stakes: Greyhound Racing in the United States,* the eighty-page report includes facts and statistics gathered as a result of research conducted over a thirteen-year period.[2] Facts include:

- Greyhounds begin racing at eighteen months of age, and race until they are three or four.
- Racing dogs generally compete every four days.
- There are an estimated 300 greyhound breeding facilities in the United States; female greyhounds are artificially inseminated and have average litter sizes of 6.5.
- Since 2008, 11,722 greyhound injuries—including 3,000 broken legs—have been documented nationwide; other injuries include fractured skulls, broken necks, and electrocution.
- In Florida, a racing greyhound dies every three days.
- Greyhounds are fed 4-D meat from diseased animals as a means of reducing cost.

Christine and Kelsey at St. John's Seminary in 1992, the day before the accident

I credit the inspiration for GREY2K USA to my dog Kelsey. Back in 1992, Kelsey and I were struck by a speeding train while out for a walk. Kelsey had managed to pull us slightly off course, thus preventing a head-on collision and saving our lives. When I awoke from a coma, my first words were, "How's Kelsey?"

Kelsey had suffered a broken hip in the accident but she lived until the age of fifteen. She stayed by my side and helped me through my rehabilitation and four years of evening law classes. She died a few days after I finished law school.

I made a promise while in the hospital that if I were ever able to walk again, I would devote my life to helping dogs and that Kelsey and I would do this work together. It is because of Kelsey that GREY2K USA exists. It is Kelsey who continues to motivate me to work for her fellow dogs every day.

At tracks around the nation, racing greyhounds routinely face the risk of serious injury or death at every turn. The most common injuries are broken legs, although tracks also report spinal cord seizures, paralysis, head trauma, puncture wounds, and death by heat stroke and cardiac arrest.

Racing greyhounds are kept individually confined for twenty or more hours a day inside small, barren cages. There are no toys for them and no playtime.

Beyond the confinement, injuries, and fatalities, in the eyes of the racetrack promoters, a dog is nothing more than a short-term investment. Even the fastest dogs can only race for a few years and during that time they are expected to generate enough profit to make up for the cost of their food and housing. At times, the pressure to generate profits leads to negligent care, outright cruelty, or the use of drugs to alter a dog's performance.

GREY2K USA continues to work to get to the root of this problem and close down dog track racing as quickly as possible. Since our foundation in 2001, the Association of Racing Commissioners International reports a 68 percent decline in wagering on dog racing. There were once nearly fifty tracks in fifteen states; now there are twenty-one facilities in seven states. Ending dog racing is really what we need to do because as long as greyhound racing continues, dogs will continue to suffer.

Chapter Seven
SARAH AND MATT

My niece Sarah loves dogs. Her dogs Sammy and Bow are an integral part of who she is, what she does, and decisions she has made throughout her young life. After working as a vet tech, she went on to become certified as an animal cruelty officer and animal control officer. "The work I do has everything to do with Bow and Sammy. Seeing their faces and knowing so many dogs don't have a bed to sleep in, or even a home, breaks my heart." This passion and love for dogs took Sarah to new heights—literally and figuratively—and, to tell that piece of her story, she introduced me to her friend Matt Kiener. Matt shared the story of his journey with dogs as well as the story of his organization called FlyPups.[1]

WHEN I BEGAN FLYING IN 1991, IT WAS A HOBBY. AT THE TIME, there were two great loves in my life: flying and my girlfriend, Jess.

Matt, Sarah, and Piper readying the plane
for a rescue flight
(Photo: Photography by Sharyn)

I had an engagement ring for Jess but promised myself that we wouldn't get engaged until I got my private pilot's license. Too many people had told me, "I always wanted to get my private pilot's license but then I got married," and that wasn't going to be the end of my flying story. Thankfully she waited, and the day after I got my private pilot's license, Jess and I got engaged.

Jess loved dogs, and in the early years of our marriage, we worked on a fifty-acre farm in New Jersey. Surrounded by all this beautiful land and having the ability to work from home, there was no reason for us not to get a dog.

I didn't grow up with dogs and at the time was under the misconception that a rescue dog would be a problem. My belief was that bad dogs ended up in rescues, and that if you wanted a good healthy dog you had to buy it. So that is what we did. The first dog we got was a beagle puppy we named Squire.

Squire is now fourteen years old and he is my best friend and constant companion. He has made me smile more than any human being I can think of and through him I have learned what it means to truly love a dog.

So now I had three great loves in my life: Jess, flying, and dogs.

Jess understood my passion for flying because she too had a passion: training horses who had outlived their racing career for Three-Day Eventing, an equestrian triathalon where a horse and rider compete in dressage, cross-country, and show jumping.

All equestrian events carry some risk. I wanted to support Jess with her work and also wanted to be able to do more than just yell "Call 911!" if there was ever an emergency at one of her events, so I decided to train as an EMT. At one of my EMT classes, I met a young woman who introduced me to her sister Sarah. Sarah is a unique individual in many respects and she also shared my love of flying and dogs.

About that time, a friend called and said he had committed to a dog flight but wasn't able to do it. He wanted to know if I could help. I had no idea what he was talking about so he explained that there were five six-week-old shepherd-beagle-English foxhound mix puppies being rescued from a high-kill shelter in North Carolina. I would fly the third and last leg of that trip to bring the puppies from New Jersey to their final destination in New York State.

The day the plane arrived at Sky Manor Airport in Pittstown, New Jersey, Jess and I met the plane and the puppies. Since my attention needed to be on flying, I needed someone along who could handle the puppies should something happen in-flight. Since Sarah loves to fly and is well trained and capable with puppies, I knew she would be a good person to have along for the ride.

We flew the puppies from New Jersey to New York State. On arrival at the airport, we brought the puppies to the FBO (fixed-base operation) where we were met by the people from the rescue group.

The puppies were permitted to run around in the FBO while we got organized. At one point, I needed paperwork from the airplane. Just before opening the door to walk out, I looked down at a puppy who had left her siblings and followed me.

I picked her up, looked in her eyes, and jokingly said, "You want to come home with me?" She licked my face so I did the only logical thing I could think of: I called my wife, and when she asked how it was going, I laughed and said, "Great. I'm bringing one home."

"Are you serious?" she asked.

"Yes," I said. "I don't have a choice."

There is a joke amongst our community that a mission has "gone bad" when the pilot adopts one of the dogs. So my first rescue mission was a mission gone bad. In reality, it was a mission that changed my life.

There are days when you feel something significant has happened in your life. Most days, you may change a degree or two but some days you experience a fifteen- or twenty-degree change. This was one of those days.

At the time, I had a small two-seater plane, so if I wanted to do this work, it would mean getting a bigger plane. The plane I needed was a Piper Saratoga, which cost ten times more than my current plane. To make it happen, I needed to stay focused. On the flight home, I named the puppy Piper, knowing that every time I said her name it would keep me focused on my goal.

I didn't want to force anything on Squire since he ruled the roost. Squire had always been more interested in the human at the end of a leash than the dog so I needed to make sure Squire remained happy and comfortable around Piper

Squire welcomed Piper as much as could be expected. Squire was ten at the time and since he and the puppy had very different energy levels, we let Squire walk or run around the farm while Jess took Piper for a hike. They both slept on our bed and everybody settled in and was happy.

Six months later, I bought the Piper Saratoga.

In the meantime, I began to see what was involved in—as well as the demand for—this work. I was getting calls from people telling me they had a litter of dogs but if I couldn't be there by the end of the week, the dogs were going to be destroyed.

Finding myself in some difficult situations and beginning to realize I needed help to make this happen, I got together with my wife, Sarah, and two other friends, Buck and Steve, and formed FlyPups with the intent of trying to rescue as many dogs as feasible by transporting them from desperate situations to non-kill shelters where they can be nurtured and prepared for adoption.

Sarah and I did most of the legwork in the beginning. We found an attorney who was passionate about our mission and volunteered to handle the paperwork for our 501(c)3 to make us an official non-profit organization.

Finding rescue missions is never difficult. What can be difficult is finding the time and the funding. I currently work as a property manager seven days a week but am still able to do a few flights every month. Every round-trip flight from New Jersey to North Carolina costs approximately $600. This is a bigger plane and it costs more to fly, so funding flights is an ongoing effort.

The flip side of having a bigger plane is I can transport more dogs. I typically fly a minimum of six dogs but prefer a dozen or more on each flight.

Most of our rescues are from southern states where there are more high-kill shelters. There is one shelter in North Carolina that has a 92.4 percent mortality rate. More dogs would make it to no-kill shelters and forever homes if they could be transported, but getting the dogs from here to there is often the biggest obstacle.

Thankfully, there are many people who transport dogs using relays or big vans for long hauls. However, some dogs are too fragile and a drive like that wouldn't be in their best interest.

Flying dogs whenever possible is the way to go because dogs transport so easily by air. They are almost always asleep by the time we get to altitude and the flight, which typically only takes a few hours, is so much easier on them than a long multiday car ride.

On a typical rescue mission, I am just the pilot. Finding dogs homes and making other plans is all arranged by the shelters. Sarah is integral in the smooth operation of our missions. Between her love of flying and dogs, she is the perfect combination for the work we do.

I got a call once to pick up twenty-seven Chihuahuas in North Carolina. Three found homes before I got there so I only had twenty-four Chihuahuas to transport. The dogs had been living with fourteen other dogs in an elderly couple's home. The wife had passed and the husband was on oxygen and in a wheelchair. The county was going to destroy them because they simply didn't have room for all of them. A Chihuahua advocate called me and I said, "I'm on my way. "

When I landed with the Chihuahuas there were several vans waiting for the dogs along with reporters and TV cameras. They surrounded the plane when I taxied onto the ramp. It was great to see all the excitement but, more importantly, it enabled all the Chihuahuas to be adopted almost immediately. A few dogs had health issues that delayed their adoption but they, too, went to forever homes as soon as they were able.

I once got a call about a Great Dane in Maryland that needed to get to Ohio. Typically, I don't do a rescue flight for just one dog but it was amazing to see how it came together. First, we learned of four dogs in Ohio: three needed to come to New Jersey and one needed to get to Florida.

After flying to Maryland to pick up the Great Dane, we flew to Ohio and picked up the four dogs. Three came to New Jersey and the one remaining dog flew to Florida with me. In Florida, I picked up fourteen dogs and then a fifteenth dog in Virginia on the way home. One dog came back to New Jersey but the other fourteen went to Reading, Pennsylvania, where they were trained as veteran service dogs. On that flight, we not only saved dogs, we also helped eight veterans. Those are golden days.

One of my most memorable calls was about a pit bull who had been used as a bait dog for dog fighting. A police officer had found the dog lying in a ditch by the side of the road, and a surgeon donated his time and skills. The community in Pennsylvania rallied and volunteers really got behind this dog. There were a lot of extraordinary measures taken for this pit bull.

The policeman named the dog Radar and he really was the sweetest dog you can imagine. When I got the call, Radar had already been through about a year of surgeries and healing and needed to be flown from Pennsylvania to Ohio where an animal behaviorist had agreed to donate his time to continue training and working with Radar.

Flying into the airport to pick up Radar, there were about thirty people who had come to see him off. It was very emotional and extremely touching. Since there hadn't been a lot of people who had handled Radar, they all wanted to make sure I was properly introduced to him since I would be the one introducing Radar to the behaviorist in Ohio.

I got down on the ground and Radar took off running towards me. He raced right up to me and engulfed my nose with his tongue.

That is one of the coolest things about what I do. The dogs know you are there to help them and that you are bringing them to a better place. They just know. Radar knew, and Chuck the behaviorist had such success with Radar that he now uses him to train other dogs.

One of the roughest transports I have ever done was following a call I got from a woman in North Carolina. She had learned of a man who had a bunch of dogs chained up outside and one of the dogs had a litter of puppies.

This was in the vicinity of the high-kill shelter with the 92.4 percent mortality rate. The woman knew with the last litter, the man had taken the puppies to the shelter and they had been destroyed. That was fine by this man. What wasn't fine, in his mind, was the disapproving look he felt he got when he brought the puppies to the shelter. With the new litter, he decided to put the puppies in his basement. His reasoning was that by waiting for the puppies to get a little older, he could then take them to the shelter without judgment or any disapproving glares. When the woman approached the man about taking the dogs, he was fine with it. He didn't care about the puppies and was just waiting to eventually take them to the shelter anyway.

When I got the call, the puppies were four or five months old and had spent that entire time confined in this man's cold, damp dirt-floor basement, living in their own feces and urine. The puppies' first trip to the

Sarah with Squire and Matt with Piper. Relaxing on the ground is Apple, Matt's boss's dog, who lives on the farm with Matt, Jess, Squire, and Piper.
(Photo: Photography by Sharyn)

vet was also the first time they had ever seen the light of day. They kept cowering and were so afraid. Despite being on leashes, they kept trying to run under the car to hide.

When I arrived with the plane it took us over an hour to get the six puppies on the plane. Normally when we are loading the dogs up at the airport, the dogs understand it's a good thing. But that particular batch of dogs was tough. I saw how afraid and hurt they were. I knew they were going someplace better but they didn't know that. They needed to be reassured. By the time we landed, they had begun to understand they were out of that place and that things were finally going to be better for them.

Much of the success of every flight can be credited to the group or organization who arranges the flight. Every step of the way requires a lot of communication and coordination. For example, just one small aspect of my transporting the dogs is knowing the size and weight of each dog. This way I can calculate the size and exact layout of the crates in my plane to determine how many dogs I can bring back.

One of the organizations I have worked with is Home for Good Dog Rescue. When they commit to a dog, they commit to a dog. If the dog needs medical care, it gets medical care. They are extremely organized and their flights are well coordinated on both ends. When I arrive in South Carolina, I am met by their local staff and volunteers who unload the supplies I bring down. They then help load the pups on the plane for transport to New Jersey. After the short flight, staff and volunteers in New Jersey are quick to unload and process the pups so they can spend the night, if possible, in a foster home. It is an easy, effortless transition for everyone, especially the dogs.

I love aviation and I love dogs so to be able to combine the two has been amazing. To know I am saving these dogs from being destroyed and bringing them to a loving home, possibly helping a veteran, and bringing people the same joy and love I have been given by Squire and Piper is a win-win-win situation.

HOME FOR GOOD
DOG RESCUE

After hearing about Home For Good Dog Rescue from Matt at Fly-Pups, I contacted them and several weeks later found myself sitting in their office in Berkeley Heights, New Jersey. They are a wonderful organization whose mission is to rescue dogs from high-kill shelters in the South, nurture them in their network of foster homes, and ultimately get them into loving homes for good. The following is from my conversation with the founders, staff, and several volunteers from Home for Good Dog Rescue.[1]

"THIS ALL BEGAN AFTER MY DOG, MANCHESTER, WAS HIT AND killed by a car five years ago," explained Toni Turco, one of the founders

(L to R) Home for Good Junior Ambassadors Rachel, Nora, and Anna

of Home for Good Dog Rescue (HFGDR), a 100 percent foster-based non-profit located in New Jersey. "At the time, I had been working on Wall Street for over twenty years. After Manchester died, I began working with a rescue organization and that, ultimately, was the beginning of HFGDR."

Rich Errico, co-founder and treasurer of HFGDR, added to the story. "I had been working on Wall Street for twenty-five years.

Shortly after Toni Ann started volunteering for the rescue organization, she called to ask if I wanted to help. Soon we were both volunteering, and within six months, Toni Ann was in charge of their adoptions and I was in charge of their spay and neuter program.

"We volunteered for several years and learned a lot. Then one day while sitting in Toni Ann's dining room with a couple of other volunteers, we started talking about starting our own rescue organization." In August 2010, HFGDR was started.

"In the beginning," Rich explained, "it was Toni Ann, six volunteers, and me doing adoption events out of Toni Ann's living room. Today we have over 160 volunteers and seventy foster families and have helped over 3,700 dogs find their fur-ever homes.

"Eventually our jobs got in the way of doing rescue work so we both retired from Wall Street. It is the best thing I have ever done in my life. I had to make adjustments to my lifestyle and probably work over 100 hours a week now but I wouldn't trade it for the world. When the day is over, you know you made a difference to a family or a dog and that is something you can't put a price tag on."

Dogs are rescued from South Carolina and Georgia, which are both overflowing with unwanted dogs on the brink of being euthanized. The dogs are transported by van or on volunteer pilot rescue flights to New Jersey, where they are taken in by volunteers who bathe and feed them. An HFGDR veterinary technician thoroughly examines each dog before it is paired with a foster family while awaiting adoption into a loving home.

Rich said, "Every year, we take a group of volunteers and staff down South. One of the first things I tell them is that we are going to be there for four or five days and visit up to ten shelters and see thousands of dogs. I explain that we can only save about 100 dogs and even though when we leave most of the rest will be put down, they can't dwell on that. The only way to keep your sanity is to focus on the ones we save, not the ones we left behind. I have never seen a volunteer or staff member come back from that trip and not be affected in some way."

Knowing that young people are the future of rescue work—and their organization—HFGDR started a Junior Ambassador Program. "On our most recent trip," Rich said, "we spent ten days down South and the girls were up every morning by 6:00 or 6:30. We never had to tell them what to do. They would begin cleaning kennels or socializing the dogs. They even cooked breakfast one morning. Their parents should be very proud because they are amazing young women and we are hopeful they will continue working with us."

Rich then introduced me to three young women: Anna and Rachel, both fifteen, and Nora who is fourteen. They each told me about their experience on the Junior Ambassador Program trip that summer. We'll begin with Anna's story.

Two years ago, my family adopted a Chihuahua mix from Home For Good Dog Rescue as a friend for our schnauzer. At the time, I didn't know anything about volunteering but my friend Rachel started fostering dogs, and when I asked her about it, she told me about Home for Good Dog Rescue.

I started volunteering about a year ago and this summer got to take part in the Junior Ambassador trip. It was my first trip down South and it was life changing.

We visited a lot of different shelters and even saw backyard breeding where breeders can keep over twenty breeds of dogs in chicken wire enclosures. Unaltered males and females of the same breed are kept together in a cage and the dogs are rarely, if ever, allowed out of their enclosure. In addition to the claustrophobic conditions, the dogs don't always have access to clean water or shade despite temperatures most days being well over 100 degrees. It was an eye-opening experience and made me understand the importance of rescue work and responsible breeding.

We visited the Aiken County Shelter but it was shut down since they didn't have the room to take in any more animals. There were over 600 animals in eighty pens and the smell was unimaginable. We pulled about twenty from that shelter, which is a lot for us, but we knew that day after day they were euthanizing dogs.

Every day we did hands-on work with the dogs. Every dog was covered with fleas and ticks so we began by bathing and grooming them and giving them flea and tick preventative. Then we spent time nurturing and socializing them.

We all had to pick a project dog while we were down there and I chose a litter of five Lab mix puppies. They were the cutest dogs in the entire world—and scheduled to be euthanized that day. All were adopted soon after we got them to New Jersey.

This trip changed me and the things I experienced will stay with me in the coming years as I pursue my career goal of becoming a veterinarian.

Next, Nora shared her perspective.

My family loves dogs and while we considered adopting a rescue dog we ended up getting our two Maltese from a breeder. A few years later, we began talking about getting another puppy and discovered Home For Good Dog Rescue. Since we were unsure whether we wanted a permanent pet we decided to try fostering.

We welcomed our first foster in August 2012 and, since then, we have had over 100 fosters in our home and also adopted our own dog, Otis, from Home for Good.

Otis was a seven-week-old, six-pound almond-eyed fluffball when Home for Good found him in a pen with his sibling in an outside pen in the pouring rain. Otis got very sick and needed a blood transfusion to make it through the first night. After being transported to New Jersey, he still had so many parasites that it took another three weeks of treatment before we could adopt him.

I began volunteering for Home for Good and was given the opportunity of a lifetime: to go on the Junior Ambassador trip.

My first project dog was a dog named Gump. When I first saw him, he was lying down on a cold bed and I thought he was an older, lethargic dog. However, after carefully picking him up and taking him outside, I soon discovered he was an energetic, fun-loving twelve-week-old puppy—actually the youngest puppy at the shelter—who loved to jump and play and had plenty of kisses for everyone!

Since one of the puppies in the same pen as Gump broke out with Parvovirus, they had to watch Gump for signs of the disease, thus delaying his transport in New Jersey. Luckily, Gump never got Parvovirus and one month later, Home for Good transported him to New Jersey.

Gump was adopted two weeks later by a family with three children and a 110-pound Lab. The family arranged for a trainer but, in October, they returned Gump because he had tried to bite the mom and had also gotten into a fight with the Lab.

I began to foster Gump at our house once again. Gump was now fifty-five pounds and covered in scratches and cuts from the fight. He was much more protective and acted differently. We immediately began training, and about a week later a couple saw him at an event and adopted him. However, the man brought him back in November because he was allergic to Gump.

I fostered Gump for about another month before he finally found his forever home on a farm where he runs and plays with a lovely little girl and a few doggie friends. It warms my heart every day to think that he now has a family who loves him dearly.

I have gone on two Junior Ambassador trips and they were both completely different experiences. The first year, we were always on the go. We left our hotel by 8:00 a.m. and would be at different shelters or foster homes all day long. It gave me the opportunity to see a lot of shelters and the conditions in different facilities and also to learn more about the situation dogs face down South. While some dogs are very well-maintained, there is still a high euthanasia rate and some counties didn't have an animal control.

Going down to the shelters made me realize how important the Junior Ambassador Program is and how important it is for our generation to do what it can to save animals in need. Not every dog in a shelter gets adopted or is with a foster and not all can be saved. That is why a rescue like Home for Good is so vital to help save the lives of these innocent animals.

And finally, Rachel shared her experience.

My family always wanted a dog but between our school, sports, and travel schedules, we felt it wouldn't be fair to the dog. Last summer, we decided to start fostering because we knew if we were away or there was a problem, the foster coordinator would help us find another foster family.

We decided we would foster a few dogs over the summer but didn't want to foster any during the school year. We ended up fostering the entire school year, with only a two-week break. In the past year, my family has fostered fifty-eight dogs.

The following year, I was invited on the Junior Ambassador trip. I couldn't believe I was being given such an amazing opportunity.

On our way to a shelter in Georgia, Toni Ann began telling us about a husky named Zeus. She said when he was rescued the shelter described him as a bag of bones who was so weak that he was unable to stand. When we arrived, he had been there for about a week. Although he was still very underweight, he had gained enough to support himself. I chose Zeus as my project dog.

Some dogs at shelters are scared and hide in the corner when you walk through, but most of them are so desperate for attention that they jump on the fence of their pen and bark to get a person's attention. But Zeus was different. He was relaxed, his tail wagging. His face looked happy and, even though they said he had gained weight, you could see every bone in his body.

I learned Zeus had been with a family with a lot of other dogs. All the dogs were chained outside and the family just moved them around their property. While the shelter wanted to get the dogs, legally they couldn't touch them. It wasn't until the family moved and let the dogs loose that the shelter was able to step in. Since Zeus wasn't able to get up, it was easy for the shelter to get him. The shelter was still trying to locate the other dogs.

Home for Good began to oversee Zeus's medical care. He had mange, skin problems, a severe case of fly strike, and cataracts in his right eye. He also had an indentation and wound on his face and there were flies swarming around the wound. Thankfully, he was heartworm negative, which was unbelievable considering he had been tied up outside all day.

We pulled most of the dogs from a shelter in Aiken. They had so many dogs, pen after pen of gorgeous dogs who, I am sure, were put down the next day. Up here, they would be adopted in a minute.

I have been asked countless times if it was hard to leave the dogs behind. There were so many dogs that would have made a family really happy, but we couldn't take them all. I remember what some of them did or looked like. It keeps me up at night when I think that they could have been loved if they had only been given a second chance.

But there are other dogs and stories—ones with happier endings. There was a brother-and-sister pair of shepherd mix dogs named Tarzan and Jane who had been found in a dump with their mom. The mother had been put down at the shelter because she was too wild. Tarzan and Jane had never had any human contact and were extremely scared when they were taken by the shelter.

We arrived about a month after they were rescued and Tarzan was still terrified of people. We worked with him while we were down there and when he arrived in New Jersey, I fostered him. The wound on Zeus's nose was healed but the bone in his face was still smashed. His skin looked better but his fur was still wiry from a lack of nutrition.

Initially, Tarzan was afraid of Zeus, but after a few hours, Tarzan calmed down and they became best friends. I have never seen two dogs bond so quickly. Fortunately for Zeus, but unfortunately for Tarzan, they were only together for a short time because a week later Zeus was adopted by a family who has been rescuing huskies for twenty years. It was amazing to see him with his new family and know he was going to a better place.

I am still fostering Tarzan. Even though he isn't nearly as happy now as he was when Zeus was around, his early fear of people has gotten so much better. He sleeps in my bed every night and the other day when I came home he ran down the stairs and gave me a big kiss.

Seeing the progress the dogs make is amazing, especially now that I have seen where they come from.

"This is an important part of the process," Rich explains. "It's important for them to see all aspects of the work we do. When they do adoption events up here, the dogs have been bathed and groomed. But down there it's not a cute adoption event. They see the dismal conditions where the dogs came from and, from seeing that final piece, they get a full appreciation of the work we do and how far the dogs have actually come."

Since HFGDR doesn't have a kennel facility, they sometimes have to leave a lot of dogs in shelters that require medical attention. To address that, they purchased a ten-acre piece of property in Aiken, South Carolina, that will house two buildings: the Almost Home canine wellness center and a retail space that will provide boarding and grooming services. Their goal is to have the boarding and grooming subsidize the rescue portion and make the entire operation self-supporting. There are future plans to open a small clinic that would provide veterinary as well as spay and neuter services to the local population.

"With this center, we will be able to treat dogs for conditions such as mange and heartworm and get them back to a good point of health before bringing them to New Jersey. It will allow us to save a lot more dogs and get them adopted," Rich said.

"When you see a family happily walk away with a new dog or puppy, you realize this is about so much more than doing rescue work. It is about saving a dog's life and uniting it with a family, but it is also about completing the family unit. We don't only save dogs, we help families as well."

Chapter Eight
SHIRLEY

Shirley and I were in the same Brownie troop and went to the same grammar school and high school. She was full of life and laughter, and had the most beautiful long red hair I had ever seen. In 2014, I turned sixty and decided it was time for me to cross "Learn to swim" off my Life List. Knowing Shirley was a swim instructor, I contacted her. That summer, thanks to my friend Debbie, who offered us the use of her pool, and the patience and guidance of Shirley, I learned to swim and learned of Shirley's great affection for her dogs.

GROWING UP, WE HAD STRAYS DOGS IN OUR NEIGHBORHOOD WE snuck food to since my mother wouldn't allow us to have a dog. However, my attraction to dogs changed when I was six and a dog bit me in the face at a birthday party. A year later, a St. Bernard bit me and I was rushed to the hospital for plastic surgery on my face. After that, I was afraid of dogs.

When I was twenty, I got married and my best friend LeeAnn gave me the perfect wedding gift: a kitten. I had always loved cats and was absolutely thrilled. Even though I was still afraid of dogs, my husband wanted a dog. One day he brought home a mixed-breed dog someone at work had given him. We named the dog Herbie.

I didn't know anything about having a dog, and

Shirley and the Burd Dogs
(Photo: Photography by Sharyn)

since they weren't my favorite animal, my husband took the lead in caring for Herbie. In the '70s, people didn't crate their dogs, so Herbie became very attached to me. Whenever I left the house, he would scratch at the door to get to me, so my husband decided to keep him outside.

I instinctively felt Herbie should be in the house with us but my husband took him outside and chained him up. Herbie spent his days either in the garage on a cold cement floor or outside, even in the coldest weather. It tore my heart apart to see him out there, so on cold days I would rush home from work to get Herbie into the house. Thankfully, my husband allowed him to come into the house at night and sleep between us in our bed. I often wondered if Herbie was confused why he was treated so differently at night than he was during the day.

The SPCA came by once because Herbie was barking all day while we were at work but nothing changed. It was very difficult for me, but I simply wasn't strong enough to stick up for Herbie or myself.

Herbie was a high-energy dog and would have done really well on a farm where he could run and get some of that energy out. But this was his home and I loved spending time with him so I signed us up for obedience classes. Herbie was a model student and would look at me, eyes glowing and tail wagging, waiting for my next command. He simply wanted to please me. The classes were a fun way to get his energy out, reinforce our love for one another, and, most importantly, taught me about the type of relationship that was possible between a dog and me.

One day, my husband and I were at a mall when we saw a mixed-breed husky. We adopted her and named her Ginger. My husband felt having Ginger would help us (or at least me) not feel so guilty about keeping Herbie outside all day but how does it help when you now have *two* dogs tied up all day in the backyard? I continued to struggle between what my husband was doing and what I felt was the right thing to do. For years, I carried a deep sadness in my heart anytime I thought about Herbie and Ginger and the way they were treated in their early days in our home.

Then I got pregnant. Now I had a baby, two dogs, and no idea how to handle all three of them. When my son was old enough to climb up and reach for the dog, Herbie got snappy so my husband immediately built a shed and kept both dogs outside 24/7. Even though they were in the same doghouse together, at night when it was really cold, I would hear them crying, wanting to come in. I begged my husband to let them in the house but he said he didn't want the house to get dirty from the dogs.

It was absolute torment. I remember bringing food out to them, tears streaming down my face, as I turned to walk back into the house. In those moments, Herbie and Ginger looked at me with such compassion and understanding that I know they understood that I, like them, was in a difficult position.

Ultimately, the fact that we were sharing the same reality in many ways brought the three of us even closer. When my son turned four, I began taking Herbie, Ginger, and my son for really long walks every day. The dogs loved going for walks with me and we were growing closer and closer every day.

When Herbie turned sixteen, we found out he had cancer. The vet said at some point he would have to be put down so I took him home and spent as much time with him as possible. We continued to go for walks but also began sitting in a field together, just Herbie and me. As I held him, I apologized for all that had happened, for not being strong enough for both of us and especially for not doing what I wanted to do over the years. Sometimes I held him so tight that it felt like we were one being; in those moments, there was a connection I never before knew existed. In those precious moments with Herbie, I was filled with the most wonderful feeling and came to intuitively understand and accept that Herbie would pass, I would get divorced, and that, through it all, everything was going to be fine.

The easiest way for me to explain the feeling is if you have ever meditated. There are days you feel so connected to God (or Source or Spirit or whatever you want to call it). That is exactly how it felt, and at the end, there were so many times I connected like that with Herbie. I cherished every moment we spent together.

When the time came for Herbie to be put down, I had no idea what was about to happen. The vet said I could come in and hold Herbie, which seemed like a good idea, but my husband discouraged me from going in. He said he would never want to see anything like that so, based on my husband's advice, I decided not to go in with the vet and Herbie. Instead, I sat in the next room sobbing, waiting for the vet to come tell me Herbie had passed. To this day, I wish I could have held him to his very last moment.

Several months after Herbie passed, we got another dog, a Shih Tzu we named Cassie. From the first day she came into our lives, Cassie was my best friend. Being a small dog, I could take her with me everywhere I went. We were inseparable until Cassie turned three and my husband and I separated and my son and I moved in with my parents. Living with my parents meant the dogs had to stay with my husband. Twice a day, on my way to and from driving my son to school, I stopped at the house and took care of the dogs. It was heart-wrenching to leave them every day.

After the divorce, my son and I moved out of my parents' house. I also met a wonderful man named Kim and slowly my life and circumstances began to change. Not only had I found a happy ending to my story with Kim, but slowly, over time, all of my dogs were once again living under my roof.

Kim loved dogs, but when we met he didn't have any. My ex-husband wanted to keep Ginger and I wanted to keep Cassie. Cassie had just had puppies and my ex also wanted one of her puppies. I gave him one but, a few months later, he gave it back saying he couldn't handle it so we gave the puppy to Kim's mother, Mabel.

Night after night, I would lie in bed and think about Ginger, knowing she was probably tied up outside all alone. I finally called my ex-husband and said we needed to talk. We met at a restaurant and I could see he was nervous as I walked to the table. As soon as I sat down I said, "I want Ginger." He looked at me, relieved, and said, "Okay." Ginger came to live with us that same day.

Kim and I married and built a home near his mother on the family's land. I was thrilled to have Ginger back and she lived happily with Cassie and us in our new home until one night, about two years later, when she died peacefully in her sleep.

We offered Cassie the opportunity to be with Ginger's body before we buried her in our yard. She spent a few minutes sniffing and saying goodbye to Ginger then walked away. I got the feeling that Cassie had accepted Ginger's passing and didn't feel the need to keep looking back.

Cassie was such a sweet, smart dog. The following year, after finding a championship breeder, we decided to breed her again. At one point, we had four generations of her family living together under our roof: Cassie, Hey Jude, Penny Lane, and Honey Pie. Every dog we have now is a descendant of Cassie.

When Cassie turned sixteen, we had a Sweet Sixteen party for her. The local newspaper did a story about the party, calling it "a howling success"—and it truly was. Everyone brought presents for Cassie and we had doggie ice cream and two bone-shaped cakes: one for the dogs and one for the humans. Some people lived over an hour away but everybody came with their dogs—many of whom were Cassie's pups. Everyone filled out a tag with their pet's name and birthdate so people could figure out if their dogs were littermates. Looking around and realizing that Cassie was responsible for most of the dogs in the yard and seeing the joy they were giving their owners was very emotional.

Two years later, Cassie passed at the age of eighteen. Over the course of her lifetime, Cassie was a mother to twenty-three puppies and grandmother to another twenty-three. When we first bred Cassie, I had never witnessed a dog being born and was extremely nervous. I read, asked questions, and learned everything I could. Then all of a sudden, it was time and I was the one helping deliver her puppies. I did it—and then I did it a bunch more times. We had lots of healthy puppies born in our home and every time was just as exciting as the first.

When you take that wet puppy, cut the cord, and assist the mother to clear its nostrils and get it dry and warm—honestly, there is nothing like it. When you get that hands-on experience, you become incredibly close to the puppies and their mother. Sometimes an inexperienced mother doesn't have a clue what she needs to do with the puppy or she is tired or overanxious. I have seen the grandmother of the puppy step in and assist with the first puppy being born. When she does, the mother suddenly realizes her role.

The miracle of life never ceases to amaze me. It's the middle of the night and you haven't slept but the mother is looking at you as she's giving birth. Her eyes are filled with pain so you quietly and gently hold her belly during contractions and sing softly to her. There is nothing you wouldn't do for that mother. Then, as the puppy begins to nurse and the mother looks up at you with pride and love it's a magical moment. There is a very special bond—especially between the mother and me—that is difficult to explain. I cherish that moment every time it happens and it always reminds me of the birth of my own son and how much I cherish that moment in time.

For the first twelve weeks, puppies are like sponges and I believe it is my responsibility to make every puppy the best it can be for its new home and family. We have been lucky since most of our puppies go to friends, relatives, or family, but there are still tears of both sadness and joy when they leave to go to their new homes.

My son, BT, and his wife, Michelle, have two Shih Tzus who are both descendants of Cassie. His dogs have a very loving and happy home and I am extremely proud of BT, Michelle, and our "grandchildren." I can always see the spark in BT's eyes when he talks to his dogs and I am immensely proud that, despite his early exposure to having a dog, he grew up knowing right from wrong when it comes to caring for an animal.

Today we have Penny Lane (the oldest at fourteen), Honey Pie, Winston, and Day Tripper, who just had puppies. We still only go to a championship breeder and Cassie, Hey Jude, and Penny Lane are all certified therapy dogs.

Hey Jude, Penny Lane, and I were part of a special program at a school in our area. The program, called ROCK (Reading Out-loud Creates Knowledge), involved third-grade students reading out loud to dogs.

Several TV stations and newspapers interviewed the students, teachers, and parents about the program. When they asked the students what they liked about the program, many said, "The dogs don't laugh at me if I make a mistake when I read." The dogs are a non-judgmental audience and allow the students to read at their own pace and ability.

One mother said her son always enjoyed having someone read to him. "Reading on his own was something he felt forced to do but now, with the dogs, he wants to read."

Over time, an entire program was devised around the dogs that included reading, writing, artwork, and other activities. On holidays, I dressed the dogs in outfits. Whether it was Valentine's Day, Thanksgiving, Halloween, or another celebration, we had an appropriate outfit. The dogs would strut into the school excitedly as they walked down the hall to the classroom. The students loved the program and the dogs, and I still have the thank-you notes they wrote to Hey Jude, Penny Lane, and me.

When we started working in the ROCK program, Hey Jude was already a certified therapy dog but I was still training Penny Lane. The students practiced sit, stay, and come with Penny Lane and felt like they were part of her ultimately getting her therapy dog certification.

Both breeders I have worked with over the past twenty-five years have told me that some dogs are more spiritual than others. Penny Lane had a spiritual quality about her—maybe because she was the oldest dog or maybe because that is who she was. I saw it firsthand with Kim's mom, Mabel.

When Mabel was in her eighties, she sold her house and built an addition onto our house. She and her three Shih Tzus (all descendants of Cassie) moved in with us so we could care for each other. Mabel fed, helped care for, and interacted with all the dogs every day. When she entered the room, all eyes were on her. If one of them wasn't feeling well or had puppies that needed extra TLC, Grandma was always there with open arms and a warm heart. She loved being with them and they adored her. After living with us for eight years, she passed at home after a short battle with cancer. Before she passed, I was blessed to witness the connection between her and Penny Lane.

Two weeks before Christmas, I put up a small Christmas tree that Kim's mom could see from her bed. She loved angels and I was hanging her angel ornaments on the tree when Kim came home from work. Knowing it was getting near the end, I told him it may be a good time to say anything he needed to say to his mom. Kim went and sat next to his mom, talking softly about when he was little and they played "This little piggy went to market" together. Mabel lay there with her eyes closed as Kim, his voice shaking, continued to quietly talk and reminisce and tell his mom repeatedly how much he loved her.

As Kim got up to leave the room, I decided to stay and finish decorating the tree. All the dogs went back downstairs with Kim, with the exception of Penny Lane. She kept pawing at the bed, insistent that she wanted to get up on it. That wasn't normal behavior for her. Since she wouldn't stop, I put her on a loveseat about three feet away from the bed. Immediately, she went to the edge of the loveseat and continued to insist that she wanted to be near Kim's mom. I finally picked her up and brought her over near Mabel. Since Mabel had become very sensitive to touch, I held Penny Lane there for a few minutes. When she finally settled down, I put her down and went back to decorating the tree. All at once, Penny Lane jumped up, ran over, and once again insisted on getting up on the bed. I walked over and Mabel had passed. Penny Lane continued to whine and bark, pawing to get up on the bed, so again, I picked her up to be near Mabel and immediately she calmed down. It was as if Penny Lane knew what had happened and wanted the chance to say goodbye to Mabel. The spiritual connection Penny Lane had with Mabel was unique and beautiful to witness.

I see that same connection beginning now with Winston. What is interesting is that when Winston was born there was a family who wanted to adopt him, but the day I delivered him, I had an instinctive feeling it wasn't the right home for him so I kept him. Now that I am older and more aware of the spiritual connection I have with some of my dogs, I realize that my intuitive feeling that day was probably my first connection of spirit with Winston.

As soon as I begin to meditate, even if he is outside or sleeping, Winston finds me, and when he does, he needs to be touching me the entire time. When I am able to connect to God (which is what I believe happens when we meditate), Winston sits and leans against me. The spiritual connection I experienced laying in the field with Herbie and saw between Mabel and Penny Lane I now have with Winston.

Ten years ago, I had another type of experience that helped me evolve and heal from something that happened with Herbie.

When Hey Jude was about twelve years old, she suddenly stopped eating and began vomiting. We took her to Dr. Sam, a local veterinarian who had the ability to do an on-site ultrasound (something other local veterinary hospitals weren't able to do).

Based on what we told him, Dr. Sam suspected Hey Jude had a blockage and, quite possibly, a tumor. He told us we could take her to another veterinary hospital about an hour away or he could open her up to try and determine what was going on. Since we both really liked and trusted Dr. Sam, we gave him permission to proceed.

Kim was extremely upset and decided to take a walk to calm down. Since it was after-hours, I appreciated the peace and quiet in the office as I sat and waited. Dr. Sam came out and asked if I wanted to see what he had found and, after suiting me up for surgery, he brought me in. Hey Jude was still sedated on the operating table and Dr. Sam showed me that she clearly had cancer. He said he could close her up and we could take her home and enjoy whatever time we had left with her, or he could put her down while she was still on the table. Another option, he said, was to take her to a large veterinary hospital about an hour away.

About that time, Kim came back. We were both in shock but decided to have Dr. Sam staple her up and rushed her to the other veterinary hospital. The hospital gave her a few days to regain her strength before performing surgery to remove what they could of the cancer. We thought that was the end of the cancer and took her home to heal. Instead, on a follow-up visit a few weeks later, the hospital told us the cancer was growing and suggested we begin chemotherapy. Since we didn't want to put her through that, we took her home.

Hey Jude grew weaker and weaker and finally we saw the look in her eyes. We decided to go back to Dr. Sam because he had been so wonderful to us and we wanted him to do it. I held her and it was a beautiful experience—and through that experience I was also able to heal the long-standing guilt and grief I had been carrying about not being there for my first dog, Herbie, when he was put down.

Ten years later, the feelings are still as strong and powerful as they were on that day. I am grateful for that experience because through it, I began to understand the importance of honoring the natural cycle of life and death, of allowing nature to take its course, and understanding if what you are doing is for you—or your dog.

My world, and my dogs' world, is the complete opposite of what it was years ago. Back then, the dogs mainly lived outside but now they are in my house, and in their first few weeks of life, in our bedroom. Back then, I was told that dogs were just animals, but through my experiences with our dogs, I have evolved to a point where our dogs are our kids and we treat them as such.

My dogs have helped me heal and I have become a more spiritual

(left to right) Penny Lane, Winston, Honey Pie
(top) Day Tripper
(Photo: Photography by Sharyn)

person because of my dogs. They have taught me lessons and led me to find answers to long-standing questions I had about myself and life. I have grown, changed, and evolved thanks to my dogs and I am forever grateful to and blessed by my dogs.

READING EDUCATION ASSISTANCE DOGS® PROGRAM

To learn more about programs for children reading to dogs, I reached out to Intermountain Therapy Animals (ITA), a non-profit organization whose mission is to enhance the quality of life through the human-animal bond. Their Reading Education Assistance Dogs® (R.E.A.D.®) Program improves children's reading and communication skills by employing a powerful method: reading to a dog, but not just any dog. R.E.A.D. dogs are registered therapy animals who volunteer with their owner/handlers as a team. The following is from a conversation I had with ITA's executive director, Kathy Klotz.

INTERMOUNTAIN THERAPY ANIMALS[1] WAS STARTED IN SEPTEMber 1993, and at the time was affiliated with The Delta Society (now Pet Partners[2]). While we have been independent since 2007, we still think Pet Partners is the best of the national therapy licensing organizations

because, like us, they focus on the whole relationship and advocate training the human end of the leash. With Pet Partners, therapy teams are retested every two years to ensure they still have the skills they need to be safe and effective. Their professional approach has also helped therapy animals gain credibility in medical settings.

In 1999, one of our board members, a nurse, called me and said, "Do you think the benefits we see working with children in hospitals would translate to reading?" As soon as she said it, it was one of those moments where you wonder why no one had thought of it before. Why didn't such a program already exist?

We started a pilot Reading Education Assistance Dogs (R.E.A.D.) program in November 1999 at the Salt Lake City Library. It was for four Saturdays and they were so thrilled with what they saw happening that we ended up on the front page of the *Wall Street Journal* before the four weeks were even up.

After that, we started getting calls from around the country so we began working on a training manual. In January 2000 we started the program in an elementary school, and last November we celebrated our fifteenth anniversary. We now have 5,000 registered therapy teams in all fifty states and fifteen other countries.

The two major venues for the program are elementary schools and libraries. While we have worked with many populations and age ranges, our focus is on kindergarten through third grade because we want children to get a strong foundation in reading. Studies have shown the importance of a student learning to read by fourth grade, not only for the sheer enjoyment of reading but also to help them academically, professionally, and economically throughout their life.

We didn't invent the concept of reading to a dog—people have been doing that for years—but we were the first to build a structure that employs therapy animals in a true literacy support program. R.E.A.D. has inspired a lot of imitators with children reading to dogs, but our hallmark is how we support the child's efforts. If the child gets stuck, obviously a dog can't help them past the problem, so a wrong pattern or difficulty can actually be perpetuated, or the child can feel frustrated. Therefore, our handlers are trained in how to support a child appropriately and use the dog in ways that support the students. Every handler is adept at speaking for their dogs and the kids believe the dogs aren't just listening but are actually riveted to the story. We have so many pictures of kids turning the book so the dog can see it. We can teach dogs to focus on a page, but what makes it effective is how the handler responds in a situation.

While making one of our first training videos, we filmed the ten-year-old son of one of the librarians. He didn't have a problem with his reading skills and, at the time, was reading a Harry Potter book to the dog. At one point while reading the book, the handler asked the boy if Lord Voldemort was a good guy or a bad guy. The boy told the handler and the handler turned to the dog and said, "Rover, he's a bad guy." Then they sat and talked about what makes someone a good or bad guy.

After the filming ended, they asked the boy what he liked the most and he said, "I really liked when Rover wanted to know about Lord Voldemort."

We had another handler who had a mini-dachshund she had taught to sneeze on command. One day, a fourth grader was reading and said, "And the ladies all had *bananas* in their hair."

The handler, knowing the girl had used the wrong word, gave the signal to Biscuit to sneeze. When she did, the handler said, "Biscuit is wondering why the ladies had bananas in their hair?"

The little girl stopped, looked at the book again, then turned to the dog and said, "Oh Biscuit, I'm sorry, they had *bandanas* in their hair." Turning to the handler, she said, "Boy, she really knows her stuff, doesn't she?"

Another reason the program works is because many children's learning difficulties in school aren't because of an intellectual deficiency. It's fear. As educator William Ayers said: "Fear can destroy intelligence." Even if you are reasonably intelligent, when the teacher calls on a student, their mind may go blank or they may be afraid to speak in front of the class.

The dog and handler are attentive, non-judgmental, and allow the child to proceed at their own pace. They create an atmosphere that is relaxing and has physiological benefits that carry over well beyond the moments when the child and dog are together. A study conducted with children in an oncology unit showed that those who spent one hour with a therapy dog needed less pain medication for eight hours afterwards. It is scientifically sound. Being with an animal floods your body with oxytocin and is one of the explanations behind people's attractions to animals.

We hear the same kind of comments from the children all the time: "The dog never laughs at me." "I stutter and the dog doesn't make fun of me." "My mom tells me to hurry up when I'm reading. The dog never does that." "If I make a mistake, the dog won't go tell my friends."

Parents tell us how their son or daughter goes home, talks about the program, and for the first time wants to find a book to read. One woman told us her son pulled up a chair and sat and read to a picture of his R.E.A.D. dog they had on their refrigerator.

The things we see and hear happen are amazing and the results are significant. The kids in our first pilot elementary school program spent one school year reading to the dogs. They were different ages and were there for different reasons. Some were struggling with reading, others were struggling with emotional or family issues, and for some English wasn't their first language. Despite their age or reason for being there, every single student went up two to four grade levels in reading skills that year.

The idea is to get a child to learn to love books and come back eager to read again. Oftentimes, it is one significant relationship with someone who pays attention and cares that allows learning to occur and allows the child to make incredible progress. In our program, that someone is a dog.

Chapter Nine
SHARI

My niece Kelly sent me a text: "Want to meet at Factory Fuel Co. for coffee?" Hmmm . . . let me think . . . a chance for a great cup of coffee, delectable pastries, and time with my niece? I couldn't get there fast enough. While waiting for our order, I noticed a cup on the counter that said "Donations for James's Service Dog." I asked the young woman behind the counter about it. "It's for my son. He's eight years old and has type 1 diabetes. We're trying to raise enough money to get him a diabetes alert dog." I knew nothing about type 1 diabetes or the dogs but I do now thanks to Shari, James, and Roman. Theirs is a beautiful and important story that I am both honored and blessed to bring to you.

FOR THE FIRST THIRTEEN YEARS OF MY LIFE, MY FAMILY ALWAYS had a dog. The last dog we had growing up was a yellow Lab named Susie who was the sweetest dog and the absolute love of our lives. When my brother, sister, or I walked into the room, Susie would smile and wag her tail, and it was comforting to know how much she loved us.

Roman

One day, while out with some friends, my dad came and found

me. He was a loving man but rarely cried. That day my dad was sobbing as he told me Susie had tried to jump over the gate in our kitchen, had a heart attack, and died.

I still remember how I felt at that moment. It felt like someone in our family had died. We all had a difficult time getting over the loss of Susie, so we never got another dog.

After I got married and had children, we were too busy to get a dog. Then, in December 2012, something happened that changed our lives and our minds.

For about a week, my son James was extremely sick and lethargic. He didn't want to eat but was extremely thirsty. Originally, I thought he had a really bad case of the flu, but by the end of the week he had lost ten pounds and was getting sicker. He was also drinking a ton of water. One night as I sat up with him, he just kept drinking water and vomiting so my husband and I decided it was time to get him to the emergency room.

I phoned my mom to tell her what was happening and before we hung up, she said, "I just hope it isn't diabetes." I didn't understand what she meant because diabetes had never crossed my mind.

Within minutes of arriving at the hospital, James was surrounded by nurses and hospital staff. When I looked at James, I began to panic because he looked like he was dying.

The doctor came in and said James's blood sugar was over 1,000 and that he had been hours away from dying. He also told me my son had type 1 diabetes.

Thinking I knew about diabetes, and confident we would be able to handle it, I asked the doctor if we could go home. The next day was James's birthday.

The doctor looked at me and said, "You are not going home. James is going to be in the hospital for a while." James was transported to another hospital.

Type 1 diabetes didn't run in our family and I didn't know anything about it. The first thing I learned was that I was familiar with type 2 diabetes, which is *very* different from what we were dealing with.

Type 2 diabetes (T2D) is a metabolic disorder where a person's body produces insulin but is unable to use it effectively. T2D is usually diagnosed in adulthood and does not always require insulin injections.

Type 1 diabetes (T1D) is an autoimmune disease where a person's pancreas stops producing insulin. It typically strikes in childhood, adolescence, or young adulthood and lasts a lifetime. To survive, people with T1D must take multiple injections of insulin daily or continually infuse insulin through a pump.[1]

After a two week-hospital stay, James came home. I continued to learn more about type 1 diabetes and how it impacted James, learning what he could and couldn't eat, how to monitor his levels, and that he would be dependent on insulin injections. I can't even look at a needle and couldn't believe I was now going to have to start giving my son injections.

One night, I had a dream that a dog was going to save James's life. When I woke up, I recalled the dream but thought it would be a family dog since I didn't know about diabetes alert dogs (DADs).

We rescued a three-month-old Lab mix named Lincoln. He was sweet, cute, and loved the kids but before long we began seeing signs of aggressive behavior. We didn't want to send Lincoln back to the shelter but we were concerned about the aggression and didn't know what to do. I started praying for guidance.

A few weeks later, a woman at my church told me about a friend of hers who had a child with type 1 diabetes. She said they were doing a fundraiser to get a service dog for the child. That was the first I ever heard of a service dog for type 1 diabetes. I connected with the woman on Facebook and began to follow their journey. In addition to being the mother of a child with type 1 diabetes, she was also a nurse and a huge help in explaining exactly what a diabetes alert dog does and how important they are to both the person with type 1 diabetes and their family.

Then it clicked. I understood my dream and began researching diabetes alert dogs.

Lincoln was still showing aggressive tendencies and we now had concerns whether he would get along with another dog. The problem was we were already attached to Lincoln. We wanted him to be where he was meant to be, so once again I started praying.

A few days later, a friend told me they were looking for a dog since they recently had to put theirs down. I told her about Lincoln and as soon as she met him she wanted him. Even with our concerns, it was hard to let Lincoln go but knowing he was going to an amazing family helped. We still visit Lincoln, and I believe I rescued Lincoln not for us but for that family.

As we continued to research service dogs, we found Brooks Labradors in Texas. We were impressed with everything we read about them but found out they had a four-year waiting list for a dog. The other option was to go down every month to train our dog along with them. Neither option worked for our family. We couldn't afford monthly flights back and forth to Texas, and we didn't want to wait four years to get a dog for James, so I asked them to refer us to someone.

They referred me to a woman named Debbie Kay who has been working with dogs and scent detection for years. Debbie said she would have someone call us and I hung up the phone thinking, "If it happens, it happens. If it doesn't, we will move on and figure something else out." Before talking to Debbie, every door was shut and every avenue was blocked, but after talking with her, things happened quickly and smoothly and everything began to fall into place.

Within a day, I got a call from Becky Causey, a breeder and DAD trainer in West Virginia. Becky said she had a dog already trained we could have immediately or we could have one from a litter that had just been born. The cost for the already-trained dog was between $20,000 and $25,000; the cost for a puppy depended on how much training Becky did and how much training we wanted to do.

When Becky told us the puppy had been born on January 7 I knew we were meant to have him because that's my birthday.

Becky and I talked for three hours about the dog, James, and our family. She said we could choose a name for the puppy so James and my husband picked Roman because they felt the puppy would be like a Roman soldier watching over James.

We went down to meet Roman and participate in four days of training. I was worried knowing James is eight and this was a big responsibility for him, but as soon as the training started, James did it all. He made sure Roman walked next to him, didn't eat food off the ground, sat when he told him to, and was focused on and aware of him. Roman was still a puppy and I knew it took a lot of concentration and work on both their parts, but James really took the initiative and he and Roman did great together. It was amazing to witness.

James working with Roman
the first time they met

James is so in love with Roman. We can't wait to bring him home. We initially wanted to do some of the training ourselves but, with four children, we decided it was wiser to allow Becky to continue working with and training Roman. We believe it is what is right for our family and for James, so we are doing everything we can to raise the money to bring Roman here.

Having Roman is going to be such a blessing. James has reached a point where the doctors are getting concerned. He is showing signs of puberty at eight, which the doctors feel is too young. They are watching him closely to see if any of this will impact his diabetes and to see if it could be a sign of something else.

James has been having a lot of highs and lows with his blood sugar. One week it is all lows, the next week it is all highs, which can cause damage to his internal organs. Like any parent, we want to keep his body strong and healthy.

The lows are another kind of worry. Many people die in their sleep from a low reading so nighttime is the scariest for my husband and me. Recently the doctor, after looking at our chart of his readings, asked us how many times we checked James at night. We realize we are doing a lot of nighttime checks but we are so scared. We would hate for that one time we thought he was fine to be when he is not. It's not fun having to test him all the time but it is what has to be.

For us, having Roman will be huge. He will be one more tool in letting us know how James is doing and will help us, and especially James, have a more normal life. James is really good at football and I want him to be able to have a chance to play in middle school or high school. I want him to be able to do things other kids do. Roman will bring us one step closer to James having that kind of life.

DIABETES ALERT DOGS AND DIABETES ALERT DOG ALLIANCE

To understand how a diabetes alert dog is trained and how it helps someone with type 1 diabetes, I turned to Becky Causey, the breeder raising and training Roman for James. Causey Labradors[1] has been breeding Labrador retrievers for over twenty years for both show and as service dogs, and their Labradors excel in scent detection work and medical detection as well as obedience and agility. Her story and journey with these dogs—and this disease—is fascinating.

MY GRANDFATHER BRED AND COMPETED WITH GERMAN SHORT-haired pointers and my father bred Brittanys. At age seventeen, I began competing with Brittanys but they love to run and run—all the time, all day long. I wanted to do activities like obedience, so two years later I transitioned to working with Labrador retrievers and have been working with and breeding them now for over twenty years.

I am a teacher by trade and trained dogs and taught obedience classes for years in my spare time. I was also boarding dogs

Becky with Daisy, a DAD
who belongs to her son Mac

and breeding Labs. When my children entered high school, I was busy breeding, showing, competing, and training dogs and finally decided to quit teaching and work with dogs full time.

A friend had created a workshop for diabetes alert dog (DAD) trainers. Because of my experience with dogs and as a teacher, she wanted me to attend and give her feedback.

I loved the workshop.

At the time, I had two friends whose children had type 1 diabetes. I watched the children grow up and knew all they and their parents went through. I knew the children could go from being completely fine to being in a life-or-death emergency in a matter of minutes. My initial thought was how wonderful it would be to help those families, and I couldn't wait to start training some of my younger dogs and puppies.

Being new at the DAD training, I knew there would be a learning curve and that my first DAD dog wasn't going to be perfect. I knew the more I trained, the more my skills would improve. The fact that someone's life might depend on this dog scared me and so I decided the first two dogs I trained would never be sold as a DAD.

The first dog I ever sold went to a little boy with type 1 diabetes. His mom, a single mother, also had a six-year-old daughter and was having a hard time making ends meet. Thankfully she had a wonderful church and family who fundraised, and the little boy got the dog just before his third birthday.

The day I delivered the dog to the family, the mom and I were reviewing the training guide and some last-minute details with the dog while the little boy played downstairs with his sister. When his mom called him upstairs, as soon as he came into the kitchen, the dog alerted on him.

The mom immediately said, "That can't be right. He ate right before you came over."

"This is all part of the training," I assured her. "Why don't you test him just to see."

As the mom began to test him, the dog continued to alert. The test results showed a reading of 68 (the ideal range is generally 81–120). The mom was astounded.

The following week, she called me, crying. "I had to call because I am freaking out right now. This dog just saved my son's life.

"We had lunch and I put him down for a nap. After naptime, we were going to drive into Pennsylvania, about an hour away. He slept for twenty minutes then woke up, fussing. I decided we would get in the car and start driving because he would probably just fall back to sleep, but the dog began pawing at me. I ignored her but she got more and more frantic so I tested him and he was below 50. There was no reason for him to have dropped that fast. If we didn't have the dog and I had just put him in the car and driven to Pennsylvania, I don't know if he would have woken up when we got there."

A diabetes alert dog is specifically trained to alert the handler to glucose levels that are out of the safe range. Typically, dogs are taught to alert to low glucose levels because if it isn't corrected quickly it is a life-threatening emergency. DADs are trained with saliva samples gathered when the glucose level is low. In general, diabetics are considered to be low if their glucose reading is 80 or below. We take samples from diabetics whose glucose meter reads 80, soak a cotton roll in that saliva, and train the dog to find it. When glucose is low, the DAD will alert the diabetic (or a parent for a very young child) using a specific alert signal. Usually this is a pawing action because it is both visual and physical and doesn't disturb others nearby. DADs don't replace medical testing or medical devices but they do offer a safety net and one more layer of protection to alert an individual or family that something may be going on.

It takes about eighteen months to fully train a DAD. Most days, we work with them several times throughout the day. Because of the amount of time it takes to train the dog, the cost for a fully trained DAD is usually around $20,000. Often the people with the greatest need for a dog are those who can least afford it. Many are families who are using all of their disposable income to pay for diabetes supplies, better nutrition, babysitters, and such.

Roman has already learned to find the diabetic scent and alert me by pawing, which is what he'll do when he goes to live with James. They are a great family, very kind and loving, and James is just the coolest little guy, always grinning from ear to ear. They have three other children so

I am really honored to be training Roman and excited for the time when he can go live with them.

Roman is a Labrador retriever. Labs have all the traits we need and are well suited to service work. At between fifty to sixty-five pounds, they are a nice size—sturdy but not so big that they are in the way. Labs have a good solid work ethic. They want to do a job, are eager to please, and are also designed to work with their nose, always keeping them to ground, sniffing.

Some trainers go to a local shelter or rescue and adopt dogs, and for some, that works. Personally, I want to know as much as I can about the health of the dog's parents, grandparents, and going back generations. I invest so much time, effort, and money into a dog that I need to start with the best possible puppy. I want the dog to be able to work for twelve or fourteen years and not come up with a family history of disease. Since I use dogs I have bred, there are five generations of really healthy dogs behind this puppy.

Two years ago, life took an interesting turn for our family. My son, who was fifteen, had been sick for about three weeks. We had been to the doctor twice and he told us there was a nasty virus going around that winter. After about three weeks, my son ended up in the emergency room and was diagnosed with type 1 diabetes. He ended up spending eight days in the ICU.

As I began to process what the doctors said, I picked up my phone and started texting my clients. "You are never going to believe what is going on. I need you."

On that day, I joined the ranks of my clients. I thought I knew what families went through and what their daily life was like, but in reality I had no idea. I thank God for setting me up with this great support system that taught us about managing the disease and transitioning into life as a diabetic family. Even though my son is older and self manages, it is exhausting. There are times when we go three or four days without a full night's sleep.

About three weeks after my son came home, our family was sitting on the couch watching a movie. For us, family includes the dogs. When I train a dog, they are not kept in a kennel since I believe a service dog needs to be in a home and live with a family.

On this particular night, we had six dogs relaxing and napping as we watched the movie. It wasn't that long after dinner but suddenly two dogs began staring at my son and became very preoccupied with him. These particular dogs had been trained on the diabetic scent but the scent was usually on me as their trainer. They had never been taught to train on my son but they continued to stare at him. I turned to my son and said, "Are you low?"

"Mom, we just ate. I'm fine."

The dogs continued to get more and more anxious. When they began pawing at him, I told my son. "I think they're trying to tell you something."

"We just ate. I'm not active. I'm fine," my son said. "I don't want to stick my finger again."

The dogs continued to pace in front of him for another twenty minutes so I finally made him test. He was 115, which was on the high end of normal but still normal. My son turned to me, smiled, and said, "I told you."

The dogs continued to fuss but since he had tested and was fine, I put the dogs in their crate, where they continued to fuss. About fifteen minutes later, my son turned to me and said, "I don't think I'm okay."

I got his test kit. He was at 58. Many diabetics' glucose levels don't drop that quickly but this a normal pattern for my son. Sometimes it happens in a matter of minutes. I kept those dogs for my son and they pick up on any changes about a half hour ahead of time and alert him.

Their alerts differ if he is having a rapid drop as opposed to when he is low or experiencing a casual drop. With a casual drop, they do a nice gentle pawing to alert. With a rapid drop, their behavior is almost frantic, a whole body reaction: their entire body gets tense, their eyes are huge, and their ears and tail are in alert mode.

Many, but not all, of the dogs I train go to children. Two years ago, I met a woman in her fifties who had been a diabetic since she was six years old. She said the only time she ever got a break from taking care of and monitoring her diabetes was when she was in the hospital—and she had been in the hospital six times in the past four months. I learned she never left the house and had been in the same clothes for days. It was obvious she was losing her will to live.

Her daughter was in college but called between every one of her classes to check on her mom. If she didn't answer, the daughter panicked, so she decided to get her mom a DAD.

After the woman learned about the DAD, things began to shift. I think the woman was tired and felt alone in her world and the dog represented hope and companionship. She wanted the dog so badly that just the idea of getting a dog was a catalyst for her to begin making some major changes. She lost fifty pounds, got two jobs, started fundraising, and got her dog. She now has a companion who goes everywhere with her, which has helped with her depression and feelings of isolation.

That isn't unique. For many, the companionship the dog provides can be just as important as the medical alert. They need someone who doesn't judge or ask questions but is there just to love them.

I cannot tell you how much I love these dogs. I cry every time one leaves to go to their new home and family. I probably caught them when they were born and have spent so much time with them. I know they are going to do great things but when they go a little piece of my heart goes with them.

It constantly fascinates me how in tune the dogs are with their people. It is hard to explain to someone who hasn't seen it but what they can do is truly a miracle. It means a lot to me what these dogs do and what it means to people. There is nothing better than waking up in the morning to a text from someone telling me their dog woke them up at 3:00 a.m. because their or their child's levels were low.

Everyone would like to make a difference in the world. We all would like to get up, go to work, and come home knowing we have helped someone. That is the most rewarding feeling. For me, when someone calls me crying to tell me, "This dog saved my baby's life," it is that feeling times a thousand.

In recent years, there has been an increasing number of stories in the media about diabetes alert dogs (DADs) and the work they are doing with individuals diagnosed with T1D. These stories have understandably driven up the demand for DADs, which unfortunately has also driven up the number of unscrupulous or inexperienced DAD providers. The Diabetes Alert Dog Alliance, with its high standards of integrity and ethics, is work-

ing to protect consumers and families. Bill Creasy, treasurer and board member, explained how the Diabetes Alert Dog Alliance helps families.

The Diabetes Alert Dog Alliance[2] is a non-profit dedicated to education, research, and promotion of the finest diabetes alert dogs (DADs) in the world. Our mission is to create an alliance between breeders, trainers, and consumers offering resources on diabetes alert dogs. People, especially those with a child with type 1 diabetes, are so desperate to help their child that they'll do anything they can. They want help and support—and they want it *now*. Since our trainers agree to rigid testing and certification criteria of their dogs, it may take them up to eighteen months to design and train a DAD for an individual or family. This timeframe may make a family particularly vulnerable to unscrupulous or inexperienced individuals or organizations who tell a family they have twenty or more dogs ready and waiting for a family. If the individual or family has the money, they have a dog.

What may seem like a dream scenario in reality is often a nightmare. Many individuals or families are given a dog that has cost thousands of dollars yet is completely incapable of alerting on a patient as promised. Even worse, their contract, or lack thereof, often means the individual or family, who may already be struggling financially, is unable to get a refund.

We recently learned of a three-year-old boy with type 1 diabetes. His parents are well educated and hired someone to train a DAD for their son while they fundraised for the $25,000 needed to purchase the dog. The trainer brought the dog and stayed for three days and showed them two or three things to do with the dog. After the trainer left, the dog started barking and growling at the husband. A week later, it bit their daughter. The trainer refused to come get the dog, wouldn't offer any support, refused to answer their emails, and ultimately blocked them from their Facebook page. They were told they would not be getting any money back and ultimately had to have animal control come pick up the dog. They have since filed a complaint with their State Attorney General only to discover there are thirty other complaints pending against this person.

The Diabetes Alert Dog Alliance is hoping to protect consumers from such situations and providers. The Alliance has established the first-ever training standards for DADs as well as a certification test. We expect all trainers to train dogs to this level of perfection before being placed with a family. We are here to educate consumers and help them understand the kind of questions they should be asking and the kind of work they should expect from their DAD.

A good dog is one that does its job but the consumer needs to be very clear before purchasing a dog that they define what that means. The Alliance suggests contacting several people and doing cross-checks and comparisons, asking for proof of any claims regarding parentage or performance. Make sure any and all health issues are addressed in writing and that *your* expectations are clearly met.

The DAD Alliance carefully screens every one of the breeders, bloodlines, and trainers who are listed with the Alliance. Our goal, and yours, is to make sure you find a dog who is a correct fit and who will hopefully live a long, happy, healthy, and successful working life with you, your family, and especially the individual with type 1 diabetes.

Chapter Ten
BARBARA

Barbara and I met back in 2009 on Facebook. Our common link at the time was that we had both written a book about Alzheimer's: mine was about caring for a loved one with Alzheimer's and hers was a children's book about a dog that visited a care facility for individuals with Alzheimer's. Barbara was one of the wise, wonderful people who reached out to me with compassion and understanding after Brooke passed. Her journey with her dogs is a sweet and tender story and together they have changed the lives of many dogs and their owners.

AFTER BEING MARRIED FOR TEN YEARS, I CONVINCED MY HUS-band, John, to get a chocolate Lab named Cassie Jo. I had dogs as a young girl but Cassie Jo was the first animal I loved and cared for as an adult. Three years later, out of the blue, I decided to get a wiener dog.

John, stunned, asked, "Why a wiener dog?" Honestly, I couldn't come up with a good reason other than that they were cute. Even though he wasn't on board with the idea, I started searching for a red, short-haired smooth dach-shund. After finding one about two hours away, I told John and

Frankie and Barbara

he was really upset. He didn't want another dog so I agreed to just go look.

John, knowing better, still held out hope, but later that same day, I brought Frankie home. For the rest of the weekend, John and Cassie Jo were mad at me, but by Monday they had fallen in love with Frankie, too.

The first six years with Frankie and Cassie Jo were great. Initially, Frankie was difficult to potty train. It took me nine months, which can be pretty typical for dachshunds. Even after they're trained, if it's raining or snowing out, they can refuse to go outside and might relieve themselves in the house. That said, they are still smart dogs.

When Frankie was six and a half, John and I decided to take a short vacation to Florida. Frankie and Cassie Jo stayed at a kennel and John and I began our drive from Wisconsin to Florida. The third day of our trip, my sister-in-law Lori, who was my emergency contact for the kennel, called to tell us she was at the vet because Frankie had been hurt. She said Frankie had tried jumping onto a container inside the kennel, perhaps to see Cassie in the kennel next to her, and fell onto the cement floor. The fall caused a disc in her back to rupture.

The vet told me Frankie wasn't moving her back legs at all. Thankfully he knew about disc disease and knew Frankie needed to have surgery right away, so Lori drove one hour to the nearest veterinary hospital that could do the surgery while John and I hopped in our car and headed home.

My mind was spinning. We knew there was a 10–30 percent chance the surgery would allow Frankie to walk again. If we did the surgery and she didn't walk, what then? What quality of life would she have?

The surgeon explained it would take three months before we knew the final outcome of the surgery. After three months, if Frankie showed no signs of improvement or was unable to walk, we would need to make a decision about a wheelchair.

That was the first I learned about dog wheelchairs. I couldn't picture what the wheelchairs looked like. While I was happy knowing there was an option, it was hard for me to imagine Frankie being in a wheelchair and never walking again on her own.

After surgery, Frankie had physical therapy and acupuncture and we also went to a vet who specialized in intervertebral disc disease (IVDD). Despite everything we did, it wasn't meant to be. Frankie was never going to walk on her own again.

It was difficult for me to accept and equally hard to imagine Frankie in a wheelchair. I thought people would judge me and think it was mean or cruel to put my dog in a wheelchair. But I loved her so much, and even though her legs were paralyzed, she was still Frankie. She was still eating and playing. She was still happy. She was getting around fairly well by dragging her back legs behind her but I knew a wheelchair would help her get around even better, so I decided to at least try.

I contacted Eddie's Wheels in Massachusetts and ordered a custom wheelchair for Frankie. Once it was ordered, I started to get really excited that Frankie would become mobile again. The day the UPS man dropped it off and we saw it was completely assembled, I jokingly said to my husband, "Open box, take out wheelchair, insert dog, and watch her run." I really thought Frankie would know what to do once she was in the wheelchair.

Instead, Frankie stood frozen like a statue. She didn't have a clue what to do so I took treats and placed them several inches apart down our sidewalk. As Frankie started rolling to get to them, I placed the treats further and further apart until, before long, we were running down the block.

Frankie was happy to be mobile again and it was such a joyful moment. I get that feeling every time I see dogs walking in their wheelchairs. To me, it's magical. Just like with humans, dogs are lucky to have options we didn't have years ago.

Afraid of what people would say or think, I was apprehensive to take Frankie out in public. While a few people stared, the majority thought it was wonderful. Over the years, people said it was awesome that Frankie was once again mobile and thanked me for taking such good care of her.

One person, a breeder, said she did not think Frankie should have gotten a wheelchair. While she understood it was a quality of life issue she felt Frankie was no longer a perfect dog. That stopped me in my tracks. I lived with Frankie and knew she was happy. Had she been miserable or without a good quality of life, I would not have made her go through that. Ultimately that woman and I simply had different beliefs, but it was also a huge lesson for me. There is no such thing, as this person suggested, as a perfect dog, just as there is no such thing as a perfect person. Yet in society we often want everyone and everything to be perfect.

In Frankie's eyes, she was beautiful just the way she was. She wasn't embarrassed or upset she was in a wheelchair; she was happy and acted like a Great Dane.

When I was in my forties, I began writing, never imagining my first book would be a children's book or that Frankie would one day be paralyzed. However, I wanted children to understand we all have challenges. Like Frankie, we can all face and overcome those obstacles or beliefs by being positive even when life does not go as we planned.

As soon as I started writing the book, it felt right. Despite my belief in the book, I had no idea how to go about writing it so I prayed. "Okay, God, if you want me to do this I'll start writing, but you need to guide me the rest of the way." From that point on, it was effortless and everything fell into place. Before I knew it, *Frankie the Walk 'N Roll Dog* [1] was written, illustrated, and published.

At the time Frankie became paralyzed, Cassie Jo had been gone from our lives for nine months and we had brought home a yellow Lab puppy, Kylie. I had been training Kylie to become a therapy dog but, with everything we were going through with Frankie, the training had been put on hold. Then I realized it was Frankie who was meant to be a therapy dog.

With my first children's book published and Frankie a registered therapy dog, we began going to schools and libraries together. We visited a local hospice facility and a wonderful place called Libby's House that cared for Alzheimer's and dementia patients. Our experience there led me to write my second children's book, *Frankie the Walk 'N Roll Therapy Dog Visits Libby's House.*

Those were truly the best five years of my life. There was no question in my mind I was right on purpose, doing what I was brought here to do, and Frankie was touching so many lives.

I had also begun working on a memoir about my journey with Frankie. Titled *Through Frankie's Eyes,* it was geared towards adults because my hope was to instill in people the understanding that every one of us has challenges, big and small, and how those challenges can impact a person's life. In June 2012, before completing the memoir, Frankie passed. That was probably one of the hardest times in my life. I cried every day for four months.

I always knew when Frankie was no longer with me I wanted to get another dog with IVDD and in a wheelchair. My husband and I never had children and I realize part of my purpose here is to care for special-needs dogs. Three months after Frankie passed, we adopted a little black and tan dachshund with disc disease named Joie (pronounced "Joey").

The Wisconsin Humane Society, knowing my work with Frankie, connected me with a film producer named Jeff. Jeff was filming a movie called *The Surface* in Milwaukee and wondered if I knew someone who had a dog in a wheelchair. I was thrilled to tell him about Joie.

Joie and I went to Milwaukee in August 2013 where she was in a short family scene. It was exciting to see my little Joie in her wheelchair up on the big screen.

Sadly, a week later (and after only having Joie with us for ten months), we had to put her down. At the time we got Joie, no one knew she had a lot of internal problems and was in a lot of pain. That was a really hard time because Joie died only thirteen months after Frankie, so I was now grieving two dogs.

In her own way, and through the film, Joie is educating people about dogs in wheelchairs and that they can live a quality life if given a chance. It is quite amazing when you think about how life has a plan for each of us—and life certainly had a plan for Joie.

Despite loving the work I had been doing with Frankie, over the years, as Frankie slowed down, there was a small voice inside me that was steadily getting louder telling me I wanted (and needed) to slow down, too. Frankie and I had done over 400 school visits and logged over 250 therapy visits and I was tired.

And that was Joie's gift and lesson to me. Through Joie, I began to take time and give serious thought to my next step. Sitting in stillness, I began to listen to my heart and the voice within. Thanks to Joie, I realized our purpose in life is to try to simply be happy each and every day no matter what we are doing. It is about enjoying and living every day in a way that is meaningful. I learned to let go of what *was* to allow what *was next* to come in and unfold. Probably the most difficult lesson to learn and biggest blessing from Joie was to let go of the fear of judgment of others. Joie was here such a short time but her gifts and lessons have changed me and my life.

Joie on the set of the movie *The Surface*

Four months after Joie passed, I adopted another special needs dog. Gidget has IVDD and even though she is sometimes wobbly when she walks, at this point, she doesn't need a wheelchair to get around.

When Frankie was getting ready to transition, a dear friend of mine said, "She has so many fans. They are going to want to do something for Frankie when she passes."

I was stunned. That thought had never crossed my mind and I said, "Do you really think so?"

My friend said she did and suggested I set up a memorial fund. Still unconvinced, I took her advice and started the Frankie Wheelchair Fund. I also founded National Walk 'N Roll Day, celebrated every September 22 in conjunction with an annual fundraiser for the Frankie Wheelchair Fund.[2]

Just as my friend predicted, after Frankie passed, we received $2,600 in memorial donations from people all over the world. I was incredibly touched. With that money we were able to keep Frankie's legacy and work alive and also help six small dogs get wheelchairs. To date, we have helped forty-three dogs in need of a wheelchair that otherwise may have never had the chance to have one.

I am an introvert by nature, but through my work with Frankie, I learned to be an extrovert. There are things I am doing now I never dreamed were possible, such as public speaking. Everything has been fueled by my passion for what I was doing and wanting to get my message out into the world. Who I am today is in large part because of Frankie.

Frankie, the Walk 'N Roll Dog
(Photo: Legacy Studios)

I believe part of my purpose is to educate the public about IVDD. When everything began happening with Frankie, Facebook and social media were in their infancy. However, through those networking avenues, and my blog, my name is out there and I am contacted by people whose dogs had "gone down" (meaning they lost use of their back legs). Since many vets were not familiar with IVDD, they advised owners to put their dog down. Thankfully, many owners, believing there was another way, searched online and found me. I have helped hundreds of people through the process of how to care for and live with a dog who is paralyzed. I have also guided them to Dodgerslist.com, a wonderful organization that is educating the public about IVDD.

I was blessed to have Frankie in my life. Thanks to her, I learned about myself, grew stronger, and became a much better person. I truly believe Frankie came to Earth with a purpose and a message and chose me as her partner to get that message out. When she was here, Frankie was a gift to so many and she will continue to be a blessing to me and many others for years to come.

✦⟁ EDDIE'S WHEELS AND ✦⟁ DODGERSLIST

Curious about the wheelchairs that Frankie and other dogs were using, I contacted Eddie's Wheels and spoke with Leslie Grinnell, one of the founders of Eddie's Wheels.[1]

EDDIE AND I HAVE BEEN LIVING WITH DOGS WITH DISABILITIES for over twenty years but our lives were totally transformed by our well-loved, extraordinary blue Doberman, Buddha. Everything about Eddie's Wheels is a result of Buddha's magic.

When Buddha was ten, she lost the use of her rear legs due to spondylosis and disc disease. She wasn't in any pain or depressed, she was simply unable to use her back legs. At the time, there were two options: risky surgery or euthanizing her. Instead, we began giving Buddha an anti-inflammatory and nightly massages—and Eddie, a mechanical engineer by trade, built her a wheelchair.

Dog in a front-wheel cart designed and built by Eddie's Wheels

That was in 1989. Since then, Eddie's Wheels has built wheelchairs and helped restore the quality of life for over 20,000 dogs. In the beginning we were seeing a lot of degenerative myelopathy, which was a bit of a mystery back then because the dogs weren't in any pain, there was just a

125

gradual loss of function. It was also a disease that was misunderstood and misdiagnosed up until 1998. The most recent study that had been done was in Switzerland in 1986 and they euthanized all of the dogs when they were no longer able to walk. Our work began where that study ended.

Since it is a progressive disease, we designed a series of upgrades and options to compensate for increased weakness in a dog. That allows the owner to have a little control over the situation. It also allows them to continue to love their dogs and allows their dogs to continue to be mobile. We also have full carts for owners who want to see their dogs through the final hospice stage of their life.

Eddie's Wheels has provided wheelchairs to pets around the world. While some customers come to our company workshop in western Massachusetts to have their dog fitted, other complete an in-depth questionnaire on our website and provide their dog's exact measurements to get a wheelchair custom-made to fit their dog.

Some of this is possible because of the American Kennel Club's breed standards. For example, if someone tells us they have a thirty-pound corgi, we know with a fairly good degree of accuracy, based on the AKC breed standards, what the dimensions of the wheelchair will be. However, we still review the numbers and look at the photographs the owner sends us. If we think there might be an error in measurement, we ask them to double check.

For the most part, the owners do a good job. They understand and want a cart that will fit their dog. Fit is very important since a cart that doesn't fit is like a person having a shoe that doesn't fit. A dog came in last week and we took a cart off the floor and tried it on him. He bumped his way right out of the cart. We tried another cart and as soon as it was on he was ready to go for a walk.

Our carts are adjustable for height and length but the width and size of the saddle is custom to the individual dog. We are the only company that shapes the cart to look like the dog. Everything is custom fitted and specific to an individual dog and its needs and has their name on it.

From the time the order is placed, it takes approximately two weeks to build a cart. Once the work order is submitted, Ed or Chris design the saddle for a rear wheel cart—we presently have over 2,000 saddle designs—or draw a blueprint for a front wheel or quad cart. Then everything goes to the production floor.

Each cart is built from scratch here on our premises and under our supervision. Think of our designs as advanced Tinker toys. We have dozens of blocks through which the bars go and are held together with set screws. The blocks are fabricated out of aluminum blocks that are milled in house. Then pieces are cut and bent into the proper shape and the pieces are welded together and the saddle is built. This step may take several days because it's important the saddle is comfortable and cushy for the dogs. Finally, the cart is assembled.

We currently have seventeen employees and they are all cross-trained to do everything from gluing pads to customizing a frame. Every one of our workers is here because they love animals and they take a great deal of pride in what we do. One of our strengths is that we have always lived with disabled dogs and our motto is: We test our products on animals.

We invented the first front-wheel cart in 2000 and it now accounts for 20 percent of our business. Last year, we made 188 front wheelcarts. In 2008, we adopted Willa and Webster, brother and sister Chihuahua-dachshund mix dogs who had been born without front legs. Willa looks like a Chihuahua and Webster is twice her size and shaped like a dachshund, so their balance points are quite different and they taught us a lot.

Webster also taught us what needed to be done for him therapeutically in addition to the cart. His malformed forelimbs are like contracted chicken wings that affect his posture and make him uncomfortable. I can tell how he leans in his cart if he needs to see the chiropractor or get a massage. His cart is part of an overall rehabilitation plan. Because of Willa and Webster, we have been able to improve our design and give better customer service.

To assist our customers with their rehabilitation plan, once a week we now have a canine rehab practitioner come to our shop to offer services such as triggerpoint myotherapy, laser, gait retraining, and massage to the dogs.

I had a man come in yesterday with a four-year-old corgi with IVDD. His vet had given him the initial diagnosis but he wasn't able to spend $7,000 on back surgery so the dog wasn't being treated. I measured the dog for a cart then I put my hand on the dog's back. I explained what I know about IVDD and told him I could feel where the dog's lesion and inflammation were located. I advised him to explore laser therapy, acupuncture, and other ways to help manage the IVDD. We went online and found him several vets who offered those therapies in his area. Finally, I pulled out the Dodgerslist information.

That was twice I'd heard Dodgerslist mentioned: first from Barbara and now from Leslie at Eddie's Wheels, so I contacted Linda Stowe, founder of Dodgerslist. Linda explained the evolution of Dodgerslist as well as the work they are doing for dogs with IVDD and their owners.

Four of my eight dachshunds have had IVDD. After spending a weekend with one screaming in pain until we could get him into surgery, I decided to try and help these dogs. I didn't know what or how, only that I wanted to do something.

I had been hearing about more and more dogs that were being euthanized because of IVDD. In 2002, I read about a dachshund named Dodger who had been taken to an emergency vet with IVDD and euthanized. As soon as I heard about Dodger, something clicked. I knew people needed to be educated and vets needed to give these dogs a chance to see if they would heal, so I started an online group and named it Dodgerslist[2] in his honor.

It started as a small group but has now grown to 15,000 people on our Facebook page and 4,000 people on the Care and Support Forum on our website. In addition to being a support group for owners and their dogs, we also print brochures and distribute them at veterinary offices, dog events, veterinary hospitals, and veterinary colleges. Our hope is by educating the public and professionals these dogs will stop being euthanized.

Dodger

When a dog owner comes home and sees their dog unable to walk or dragging their back legs and screaming in pain, they oftentimes panic and don't know what to do. We want to give them understanding, help, and hope.

IVDD is caused by disc material putting pressure on the spinal cord. A normal disc provides cushioning between the vertebrae. With the prematurely aged disc, it can begin to bulge out of shape. Tiny cracks develop and any movement, from jumping to just turning, can lead to increased disc damage. When the disc pushes on the spinal cord, it causes pain. As the nerves going to the legs become damaged, the dog may begin walking wobbly or their paws may knuckle.

Conservative medical treatment follows a protocol of limiting movement of the spine, much akin to a cast for a broken arm. Strict crate rest provides the necessary environment for the disc to form scar tissue and with time the disc material will hopefully recede. Failure to crate rest can cause the disc material to explode into the spinal cord causing severe damage to nerves. The result can be a dog dragging its legs or becoming paralyzed. While medications can provide immediate comfort from pain, reduce inflammation, and protect the stomach from extra acids, they do not heal a disc.

Surgery, if performed early, can be successful. During surgery, the disc material that is compressing the spinal cord is removed. Since the spinal cord is very fragile, the chance of a complete recovery lessens with every hour that passes. The outcome and recovery for the dog is influenced by how much time has passed before surgery is performed and how much damage has been done during that time. Surgery can cost from $5,000 to $10,000 depending on where you live so, for many people, it is simply not an option.

It is important for people to understand IVDD but it is also important for them to understand that dogs can and do recover from IVDD. Two of my dogs had surgery and two of my dogs recuperated without surgery.

Dodgerslist is trying to educate people about every aspect of IVDD including the first signs of a problem. Some dogs may show signs in advance of an episode—from yelping in pain to a slight limp. It is important that as soon as an owner sees their dog limping or in even a little bit of pain, they crate rest the dog right away so it doesn't get worse. It is also important for people to know that dogs who have already had an episode may never have another one while others will have recurring episodes.

When Dodgerslist began, it was specifically for dachshunds since the belief was that dachshunds and similar dwarf breeds were the only breeds that got IVDD. We now know there are a lot of other breeds who get IVDD and several of them are not considered dwarf breeds. Many researchers and breeders today believe IVDD is genetic. If the offending genes can be determined, genetic tests could then ascertain which dogs are carriers and the problem could be bred out of future generations of susceptible dogs.

For six years, I worked with a researcher from UC Davis in the hopes of finding the genes responsible for IVDD. We collected thousands of swabs from dogs that had IVDD but unfortunately the researcher left UC Davis before he was able to isolate the genes. This happens with many studies—either the funding ends or the researcher leaves the college or university and that is the end of the study.

It was heartbreaking when it ended because I was so hopeful. There are lots of theories why some discs calcify and harden and some don't or why some dogs have one episode and others have several but there is no hardcore proof or answer. Thankfully, research is being done now at several schools, including Texas A&M, Iowa State, and North Carolina State. Part of the hope is if they can figure this out it would help the dogs and also possibly help people with herniated discs and other forms of paralysis.

I never expected Dodgerslist to grow the way it has but somebody up above is watching over us. I believe it might be Dodger and the other dogs I have had with IVDD. Until we can find the cause and a cure, we will continue to do what we can to help and save any dog impacted by IVDD. Our motto is: Until there is a cure for disc disease, there's Dodgerslist.

Chapter Eleven
JOAN

Many moons ago, a close friend invited me to join her on a women's retreat in Kansas and said, "I want you to meet Joan. The two of you are like two peas in a pod." Joan, I learned, was the woman who had coordinated the retreat, and as Sharyn and I walked into the Circle S Ranch the first day of the retreat, a beautiful, sparkly, effervescent woman came toward me with her arms outstretched. Joan has changed my life in a multitude of significant ways. She is my cherished friend, Sister, mentor, and prayer partner and it is with immense joy and gratitude that I share her story with you.

AS A CHILD WE HAD A LOT OF LOSS AND DEATHS IN OUR FAMILY. When a parent loses a child (which is what happened in our family) they lose a part of their spirit and it is difficult for them to be fully present for the other children. In our family, animals became a place of safety and healing and were the emissaries of love we needed to keep our hearts open and to teach us the power of unconditional love.

Animals come into our lives to give and receive love. I truly believe animals find us; we do not find them. There is a higher purpose for our union and when what our souls have contracted to undertake together is finished, they

Nike

are free to leave. My dogs have given me some of my greatest joys and been my biggest teachers in the art of living and dying.

Two of my pets, Nike and Spirit, were inspirational in guiding me to my craft and life's work with essential oils.

It began with Nike, a cocker spaniel, who came into my life as a young puppy. When she was two years old, a young child accidentally sat on her and broke her back. The vet said she would never completely heal or be able to walk again. Probably needing multiple surgeries, he said she would never be the same dog and recommended we put her down.

Asking the vet for a few minutes alone with Nike, I sat with this precious little animal, looked into her eyes, and said, "It's you and me, girl. What do you want to do? I will do whatever you want." As we sat there, she gave me a sign that she, and we, could do this. It was my first experience of how dogs communicate through their eyes.

As we walked out of the room it was obvious from everyone's face that they thought I was going to have Nike put down. Instead, I said we were going home. They warned me for the next six months she would have to be carried outside to go to the bathroom and would need help in relieving herself. I said I understood and we went home.

The first thing I did was pull the mattress off my bed and that is where Nike and I slept together every night for three months. Since I worked during the day, I needed to find a way to check on her during the day. I honestly don't know how we did it but I taught Nike how to slip the phone off the hook. Every morning, I put the phone next to her and would call her mid-morning. Nike would slip the phone off the hook so I would know she was okay. At lunchtime, I came home to check on her and my landlord helped as well.

At the time, I was studying herbalism. Despite knowing the power of herbs, I had not yet begun to use them to their full potential. I noticed whenever I took Nike outside there was a particular place she gravitated towards. When we were there, she would lay in the grass and her whole attitude was different. Whenever she was in this spot, she was happier and didn't seem to be in as much pain.

I finally figured out she was lying in a field of peppermint and I learned it was wonderful for pain relief. I began making Nike some products with peppermint in them and ultimately this blend became the Peppermint Peppy Mist for our line.

After three months, I called the house one day and Nike didn't answer the phone. Even though she was doing really well, my first thought was that she had passed over so I ran home. Unable to find her, I ran down to see if my landlord had taken her out but he hadn't. As I walked back into my apartment, Nike was sitting there, tail wagging, smiling up at me. She was fine.

Nike lived to be sixteen years old and I credit her for kick-starting me on my career path. I became immensely dedicated to my work and went around the world studying and learning all I could about the power of essential oils.

I also began to study the affinity of dogs —and all animals —to know what they need to heal. Animals have an instinctual connection to the world they live in. They understand how nature supports them and know where to go to find that support when they need it. They have this amazing ability to know which tree to rub against to be soothed or what plant to lay on to help heal themselves.

Through Nike's health challenges, I learned the power of the natural world to heal and how the tools of my trade—essential oils and herbs—could help heal, nurture, and support animals as well as humans, and I began to create The Pet Alchemist, an all-natural line of pet care products.[1]

I was teaching aromatherapy classes and had an aromatherapy school in Los Angeles. I had created the pet care line, was creating products for my own company, and other companies were hiring us to produce lines for them. My days were busy and long. I was working sixteen-hour shifts but thankfully had a great crew working for me.

One day, knowing we all needed a break, I said we were going to stop working and go see the Barbara Streisand movie that was playing at the Beverly Center. As we all piled out of the car, I felt a strong instinct that I needed to go to the pet store in the Beverly Center.

I walked into the store and in the very back of the store was a tiny one-and-a-half-pound baby Chihuahua. It looked incredibly sick so I walked back to the front and asked the gentleman working if he knew they had a really sick dog in the back.

He looked at me, shook his head, and said, "Yes. We're going to put him to sleep tomorrow."

"What's wrong with him?" I asked.

"Everything."

"Can I see him?"

"We can't let anyone touch him," he said.

I asked him to please get the owner on the phone and repeated to him that I wanted to see the Chihuahua. He, in turn, repeated what his employee had told me: "We can't do that and, besides, he's going to be put to sleep tomorrow."

When I said, "What if I want to buy him?" there was silence. The owner asked to speak to his employee and told him to allow me to see the dog. I took this little baby into my arms, looked into his eyes, and told him, "You're going home with me. There's no way you're going to be put to sleep tomorrow."

The owner told me that was fine but I had to pay full price for the dog: $2,300. He also said if the dog died within the next five days, he would refund me $500.

My friends came rushing into the store to tell me the movie was about to start. Seeing me with this puppy, they asked what I was doing.

"I'm buying a dog." Pulling out my MasterCard, I bought the dog and off we went to the movies. My girlfriends and I passed him back and forth, each taking a turn holding him over their heart chakra.

The next day, I was scheduled to fly to New York to teach a course at the New York Open Center on essential oils. This was before the era of body scans and searches so I simply tucked him in my blouse next to my heart and no one ever knew he was there.

There were approximately thirty women in the class and every one of them held him that weekend. As he was passed from heart to heart, they asked me his name but I hadn't yet decided.

Just as I began teaching about the chakra system and said the word "spirit," he jumped up out of the little basket I had made for him and started making noise. I looked down, and this little dog that could barely walk was standing there looking up at me, barking.

The women all laughed and said, "He's telling you that's his name."

So, from that day on, he was known as Spirit Le Fleur, which means "Spirit of the Flowers."

Needing something to build up Spirit's immune system, I developed Ravensara Rub. It supported and built up Spirit's immune system, and it also keeps a healthy dog's immune system strong.

My niece and her dog, Terra Bella, lived with me in LA, and every day Nichole, Terra Bella, Spirit, and I went off to work together and then returned home together at the end of the day. Spirit and Terra Bella became best friends and were inseparable until I got a job offer in Kansas in 2000.

When we moved, Spirit had to leave his beloved Terra Bella behind and he grieved her for months. His entire personality changed and he started losing the hair on his back. I thought he would get over it but my husband, David, said we needed to get Spirit a playmate or he wasn't going to make it.

A friend told us about two Chihuahuas up for adoption. We took Spirit with us and the minute Sabrina saw Spirit she went over and started kissing him. From that moment on, even though she was the baby, Sabrina knew Spirit needed her and she took care of him. On some level, Sabrina took Terra's place and, once again, Spirit started becoming himself again.

Again, I believe animals come into our lives for a reason and need a role to fulfill within a home or family. Sabrina's role in our household was the caregiver. Spirit was always so fragile and Sabrina was his caretaker his entire life. When we got cats, she became their caretaker as well.

As an energy therapist, I look at the role a dog plays within a family and the conditions that exist. Through that, I begin to understand what they are here for and how to help them. Pets mirror what is going on in a household or within a person (especially the emotional energy) and come in to show us parts of ourselves that we need to (or are trying to) heal, strengthen, or awaken.

As Spirit aged, he taught me that in order for me to be comfortable with his aging process, I needed to be comfortable with my own aging process. I enjoyed aging on some level but wasn't comfortable with slowing down and not being able to do the things I once could. Animals aren't

Sabrina

afraid of aging because they're so in touch with the whole process of living and dying.

Spirit taught me that the last part of your life can still be wonderful. Just because he couldn't walk around the entire park like we once did, he could still enjoy going to the park. He still loved having little licks of ice cream. Nothing changed; he just got older. It wasn't like one stage of life was better than the other; they were just different.

Spirit also taught me the power of honoring a pet's life and process. As a woman, I always want to nurture and fix things, and as Spirit began to make his transition, I wanted to smother him. I wanted to hold him while he was lying in bed but he kept pulling away. Initially, it made me sad but ultimately taught me that I needed to let go and let him do this on his own. He taught me to allow the process and to support an animal the way *they* need not the way *I* need.

Spirit's message to me, at the time, was that the body has wisdom. He knew what was happening; he just needed me to love him and allow the process. Once I understood that, aging and dying became this beautiful process, and Spirit was able to finally pass over.

Spirit came into my life when I needed something to love and care for and he was able to leave when he knew I had learned how to do that for myself. In so many ways, Spirit taught me how to listen to the animals—and to myself. Animals will show you if you will listen, watch, and allow.

Spirit lived to be seventeen years old and was instrumental in getting me to work on an even deeper level with essential oils and plant spirit medicine and how they help dogs and their owners.

Sabrina grieved deeply for Spirit after he passed. For once in her life, we were able to focus all of our love and attention on her, but Sabrina showed me when a dog's role is finished, it's time for him or her to leave. With the cats and Spirit now passed over, Sabrina no longer had a job.

We went to the vet and he assured us that Sabrina was healthy, but two days later she passed. Sabrina missed Spirit, and although I believed I needed her, her role here was finished and she shut her system down.

As hard as that was for me, Sabrina had the most beautiful death I had ever seen. She wasn't afraid. Because of her

Spirit le Fleur in Santa Fe, New Mexico

and my other pets, I no longer fear death. Instead they have taught me about the implicit contract that exists between the spirit and body as well as the beauty and wisdom of the body to know exactly what to do and how to care for itself until the last breath.

For the first time in my life I don't have an animal. For a time, I was afraid I would shut my heart down. David and I also wondered if we will ever find another pet that would fill our hearts like our other dogs. We hope we will but we also know it is really not up to us. When we are ready, and hopefully for all the right reasons, a little one will walk across our path and we will all know without a doubt we are meant to journey on together.

We all have an unconditional love for our animals. They are so innocent and precious in spirit that you would do anything to help them through any health challenge or condition they have.

I personally cannot imagine a life without two things: animals and nature. These gifts we humans have been given are blessings that not only keep us healthy and whole, but that also keep our hearts, minds, and spirits alive with the magic and wonder of this universe.

ANIMALS AND
ESSENTIAL OILS

With many people seeking more natural ways of enhancing their and their pets' lives and health, there is an increased interest in and use of essential oils. We all want what is best for our dogs; therefore it is important to understand that essential oils, while seemingly innocuous, can be powerful and potent. To provide you with additional information about the safe and effective use of essential oils with animals, I asked Joan to share some additional wisdom and knowledge.

OUR ANIMALS ENTRUST THEIR HEALTH TO US. THEY ALSO KNOW the natural world they live in is part of their support system, so it makes sense to use nature in the form of essential oils to help keep them connected to what they instinctually know empowers and heals them.

Essential oils can be a wonderful addition to any dog's overall health. The real challenge is on the part of the human to listen and act with wisdom and caution in the use of essential oils and aromatic products. Since essential oils are potent, they must be used carefully and blended so as to safely provide relief and assistance. Different animals metabolize essential oils differently, and by and large the oils need to be appropriately diluted before use. In addition, some essential oils are contraindicated for use with certain health conditions or with certain allergies.

Many essential oils can be used in an atomizer, diffuser, or mist spray for inhalation therapy. Some essential oils can be applied topically for healing or for skin or paw care. However, when using essential oils in this manner, it's important to follow some safety precautions.

- Never give any essential oil to your dog internally.
- When applying to a location where the dog may be able to lick it, watch for sign of any allergic or negative response. Wipe the area

with a cool wet cloth diluted with mild soap, rinse, and repeat, and, if necessary, seek immediate veterinary assistance.

- If the dog begins coughing or having breathing issues (from topical or diffusion use) remove them from the area. If the symptoms persist or get worse, contact your veterinarian.

- Do not get essential oils near or in your dog's eyes. If you do, immediately flush the area with water or sterile saline solution until the area is clear. If that doesn't help, try a bit of milk, which will help absorb any essential oil residue.

- Never apply essential oils directly to your dog's muzzle area, inside nostrils, ears, mouth, or on genital areas.

- Less is best with essential oils. Allow them to work their subtle magic. Don't be tempted to think that constant spraying or use of essential oils will speed up healing. This is especially true with sensitive animals.

The beautiful thing about essential oils is that they work on the physical body while also strengthening a dog's (or person's) whole energy field. They support the animals we love and cherish while also assisting the person applying and using the products to come into balance and alignment. And they smell wonderful! I have one client who uses marjoram on her dog. She phoned me one day and said, "I love that scent. Can you get me some and put it in a bottle without a label on it? I want to give it to my husband as a cologne." Her husband loved it. So now the dog is healthy and happy—and so are the wife and her husband.

After being in the essential oil business for over thirty years, I have found the use of essential oils in the care, nurturing, and pampering of our pets can be instrumental in assisting them to live a stress-free, safe, empowering, and healthy life. Essential oils can assist in the day-to-day nurturing of your pet as well as when they are experiencing health challenges and are in need of support with ailments. Because of Nike and Spirit I have been able to help thousands of pet owners care for, nurture, and support their pets through all kinds of conditions.

If you have any questions or are unsure about the proper use of essential oils, your best path is to seek out the advice and guidance of a trained pet aromatherapist.

Chapter Twelve
CORINNE

In 2005, I attended a writing workshop in New York City and sat next to a bright-eyed woman with a smile bigger and more radiant than all of Manhattan. She held out her hand, said, "Hi, I'm Corinne," and in that instant we became forever friends. At the time, we were both aspiring authors. A few years later, we were both published authors. To celebrate, I spent a week with her and Rudy at their home in Utah. Witnessing firsthand the connection and love they share, I can say without question they are a match made in heaven and I am over-the-moon excited to share their story with you.

I ALWAYS LOVED DOGS BUT MY JOB AS AN INTERNATIONAL flight attendant required me to be gone for days or weeks at a time so it wasn't feasible to have a pet. After twenty-five years and an imminent company bankruptcy, the airline began offering extended leaves of absence. I was ready for a change. I also wanted to add more creativity and deeper meaning to my life, so I applied for a five-year unpaid sabbatical. I now had the time to do two things I'd been putting off: taking painting classes and getting a dog.

My experience with a dog was minimal because it had been a long time since I had a dog, so

Rudy and Corinne
(Photo: Juli-Anne Warll)

I borrowed other people's trusty hounds for hikes and volunteered for Utah Friends of Animals Furburbia adoption center once a week. In an attempt to find a furry four-legged friend that spoke to me, I began spending even more time volunteering at Furburbia.

The first dog the staff recommended was Bob. "Bob's our favorite," they said, smiling. Bob was skinny and scarred. He was becoming kennel aggressive after early abuses and a three-year stint in and out of various shelters and foster homes. He had fresh cuts on his face from a recent scuffle with another dog at the shelter.

I ignored their suggestion and picked out a medium-sized dog with a bent tail that I had played with earlier in the week. The staff steered me away from the dog, saying he wasn't housebroken yet, adding, "We like Bob."

"Mmmm," I told them, "I don't think so." Bob seemed wary and troubled.

The next week, I picked out a second dog and, again, they discouraged me from my choice, saying the dog chewed furniture and wasn't well socialized. Again, pointing to the tan and white mutt in the next kennel, they said, "Bob's our favorite." And, again, I ignored them and picked out a third dog.

The third was a purebred Springer spaniel. Since she had just had puppies, she wasn't quite ready to go. During the waiting period, I mentioned her to a veterinarian friend who immediately discouraged me from getting her. He told me that Springer spaniels were one of the most hyperactive breeds and questioned whether I could manage her. I insisted I could train her, and besides, she was so pretty.

The women at Furburbia looked at me again and said, "We *really* like Bob." I looked over at Bob, and at that moment, he lunged as someone knocked on his kennel as they walked by. "Look at him," I said, "he just snarled at that guy."

They encouraged me to take Bob for a walk. "Just take him outside. Take him for a walk. When he's out of the chaos of the shelter, he's a whole different dog. Just give him a chance," they pleaded.

Once outside and away from the barking dogs, Bob was indeed a different animal. We walked around the park and sat down on a bench. Bob leaned his body against me and looked at me with a soulful gaze filled

Corinne and Rudy in the studio
(Photo: Charlene Brewster)

with hope and a touch of sadness. It was almost as if he knew this might be his last chance.

The shelter told me Bob was an English pointer mix, but they didn't know much more about him. All of his teeth were cracked, broken, or missing. The vet suspected he had been chained up and beaten or attacked by other dogs and he had probably tried chewing through his chain or cage to get away. I agreed to take Bob home.

The first thing I did was change his name to Rudy since a new life required a new name. I hadn't had a dog in a long time, and both of those dogs we had gotten as puppies. Rudy was almost three with an uncertain past. I had no idea what to expect.

Rudy surprised me. Inside the house, he had perfect manners. He never made a mess, never got on the furniture, and didn't beg. I could leave a steak on the coffee table and walk back into the kitchen and Rudy wouldn't touch it.

Outside the house was a different story; we definitely had work to do. It was obvious he hadn't been in a car much, and his reaction to passersby was erratic and at times intense. I couldn't let him off-leash because he would bolt after deer and rabbits. I decided to compromise by using a fifteen-foot leash. Rudy would turn, glare at me, then hurl himself at the end of the leash at a forty-five degree angle over and over again until my hands were completely blistered. I tried taking him to the dog park but he would immediately climb the fence and take off. Instead, we started pre-dawn training sessions at an outdoor hockey rink with a concrete base and a fifteen-foot fence. We did laps and played the "Go/Come" game where I would let him take off and run, then call him back to sit and stay. It was our compromise to allow Rudy a little bit of freedom.

In a controlled group setting with trainers and other dogs, Rudy responded well, but when unleashed dogs ran up to him on the trail, he was unpredictable and aggressive. Rudy dragged me through the mud, across asphalt, and through sagebrush whenever he saw other dogs. Twice after a particularly stressful day or doggie incident, I considered taking Rudy back to the shelter, but I couldn't do it. I couldn't give up on him. My friends rallied to the cause and invited us over to their yards for doggie play dates, and I worked with a couple of trainers in private and group classes to try and socialize him. Slowly, Rudy began to improve.

One day, Julie, a professional animal communicator, said, "Rudy wants you to know he loves you so much, he would kill for you." I asked her to tell him he didn't need to go to that extreme, but it made me understand that some of his issues were simply him being protective of me. I believe he felt that since I saved him, he was going to save me, even if it was from a ten-pound Chihuahua or a dog no bigger than my wallet.

Rudy was extremely wary of men, especially men in white diesel trucks. If I dropped a pan lid on the counter, he would slink to the opposite corner of the kitchen and cringe. He didn't wag his tail for the first year and a half, and when I tried to hug him or get too close, he would cower. His lingering fear of abuse was palpable, and it broke my heart.

I loved Rudy's tan and white markings and began to make sketches of him in my journal. I tucked them away and didn't tell anyone about them. One day my friend Julie, the animal communicator, came by. She immediately started chuckling and said, "Rudy really likes the drawings you did of him this morning."

Julie also told me Rudy really liked when I painted him. "He says he thinks he's really handsome, and this is what you're here to do together. He says he's doing his part by being such a good-looking dog, and he needs you to do your part by putting it down on paper."

And that is where it all began. When I first started painting Rudy, I would stay up many nights long past midnight experimenting with shape and color. I began swiping paint on canvas trying to impart Rudy's positive philosophy and supreme "dog-ness" through pictures instead of words. I began to get a lot of support from friends and strangers, and

Rudy and Corinne reading their
book together
(Photo: Cheyenne Rouse)

then our first painting, "Don't Be Afraid to Leave the Path," sold to a collector at the annual Kimball Art Festival gala.

Rudy kept posing and I kept painting.

We spent our mornings hiking the trails near my house. Afternoons and evenings were filled with weekly obedience classes or classical music and the smell of acrylic paint and graphite.

If I was wasting time watching television or working on the computer, Rudy would come in and stare at me. He would continue to stare and then walk into the studio and sit by the easel. If I didn't respond to his lead, he would come back out and again sit in front of me and give me a strong nudge with his nose, then return to the studio and lie down next to the easel until I got back to business.

Eventually, my paintings of Rudy morphed into a children's picture book, *The Tao of Rudy*.[1] I had no artistic training or publishing experience, so everything about my creative evolution and this journey with Rudy has been magical. I received a $9,000 grant to help pay the printing costs; the first book won two prestigious awards and sold out of the first printing. Then, other artistic opportunities began to magically appear, from teaching art to at-risk children, to doing presentations and book fairs at schools, to becoming a tutor for a state-run reading program for first-graders.

Next came a bilingual version of Rudy's book followed by sales of some of the original paintings from the book. My little project also caught the attention of Chronicle Books, a major publisher who acquired the rights for a third book. The sequel, *Shoot for the Moon!: Lessons on Life from a Dog Named Rudy*, won an award and garnered positive reviews from top publications like *Publishers Weekly*.

Rudy has become a local celebrity and has appeared on local television and attended book signings. Kids often run up to me and say, "You're the lady with the dog. You're Rudy's mom!" After nine years of love and stability, Rudy is now comfortable among strangers. He enjoys his young fans, especially when they start chanting, "Ru-dy! Ru-dy!" from the playground at the school.

And the ball just keeps rolling. The third picture book led to a fourth called *Wake Up to Love!: Lessons on Friendship from a Dog Named Rudy,* and our fifth book, *Roaming with Rudy: Paris!* is the start of a whole new travel guide series and travel club for kids. It's as if some force is guiding me. That force is Rudy.

With each milestone or success, friends congratulate me while shaking their heads and saying, "We've known you for twenty years. You're not an artist. Where is all this coming from?"

"Well," I reply, "I adopted this dog . . ." And that's the truth. That is really where it all began.

How do you put into words the essence of a dog's love and their impact on your life? I never realized, until Rudy, that dogs had such a sense of humor. Rudy is funny and playful and is always encouraging me to join him in a race around the yard. I never realized, before Rudy, that dogs were so in-tune with humans. Rudy's eyes are deep and very expressive, and he seems to be able to completely tune into my mood.

So many times I get these little sparks where I feel like I can understand what Rudy is trying to tell me. Sometimes when he is lying in the beam of sunlight in the kitchen, he fixes me with a gaze of such adoration and love that is difficult to describe. In those moments, it is as if I completely understand what he is trying to tell me.

All of the wisdom in my books comes from Rudy: Take a Closer Look; Let Yourself be Loved; Follow Your Heart; Don't Be Afraid to Leave the Path; and Life is Filled with Magic and Joy! He has taught me to be quiet, to sit and listen, and to wait and be open for inspiration no matter what the source. After nine years, Rudy still looks at me in his patient, knowing way, like some kind of benevolent Swami guru.

My magical mutt has opened up a path for me that I might never have conceived of or discovered on my own. It is almost as if this legacy he has inspired is his gift to me, a lasting thank you, for taking a closer look and for giving him a chance, a home, and a purpose.

Rudy didn't drag me out of a burning building. He didn't save me from drowning in icy floodwaters or lead me out of a raging forest fire. He didn't bring me back from the hopelessness and despair of depression or drug addiction. Rudy did none of these things, but he saved me nonetheless. The truth is: we rescued one another.

ANIMAL COMMUNICATION AND INTUITION

Several people mentioned the role an animal communicator (or their own intuition) played in their journey with a dog so I decided to search for one to interview. Trusting my intuition, I was guided to Marta Williams,[1] an author and animal communicator. On the day we spoke, there were wildfires in California threatening Marta's home and animals. Although facing possible evacuation, she graciously took time to speak with me and share her insights and experiences.

MY BACKGROUND IS AS AN ACADEMIC AND SCIENTIST. I HAVE A BS in resource conservation from the University of California at Berkeley and an MS in biology and systematic ecology from San Francisco University. For many years I worked as an environmental scientist, studied wildlife in the field, and rehabilitated ill and injured animals. I looked at what was going on in the world and began to feel the work I was doing as both an environmental scientist and wildlife biologist wasn't enough to help or really change the path we were on. People's consciousness needed to change for things to

Marta with a friend's dog, Maisey
(Photo: New World Library)

change on the Earth, and as I continued to ask questions, I was led down this path.

I always loved animals and, from a relatively early age, had a keen ability to tune into people's and animal's feelings. In 1989, I learned to communicate intuitively with animals by taking classes and practicing by intuitively asking verifiable questions with a variety of animals in a number of different situations.

My background in academia made learning animal communication more difficult and also made it hard for me to accept it was real or believe I could do it. Over time, I understood this was my path and dedicated myself to learning it. Now, in addition to being a full-time animal communicator, I offer consultations, workshops, clinics, and lectures around the world.

None of that would have been possible had I not kept an open mind and a willingness to experiment. Many people are skeptical about animal communication, which I can understand because I, too, was skeptical when I first began studying communication. However, after working in this field for so long and testing myself for accuracy, I have proven to my own satisfaction the reality and accuracy of it.

I have developed a unique training system that provides individuals with the ability to begin practicing immediately with quantifiable and verifiable proof that what they are doing is real. That doesn't mean a person's rational mind and skepticism won't interfere, but it makes it much easier for them to follow the intuitive information they are receiving.

Everyone can communicate with animals but it is something you have to study systematically. The basics of animal communication are to pay attention to any impressions or feelings you are getting through words or thoughts. It is especially important to pay special attention to any feelings you may be getting.

Talking intuitively to animals is easy. What we oftentimes find difficult is listening. Begin by simply talking out loud to your animal as if he or she completely understands you. Talking to your animal this way can change the animal's behavior completely, sometimes right away.

I recommend people keep a notebook and write down everything they notice in relation to this experiment. What is happening? What do you notice? Has your animal started acting differently?

Many people question whether they actually have intuitive ability. Intuition is not something only a few gifted people possess. It is something we all have but, for many, it has been suppressed. People of indigenous cultures are comfortable using their intuition because for them it is a completely normal state of being. The same was probably true for our ancient ancestors, but modern people no longer connect with their intuition and have therefore become estranged from it.

We actually use our intuition every day. Have you ever thought about someone and then gotten a phone call, visit, or card from them? Have you ever had an unexplainable and immediate dislike or concern over someone or a situation? Have you ever known how someone is feeling, either emotionally or physically, even if you're not with the person? Anytime you say, "I have a feeling . . ." what you are really saying is you are getting an intuitive impression about something or someone.

The idea of intuitive communication with animals and nature challenges many of our long-held beliefs, especially the belief that other species are inferior to humans intellectually, emotionally. and spiritually. Through my work, it is obvious these beliefs are not only untrue but are some of the root causes for the ecological imbalances and crises we are now facing.

All animals have a constant connection with their intuition. They are able to communicate with each other intuitively and can sense a person or situation immediately, so when an animal comes into your life, they can often lead you to be more intuitive. On a spirit level, the animal may have come to guide you to do the work you are meant to do in this world and/or help you heal whatever may be holding you back in your life.

As a scientist by nature, I like to break things down and help people analyze things. In my most recent book, *My Animal, My Self,* I explain how animals are in our lives for reasons we may not necessarily see or understand right away. It is only when we delve into a deeper level that we understand there are expansive reasons for every animal who comes into our life.

The best advice I can offer for beginning to develop your intuition is to always follow your heart since that is where intuition resides. In general, following your heart will lead you in the right direction.

Chapter Thirteen
TRACY

In 1988, Robb suggested I take my sons to visit his neighbor Tracy. Two years earlier, Tracy had opened Woodlands Wildlife Refuge[1] to receive, rehabilitate, and release injured and orphaned native wildlife. On the day we visited, there were rabbits, skunks, and raccoons. This summer, over twenty-five years later, I attended an educational program at Woodlands' new location, and saw raccoons, turtles, skunks, foxes, squirrels, woodchucks, bobcats, rabbits, porcupines, coyotes, and bears being cared for and rehabilitated. Over the years, I have been inspired by the work Tracy and the Woodlands staff and volunteers do for and on behalf of animals. She is a brilliant, deeply committed, and focused woman and I was excited to talk with her about the animals in her life, especially a dog named Thelma.

Tracy at Woodlands Wildlife Refuge
in New Jersey

SOME OF MY EARLIEST memories from when I was around three years old are of all the animals we had: a raccoon, a squirrel, a duck, and a boxer named Saber. Being so young, I don't know how the animals came to live with us but I do know they were all very much a part of our family.

The squirrel lived behind a clock on the back

porch and came and went at his leisure. Nikki the raccoon lived in the house and got along with all the animals, especially Saber. Nikki often put her treats in Saber's water bowl. Since her treats were usually graham crackers, Saber's water turned to sludge. It apparently never bothered Saber because I remember many times seeing them lying together on our living room floor.

I don't remember what happened to Nikki or Saber or any of the other animals, possibly because I was so young—or possibly because I was already busy exploring and taking care of other animals. I was the kind of kid who went off by herself and walked the trails and in streams and turned over rocks and brought home tadpoles. If something was injured, I walked down to see Doc Dineen, the veterinarian on Main Street in Hampton, New Jersey. No matter what I brought him, and no matter how obvious it was that there was no hope for the animal, Doc Dineen always made time for me and whatever I brought him to examine. Here I was, a young kid, sitting in the waiting room with an animal who probably had no hope but he always took the time and explained things to me. He never made me feel like it was worthless or not a good idea to try and help an animal. He was an amazing man and role model for me, and I am forever grateful for the time he spent with me back then.

I was in my twenties when I got an Alaskan malamute named Zeke. Zeke was the first dog I was directly responsible for and had a deep connection with.

Malamutes are a strong Northern breed and very quick learners but they also have an attitude of doing what they want, when they want. While they can honestly do well in almost anything, they first have to decide whether or not they want to do it and therefore have been called, not unfairly, strong-willed. For those reasons, doing obedience training with a malamute was almost unheard of at that time. That didn't stop Zeke and me. We trained for obedience and travelled and competed in several states.

There are five levels of competition in obedience. At each level, you need to complete three legs in order to move on to the next level. Zeke had been doing really well and only needed to complete one more leg before moving on to the final level of competition, so we packed up the truck and headed to a competition in Long Island.

We checked into the hotel and Zeke immediately went into full pro-tection mode. I tried to get him to relax, knowing he had a full day of competition the next day and needed to be at the top of his game, but he wouldn't listen. Every time someone walked down the hall or he heard a door shut, he would growl. He didn't sleep at all and instead kept his nose pressed against the door, on full alert.

The next morning, we got up and drove to the competition. It was a gorgeous autumn day and I was so happy for him since this would be the last competition for him in this group. He had worked hard and I knew he was ready and could pass with ease—if he wanted to. Every-thing we needed to do was to be done off-leash, without any voice com-mands, using only hand signals. I got Zeke into position and he sat there calm, obedient, and ready. Then, before I could give him the first signal, Zeke took off running around the ring. Just as quickly as he took off, he came back and sat down in perfect position as if it never happened. Of course he was automatically disqualified but in competition you still need to go through the motions, so we did and Zeke did everything per-fectly. If he hadn't taken off in a mad dash around the ring he would have come in second and we would have completed that level of competition.

At an indoor event in Philadelphia, all of the rings were set up within close proximity to one another. About twenty feet away, in another ring, was a mastiff. Zeke took one look at the mastiff and jumped over the ring. The two of them squared off, and even though they didn't fight and no one was hurt, that was the end of that competition.

Zeke was completely loyal and obedient—until he didn't want to be loyal or obedient. He would accept his punishment without complaint because, in his eyes, it was worth it since he also got the freedom to do what he wanted when he wanted.

My best friend in the world at that time, without a doubt, was Zeke. An important relationship in my life ended and Zeke saw me through that transition. I moved into my own place and, for a long time, it was just Zeke and me.

We loved going for long walks, and one day, when Zeke was seven, we headed out for hike. It was a beautiful day so we just kept walking through the nearby woods and fields. When we came home, Zeke went into the kitchen. I assumed he was going to get a drink but instead he lay down on the kitchen floor and died. It was crazy. I called my vet and he asked if I wanted to bring him in. I decided not to go and put him through that since it wasn't going to change the outcome.

Zeke and his passing had a huge impact on me. I had been going through a bad time and Zeke was my anchor. And then, in an instant, he was gone. I was in shock and felt incredibly alone.

Before he passed, Zeke did reach the final level of obedience, which was extremely rare for an Alaskan malamute at that time.

After Zeke passed, I decided not to get another dog, and especially not another malamute. But as chance (or fate) would have it, a friend of a friend walked through my door with a malamute puppy. I named him Jake and he was wonderful, very mellow and a really good friend. Just as Zeke had been there for me during a major transition in my life, Jake was there for another major transition in my life when I began to learn about something called wildlife rehabilitation.

Because I had a lifelong appreciation for wild animals, I wanted to learn more about wildlife rehabilitation. The more I researched and learned, the more interested I became in this field of work. With a perfectly good job in the field of orthodontics, I had no plans of making a career change, so after apprenticing with other rehabilitators and passing the state criteria, I began rehabilitating wildlife as a hobby. Between my job, Jake, five cats, and the wildlife rehab, life was good.

My next dog came to me through my work with wildlife rehab and it was one of the most uncanny experiences of my life.

One hot summer day, a local police officer called to tell me there was an injured goose behind the town car wash. Normally, I don't work with birds since there are other organizations in New Jersey that do. However, since it was my hometown, I decided to help out and get the goose where it needed to be.

Arriving at the car wash, I saw that one of the officers had the goose under control. As I walked over to talk with the other officers and car wash employees, I noticed a little black terrier running around loose. I asked about the dog and suggested they either put a leash on it or put it in the office. They explained it wasn't their dog and they had no idea who the dog belonged to. They said the dog was always running loose and had already been hit once by a car in front of the car wash.

I walked over to get the goose and, turning to put it into my car, saw the terrier sitting on the front passenger seat of my car staring straight ahead. The guys from the car wash laughed and said, "I guess you're taking the goose and her, too."

Deciding she couldn't be left to run around and risk being injured, or worse, I told them I would take her home and try to find her owners.

Pulling out of the parking lot, I glanced over at the terrier. She sat absolutely still and calm, eyes staring straight ahead. Throughout the ten-minute drive back to my house, I kept glancing over at her but she continued to stare straight ahead. There was only one time on the drive when I looked at her and she looked back at me. In that moment, she had an expression of sheer excitement. If she could have talked, I think she would have said, "Yipee! A road trip!" so I named her Thelma after the film *Thelma and Louise*.

Thelma was a typical terrier with a scruffy little face and covered in shaggy grey and black fur. She weighed maybe thirty pounds. As we got closer to my house, I suddenly realized Jake—a 140-pound dog—and five cats awaited us. How in the world was I going to walk onto the property with a stray dog?

Looking at Thelma and knowing there was no turning back, I said to her, "Well, Thelma, let's see how this plays out."

Since the sole purpose of my trip had been to bring home a goose, not a dog, I didn't have a leash or anything to get Thelma into the house. I parked the car and walked around to open the door for Thelma to see what she would do. If she ran away then that was what was meant to happen.

In order to get into my house, you had to walk through the garage and over to an entryway. The entry isn't visible from the driveway but Thelma jumped out of the car, ran straight into the garage and over to the entryway, and sat at the door waiting to go into the house. I was shocked. It was as if she knew exactly where she was or had been there before.

Again, I thought, "Okay, let's open the door and see what happens." Thelma dashed in, blew past Jake and the five cats, ran around the house checking everything out, then sat down on the living room couch.

Jake and the cats looked at me like, "Who the heck is this and what is she doing in our house?"

For two weeks, I advertised to try and find her owners. Finally, one day a woman called and told me the dog belonged to their son. He had gone off to college and left the dog with them but they didn't want her.

So Thelma was here to stay, and there was never a problem. All of the animals in the house got along and I credit Thelma for that. She kept the peace simply because of her even-keeled, peaceful demeanor. Just like the day I picked her up and she sat so calmly in my car, that's how Thelma was all the time. She was always good and never bothered any of the other animals, and they never bothered her. Thelma was a sweet soul and everyone loved her and she loved everyone—which is why she ultimately became the greeter here at Woodlands.

Thelma was a home dog—she loved being home. Being a smaller dog, going for long walks wasn't her cup of tea. She would wander around the property but I never once had to put Thelma on a leash. Even though I never showed her where the property lines were, she never left the property and never had to be controlled in any way. Thelma instinctively knew where she should and shouldn't go on the property. She also never went where the wildlife were being kept, which was uncanny.

Wanting Jake to have the same freedom as Thelma, I had an invisible fence installed. Within minutes of putting the collars on Jake and Thelma, Jake took off and ran right past the fence. It stunned him for a second but he kept right on going, which is all part of the malamute mentality that says, "Okay, I got zapped but it was so worth it. I'm free!" Thelma on the other hand got zapped and sat down and stared at me. I can still clearly see the look on her face as it went from surprise and confusion to disappointment in me. It was as if she were asking, "Why do you think I need this?" I took the collar off both of them and shut the fence off—it didn't work for Jake and Thelma didn't need it.

Thelma seemed to be such an old, wise soul. I always asked her, "Who are you and what are you doing here? You know all of this so well. What's going on here?" Sometimes I wondered if she was a reincarnation of one of my best friends from childhood, Damon. Damon was an adventurous soul and growing up he and I were always off on adventures together. Sadly, Damon passed in the early '80s but Thelma had the same love for adventure. I used to ask her, "Are you Damon?" but she left here with me still wondering.

Thelma was eight when she came into my life and she died of old age when she was fifteen. A couple of years after she passed, I saw her. It was the craziest thing but it's still incredibly clear in my mind.

I was outside talking to my husband, Jeff, when, turning my head towards our house, I saw Thelma sitting in the front window. She was there as clear as day. I turned to tell Jeff and when I looked back, she was gone. I realized that moment was meant just for Thelma and me.

That was the thing about Thelma. I had dogs growing up and dogs before Woodlands Wildlife Refuge. Every one of those dogs came to me because of my love of caring about and for animals. Thelma is the only dog who came directly to me because of my work at Woodlands.

When I look back on how Thelma came into my life, it was magical, like kismet. We were brought together by that injured goose—an animal I normally wouldn't have taken to rehab. I now know it was because Thelma and I were supposed to meet. And she knew it. I had no plans or intentions of getting another dog but Thelma knew we were meant to be together. Her attitude that day, sitting on the front seat of my car, was, "I'm going home with you because I'm supposed to."

Likewise, I didn't choose the work I do with wildlife, it chose me. I had a perfectly good job and no plan or intention of changing careers but one thing led to another, and as I continued to follow my passion, it just happened. I am one of the incredibly lucky people who ended up doing exactly what they are supposed to be doing in life.

I feel so blessed. Seven days a week, I am surrounded by animals here at Woodlands. Not only do we have a high success rate of releasing formerly injured or orphaned animals back into their natural habitat but we also educate the public, as well as private groups and organizations, about the animals.

Thelma and all of the animals, both wild and domestic, are a wonderful and constant reminder to all of us of the synergy that connects us all.

Chapter Fourteen
DONNA

In 2005, a beautiful Victorian house on Main Street in my home-town began undergoing some fabulous renovations, and shortly thereafter, the doors of Main Street Manor Bed & Breakfast opened. In the ensuing years I got to know the owners, attended community and educational events at their inn, and eventually was honored to meet their dog, Quincy. Quincy was an integral part of the bed and breakfast as well as a well-recognized and beloved member of our community.

Donna, Ken, and Quincy at Main Street Manor Bed & Breakfast
(Photo: Jenna Perfette Photography)

MY HUSBAND KEN AND I always loved to travel and especially enjoyed staying at different bed and break-fasts. We talked a lot about someday buying a B&B and how cool it would be to find an inn and make it our own. After endless conversations and months of searching, we came upon this beautiful inn, took a total leap of faith, and bought it.

We made the inn every-thing we felt a B&B should be: a full hot breakfast served every morning, inn-baked treats available 24/7, the rooms dressed in vin-tage linens, beautiful china, and lacy window dressings with stuffed teddy bears on guestroom beds. To really make our place feel like home, we decided weary travelers would enjoy being greeted by a dog's big smiles and wet nose and our thirteen-year-old yellow Labrador, Beau, was the perfect guy to complete the picture.

From the day we got Beau as a puppy, he was always a very happy dog, low maintenance and with a perpetual smile on his beautiful face. We used to joke and say, "Beau is happy just breathing!" Anyone that met Beau knew that described his personality perfectly. He loved just being around people so his new role at the inn suited him quite well into his senior years.

When Beau was thirteen, his hips began giving him some trouble, but he was happy to lay on the foyer rug and have guests pat him as they came and went. His tail-wag made our and many of our guests' day. Although he struggled to get up and down a lot of the time, for the most part he was happy.

We made some modifications to the inn to allow Beau to maintain his independence. Beau loved lying in the grass off of our kitchen and watching the birds and butterflies. Occasionally, a squirrel would get his attention and he'd give a gruff old bark. Knowing how much he loved being outside, Ken constructed a wider than normal ramp, which he covered in plush carpeting, so Beau could go outside with minimal assistance. When the stairs to our second-floor bedroom became too much for Beau to navigate, the three of us began sleeping on a pull-out sofa in our downstairs family room.

The evening before Beau passed we were taking down the Christmas tree. Beau was lying in his usual spot on the inn's foyer rug watching us. There had been an ice storm that evening, but Beau suddenly became insistent that he wanted to go out. We tried steering him towards his ramp at the back door but he remained focused on the front door of the inn, insisting he wanted to go out that way. We finally opened the door and Beau went out and down the porch steps and onto the grass. We followed after him as he proceeded to walk around the entire perimeter of the property. Beau maintained a strong, steady stride as his paws crunched through the layer of ice that coated the ground. After walking around the entire property, he walked back in the front door and lay back down on the foyer rug.

We all went to bed together that night, and the following morning, Beau had a seizure. Ken was at work, so I was home alone with him. He kept looking up, trying to stand, and would collapse back down. Even though I know you're not supposed to approach a dog when they're having a seizure, I couldn't help myself. I got down on the ground and held him, kissed him, and just talked to him and told him it would be okay. I could not leave his side. The seizure went on for what seemed like forever. I waited until he was calm then called our vet.

By the grace of God, there was an office emergency that morning and Beau's vet answered the phone. When I told him what had happened, he said he would be right over. I called Ken home from work and he and the vet arrived at about the same time. Ken and I believe that Beau picked his time to leave, especially in light of his insistence to circle his home one final time. Thinking back on that night, I still cannot believe his strength and commitment to do what he wanted to do. He was always such a gentle soul, but that night he showed us just how strong he was.

There were so many things that extended Beau's life and allowed him to maintain his happy-go-lucky personality and dignity, including the ramp Ken built and the gentle quality of life afforded an inn dog, The days we spent with Beau minding the B&B together were priceless.

It was January 2006 when we lost Beau. We missed him terribly and our life was so empty without him. We talked about getting another dog, but we needed time to grieve and respect his memory and life. It took us several months to process the loss. As we began to think and talk about finding our next "child in fur," we knew there were other things we needed to consider.

When we first got Beau, we owned a house and had more regular (or normal) lives. Before becoming innkeepers, our days were more normal. Even though we both had jobs, weekends and free time was ours. With a B&B, we had little free time. We knew getting another dog also meant finding one with a personality that would fit into our lifestyle and our work. Either way, we knew our breed of choice would be another Lab, so the search began.

After speaking to a number of Labrador breeders, we found Sherry, a breeder not far from the inn. She had two females scheduled to give birth in April, which meant we could have our new addition sometime in June. We met Sherry and her brood of Labs in March and their look and temperament was exactly what we wanted—and the June timing for the puppies to join our life and home worked perfectly for us.

Sherry called in April and off we went to see the puppies. We wanted a male, and of the twenty-four puppies, there were three yellow males still available. We needed an independent guy, somebody who could be left by himself and be cool with that. Two of the yellow males were playing with each other, rolling around together and having a grand old time. The third one had gotten hold of a stick and was off by himself, lying in the grass and chewing on it. I can still picture his scrunchy face and hear his squeaky noises as he went to town on that poor stick. Watching the intensity and purpose in that face as he chewed the stick to bits, we knew he was the dog for us. We took the stick from his mouth and picked him up as he squirmed, wiggled, and nipped. Sherry marked his right shoulder with a dot of red nail polish so when we came back for him, there would be no question he belonged to us.

We decided to name him after our favorite place on Earth: the town of Aquinnah on Martha's Vineyard. It is the place we hoped to one day retire to with our puppy. While the puppy's formal name was Aquinnah Summer Dream, we called him Quincy for short.

In June, we went back to get Quincy and he was a bruiser from the beginning. He was very active and very stubborn, as puppies typically are. Quincy had his very own "Wall of Shame," which he single-handedly created over the course of several months. The wallpaper in our kitchen had a small tear in it and was beginning to lift away from the wall in one spot. Quincy never missed a thing and his attention to detail was amazing so one day, noticing a little edge of wallpaper sticking up, he began to bite at it. He would run over to the wall, rip a little piece of wallpaper off, then scamper away. And so it went. For months, we found little pieces of wallpaper all over the kitchen until Quincy developed a taste for the wallpaper and began eating it instead.

Quincy ended up ripping all the wallpaper off one wall and then began working on the drywall. Ken allowed Quincy to complete his masterpiece before covering it over with beadboard. Toilet paper was another of Quincy's fixations and he took every opportunity to grab a roll and tear it to shreds whenever he gained entrance to the bathroom.

Ken and I are strong minded and Quincy was too. The first three years we had him, Quincy was terribly defiant. It had to be his way or the highway and there was no way to make peace with him. So many times I thought about the movie *Marley and Me*, and how, just like Marley, we now had "the worst dog in the world." Being honest, I didn't like Quincy very much for the first three years of his life. He ate dirt, pruned plants, and chewed rocks and table legs. He was just so fresh and always up to something. I had heard the phrase "A tired dog is a happy dog," so I took him for five or six walks a day but it didn't matter. He never seemed to tire! He was always challenging me and would jump up and bite at my elbow or sweatshirt just because he wanted to do things his way. At times when we were out for a walk, he would just sit down and refuse to walk or move. How do you drag a 105-pound headstrong dog when you're seven blocks away from home?

But when you have a pet, you work it out—and we did. Once Quincy turned nine months, we began closing the inn once a week and took him for obedience and agility classes in the evening. He was like a sponge, learning commands quickly and was very smart—sometimes scary smart. He loved agility and learning new things but he wanted all of the teacher's attention. The teacher had to use him as the demonstration student or he would get terribly upset. If he couldn't go first, he would start yelping at the top of his lungs—it was so embarrassing! When we drove up to school in the evening for class, he could not contain his excitement, yelping and barking from the truck to let the class and teacher know he had arrived. He was a real performer and won the tail-wagging contest the final night of graduation from obedience school.

We always made Quincy a part of the inn from the time we picked him up from the breeder at eight weeks old. He even has his own page on the inn's website, which chronicled his entire life, but first and foremost, he was our pet. For the first two years of Quincy's life, he lived exclusively in our innkeeper part of the house and we only had him interact with guests while out in the yard, on the front porch, or while on a walk. We felt it was important for him to learn to be a gentleman and greet guests properly, with NO jumping up!

I will never forget the first day we allowed him into the front guest part of the inn. He stood in the kitchen doorway looking into the dining room like it was a foreign country. He kept blinking his big brown eyes and refused to set foot in that area. Finally, after we encouraged and coaxed him repeatedly, he finally stepped in and explored the dining room, library, foyer, and parlor. Quincy understood the difference between the guest area and "our" part of the inn. From that day on, Quincy knew this was a special space he could visit and enjoy, but only when and if we gave him permission.

Breakfast was a special time for Quincy because afterward we allowed him to come into the dining room to meet the guests. We called it the "Meet-and-Greet" and it was a big thing for Quincy. After everyone finished breakfast, Ken would say "Okay, Quince, we're going to do a Meet-and-Greet." Quincy would grab a favorite toy and push through the kitchen door into the dining room. He would circle around the table and grab whatever pats, hugs, and kisses he could while stealing a multitude of hearts. He was a proud and dignified dog who gently presented himself to people and sized them up in the process. He liked most people but was not a fan of children, small dogs, or cats.

Quincy had the same innkeeper work ethic as Ken and me. Besides the Meet-and-Greet, he loved and did well at every job we gave him. As security guard, he would lie at the kitchen door and bark at the comings and goings of guests. He barked when a car pulled in the driveway or left, and barked when there were folks walking by. It was quite helpful because depending on where I was in the house, I could always tell that "somebody's here" bark.

Another of Quincy's jobs was going out to bring in the newspaper. He easily grasped the task of getting our paper. The learning curve for him was in learning NOT to pick up the neighbors' newspapers on our daily walks.

I know deep down Quincy's favorite job of all was bringing in Ken's lunch bag and coffee cup. Every morning, Ken poured coffee into a travel mug, packed his lunch, and headed off to work. Every afternoon, around 4:00, Quincy would head for the back door to wait for Ken to come home. Quincy could be in a dead sleep, but somehow he always knew when it was 4:00 p.m. He would wait all wiggly and impatiently with his nose pressed to the glass on the back door. As soon as he spied Ken's truck pull in the driveway, he would bark and run out to welcome him home and steal a kiss. Then he would carry Ken's coffee mug and lunch bag into the house. It was his ritual—and he truly lived for it every single day.

Weddings at the B&B are always special days but there's a different kind of energy in the air and Quincy could always feel it. There's some tension because you want everything to be perfect for the couple and Ken and I would be busy doing a lot of different tasks. After our morning walk, Quincy would see us scattering to do our tasks and he would just lay down and relax—unless Ken was setting up chairs for an outdoor wedding. Quincy always went outside to help Ken with the chairs.

Quincy was incredibly well behaved and when the guests started coming for the wedding, he would go into his crate, lie down, and sleep for the next couple of hours. People could come in and out of the house and they never even knew there was a dog in the house. Somehow Quincy understood that he did not have to be "security" once folks were inside the inn. After the wedding ceremony, Quincy would come out of his crate and Ken would take him for a walk. Quincy understood this was his life and he played his part by being a good boy and being patient. He knew we always would make time for him once everything was done with the wedding. And that's what Quincy wanted—he just wanted to be with us.

In the car or truck, Quincy was a lunatic. Ken was especially patient with him but there always needed to be two of us with Quincy if we were driving anywhere. That never deterred us from taking him on trips or for a ride. He was well socialized and we had so many really great vacations together. Other than a conference we had to attend in Arizona, we never went on vacation without Quincy.

One of our favorite places to go for vacation is Martha's Vineyard. To get there, you must drive, then take a ferry over to the island. Whenever we were in an unfamiliar place, Quincy would get terribly upset and start crying and yelping if Ken or I walked away for even a second. On several trips to the Vineyard, the ferry guys would tease him and call him a big baby. It was sad that his separation anxiety kept him from relaxing and enjoying our off time, but it never deterred us from taking him places with us. We knew and respected his personality.

Quincy was a methodical thinker who processed everything and made a decision only after careful consideration of all the options. The greatest example of this is from something that happened last spring.

It was about 7:00 a.m. and Quincy and I headed out for our morning walk. It was trash day and one of our neighbors had put out around a dozen stuffed animals on the curb to be taken away. As we walked down the street, Quincy made a beeline for them. For about five minutes, he sniffed each and every one, picking one up in his mouth, putting it down before moving on to the next one. Finally, he picked up a small blue Angry Bird and began walking again. He carried it for several blocks and then sat down with it still in his mouth. He absolutely would not budge. I kept saying, "C'mon, Quince, let's go," but he didn't move. I knew he either had something on his mind or was tired of walking, so we turned and began walking back towards the inn.

Quincy continued to carry the Angry Bird, but when we were across the street from the pile of stuffed toys once again he sat down, never breaking eye contact with the pile of toys. It suddenly became obvious what he was thinking, so I said, "Quince, do you want to go back and look at them all one more time?" He immediately headed for the pile, put Angry Bird down on the ground, and sniffed the pile again. He picked up the green turtle, then put it down. He picked up the yellow duck, then put it down. He picked up every single stuffed animal that was in that pile, and after a final assessment of every toy, he picked up the Angry Bird and happily trotted back home. That became one of his favorite toys and I keep it in my car to remind me of the amazingly intelligent boy Quincy was.

There was a time in Quincy's life when we had Diana, a local Reiki practitioner, come to do regular sessions on him. Most dogs are extremely relaxed after five minutes of Reiki, but after a half hour Quincy was still standing up. He never completely relaxed. As a puppy, I would try to get him to relax but he never did. Even when he seemed relaxed on the outside, Quincy was still going a million miles an hour on the inside.

The last six months of Quincy's life were really bad. However, I don't want Quincy's story to be full of trials and tribulations of his poor and failing health. I do not want this story and the legacy of Quincy as our inn dog to be about his worst days. I want it to be about his best days and all the joy he brought us and so many other people.

Quincy taught us so many things in the nine and a half years we shared. He taught me to really think things through, sort out your options, and take things as they come. When I talk about him I am really talking about us, about the inn and the life we created together, because that's where the magic comes in. We had a magical life with him. He was the fun, reckless, and wild one. At the inn, and in what was often had to be a controlled environment, he brought the crazy in and it was all good. Every minute of it.

Telling the story of Quincy has allowed me to feel all the emotions attached to losing him. It is sad that eulogies and obituaries come only after people and pets are gone. I think Quincy would have loved this story of his life—and in typical Quincy fashion, he would remind me of a couple more stories about him I forgot to tell.

Following Quincy's passing, Ken and Donna wanted to place his obituary in their hometown paper. They had done it for Beau but in the ensuing years, the newspaper had changed hands and the new management didn't allow dog obituaries. I think it worked out perfectly because now, rather than it appearing to a small audience in his hometown, it will appear for the first time to a larger audience around the world.

QUINCY AROLD

Quincy was born on April 22, 2006, and began his life with us at the inn on June 11. As a puppy, Quincy's "Marley-like" nature made life interesting, to say the least.

At the age of two, Quincy was introduced to the front of the house and began meeting guests there. He enjoyed the role of Greeter and took his job as Head of Security very seriously. Quincy was well known along Main Street and loved his daily walks and attending town events. We enjoyed seeing smiles on people's faces as they watched him sit at each corner before crossing the street. Quincy had become quite a gentleman.

The nine years we had together were filled with simple daily pleasures and the best vacations. Quincy was not a fan of car rides but loved relaxing destinations. He was a wonderful swimmer and a true retriever in the water. His separation anxiety kept us close together, but we liked that. Our downtime away from the inn was precious and we made immeasurable memories.

Because of the inn, Quincy was able to meet many people and touch many hearts. Anyone who met him loved our beautiful boy. He was a stoic, happy dog whose talents were

Quincy
(Photo: Jenna Perfette Photography)

wasted on us. Quincy would have been an amazing police dog or bomb sniffer because of his attention to detail and work ethic. I always wished he could read because he seemed bored a lot of the time.

Quincy was much more of a thinker than a fetcher and that's what made him so unique. We love him immensely and he left us way too soon. Quincy's presence is, and will forever be, missed at the inn but most especially by Ken and me when we spent our off time together. He was our forever companion and our very best friend. We love you, Quincy. Life will never be the same without you.

ANIMAL REIKI

After my conversation with Donna, I reached out to Diana Fenty Davis, the local Reiki practitioner who worked with Quincy.

I LOVE QUINCY. HE WAS A TROOPER, A SOLDIER AND STOIC TO A fault. I met him for the first time when a mutual friend, thinking Reiki might possibly help Quincy, introduced me to Donna and Quincy.

Quincy was prone to take on his owners' anxiety. He wasn't sure what was happening around him but he knew his owners were worried and therefore felt, on some level, he should be worried, too. I explained to him that because he was not feeling well, his parents were concerned. He understood and immediately relaxed.

Quincy always wanted to please his parents and constantly worried he was a problem for them. I explained to Quincy that he was loved beyond words and that he could just relax and receive their love. He was such a beautiful soul and remains ever at Donna's side, trying his best to comfort her in his next life.

Next, I contacted Kathleen Prasad, an Animal Reiki teacher, the founder and director of Animal Reiki Source,[1] and the president of the Shelter Animal Reiki Association.[2] Kathleen graciously took time to share her insights, experiences, and knowledge of animal Reiki.

The word Reiki comes from two Japanese words: *Rei*, which means spirit, and *Ki*, which means energy. So

Kathleen and Dakota
(Photo: Kendra Luck)

Reiki means "spiritual energy" and is a system of spiritual practices based on meditation to help the practitioner become more present, mindful, and compassionate.

When you learn Reiki, you learn meditation practices, hands-on positions for yourself and other people, as well as breathing practices, symbols, and mantras. Reiki for humans often includes hands-on healing treatments. If someone is sad or hurt, we instinctively want to put our arm around them or hug them, and that tactile piece can be an important part of the healing process. With human Reiki, the practitioner does the hand positions and guides the treatment.

When working with animals, we use a different approach and one that takes into account their way of being in the world and their awareness of the subtle nature of things. The most important part of a Reiki treatment with an animal isn't touch (which may or may not be part of the session) but the practitioner's state of mind.

Animals are very sensitive to our emotional state. If we are in a space of anger, it can be very disturbing to an animal. The more we focus on fear and worry, the more unpleasant it will be for an animal to connect with us. The more we come from a space of humility, gratitude, and compassion, the better responses we will see from the animals. Letting go of your hands and opening your mind is the best way to support your animal's healing.

With animal Reiki, the practitioner is still and the animal guides the treatment. It's important to respect the animal. If they say no to Reiki, you need to accept it. Sometimes they simply aren't in the mood or want to play. Dogs in shelters have been cooped up in a cage and will probably want to go for a walk first so they can relax and sit with me.

Animals appreciate being given control of the session—not only by being allowed to say yes or no but by determining the way the session will unfold. It's important to begin by asking permission of the animal directly in a non-assertive manner. Make sure your body language matches this passive intention. Try to stay in a non-threatening pose or stand over them, do not initiate and hold eye contact. Let go of your expectations of how the session should go. Instead, go inward and hold a meditative space and allow the dog to come to you. There may be an ebb and flow of the dog coming and leaving. Or they may sit next to you or put a specific body part in your lap that needs healing.

Ideally an animal Reiki session will last from thirty to sixty minutes to allow for the dog to go into a deeper relaxation. It is when the body is relaxed and truly at peace that optimum healing responses can take place.

The whole purpose of the practice of Reiki is to let go of judgment, of doing and trying to fix things, of expectations and anger and fear, and to really just be. All the differences melt away and it doesn't matter that I'm human and they are a dog. When we look with our eyes, we see physical differences, but when we open and see with our hearts, we see that we are all one. I call this seeing with our Reiki eyes and it is in that openhearted place of connection where healing miracles reside and are possible.

I work with a lot of shelter animals. With Reiki, you can see animals getting better, relaxing, and being relieved of stress and you can see nervous, neurotic behaviors begin to soften.

You can sit with a dog who is completely shut down, unresponsive to any outside stimuli because of trauma, their eyes lackluster. I can sit in a meditative space and begin to see the spark come back into the dog's eyes as they feel my peacefulness and my open heart. They start to remember, "Oh, there is hope. I can get better. There is such a thing as kindness and love." Sometimes it's about simply holding hope for dogs who have given up.

For animals in hospice care, it helps create a space of peacefulness for both the animal and the people. Many times, the dog is at peace with their passing but the people are having trouble facing it. Reiki creates the possibility for everyone to be on the same page.

Anyone who has struggled on any level will tell you they always remember that special person or animal who just sat with them, without judgment or an agenda. When someone is fully present with another— be it human or animal—without trying to fix or judge them, that kind of compassionate support is the most powerful gift you can offer another being.

Animal Reiki is a way to help the healing process of an animal when they are suffering or going through a difficult period emotionally, spiritually, or physically. It is a way for the dog's person or practitioner to help and support the animal. While it's true that Reiki is a healing system, people often have expectations that if their animal receives a Reiki treatment all physical and emotional problems will disappear. While it sometimes does mean getting better, healing doesn't always mean a cure in the way the person anticipated. Sometimes it is a dog's time to pass. With the tools of Reiki, they can do so in a beautiful space of peace and balance.

I have found that dogs resistant to Reiki are usually resistant to our approach. We need to let go of judgment or expectations. Dogs are very sensitive and if they see us coming to "fix" things through Reiki, it creates a resistance with the dog because they feel you are judging them and coming in with a negative vibration. For instance, if your dog is dying and you're very emotional about it and want Reiki to "fix" the dog, you are coming at it with a preordained agenda. I experienced this with my dog, Dakota.

Dakota was the first dog I ever did Reiki with. He was an Australian shepherd mix I rescued from the Sacramento Animal Control as a puppy. Even though I learned Reiki a few years after I got Dakota, at the time, I never thought about doing it for dogs.

When Dakota was about six years old, he would come over and lay on top of my feet as I did my meditations. He had always laid *by* my feet but now he was laying *on top of* my feet. Even though I wasn't consciously trying to give him Reiki, he liked it and wanted to be part of it. Without realizing it, I was already doing animal Reiki. That was a powerful lesson.

When Dakota was a little over sixteen years old, he was diagnosed with cancer. I was devastated and determined he was going to be a miracle patient and that I was going to cure him with Reiki.

Dakota was so upset with my attitude. Even though he could no longer walk, if I tried to do Reiki with him he would drag himself away from me. I would cry and ask him, "Dakota, what are you doing? Why don't you want Reiki?"

One day, as this was happening, I put my hands over my heart. As I did, Dakota turned and looked into my eyes. Looking first at him and then down at my hands over my heart, I understood what he was telling me. He was saying, "Mom, I might be dying of cancer but I'm fine. *You* are the one that needs healing from this. You need to do Reiki on yourself." In that moment, I got it. Realizing I was sending all this panic, fear, and anger to Dakota, I began doing Reiki for myself and Dakota immediately gave a big sigh, lay down, and relaxed. It was almost like Dakota was doing Reiki for me so I could handle what was going to happen. It was as if he said, "I'm going to help you, Mom. We're going to do this together so you can get through this journey." That was so profound to me to realize that even in the midst of his terminal illness Dakota was helping me.

It often takes humans a lot to get into a spiritual space, but dogs are already there. They are so open in their hearts, so present and in the moment. With Reiki I have seen that when we work on ourselves and learn to let go of a lot of stuff, we can do a lot more to help our dogs. Many times though it is our dogs who end up teaching us about life, healing, and letting go, and that love never dies.

I would recommend all dog lovers consider learning Reiki so you can be with your dog in their space with an open heart. It will completely change your relationship with your dog and enrich the life you share.

Chapter Fifteen
MARY

Mary moved to my hometown in seventh grade. She was a sweet, quiet girl with beautiful eyes and a shy smile. After we graduated from high school, Mary moved away, but many years later we reconnected and she visited me in New Jersey. We talked nonstop during the days she stayed here at my house. She still had the same beautiful eyes and smile and was still as sweet as I remembered her to be all those years ago. I also learned about Mary's love for dogs and especially her beloved Golden Girls.

BEFORE I MET MY HUSBAND, I HADN'T HAD A DOG FOR OVER twenty-five years. I often thought about getting a dog but was single, moving around a lot, and didn't have the time or money necessary to devote to a dog. When George and I got married, Goldie, his five-year-old reddish-colored golden retriever, was part of the package and that was fine with me. Goldie was incredible and just as sweet as she could be.

Although Goldie and I bonded really quickly, it took me a while to understand dogs and what they needed. Thankfully, Goldie was patient with me. Because of the companionship and love Goldie showered on me, I remembered the wonder of dogs and fell in love with them all over again.

Goldie, the original Golden Girl

When we got married, George was in the Air Force and we lived just outside of St. Louis. Two years later, he retired from the Air Force and the three of us packed up and moved to Wichita, Kansas. After about three years, we noticed Goldie wasn't able to balance very well. After doing some tests, the vet said she had cancer in her spine. We took her home and over time her back legs would go out from under her and she was no longer able to walk.

We took Goldie back to the vet for tests one day, and I was home alone when the vet called with the test results. He said the cancer had spread throughout her entire body and that it was time. I just started screaming. George came home and we went to see her for the last time. Goldie was sitting in a cage with her whole backend shaved and we just lost it. They asked if we wanted to be there but we said no, walked out to the parking lot, and couldn't stop sobbing. Goldie had been in so much pain and even though they told us she went peacefully, to this day, I regret not staying with Goldie until the end.

I missed Goldie so much. My heart was broken and I didn't want another dog, but about a year after Goldie passed, I told George, "I need another dog. I can't take it anymore."

When we lived in St. Louis, I worked at Ralston Purina. Many of my coworkers had golden retrievers they had gotten from a breeder in Farmington, Missouri, so I called a friend and got the breeder's name and number. The breeder sent us videos of a new litter of puppies. The breeder had a different color ribbon on each puppy and George and I were both drawn to "Ms. Orange." We called the breeder to let her know which one we chose. Since the puppies were too young to separate from their mother and littermates, we made arrangements to pick her up when she was eight weeks old.

I had never picked out a dog or had a puppy of my own, so I was extremely excited. When we arrived in St. Louis, we stayed with my longtime friend and dog lover, Mary. That night, my friends from Ralston Purina threw me a surprise puppy shower and gave me every imaginable kind of dog toy and treat as well as Ralston Purina dog food—all of which added to the excitement of going to get our puppy the next day.

Mary, George, and I drove to the breeder to pick up Ms. Orange, who was now known as Casey. We placed Casey on the back seat in a little box filled with soft, cozy towels and blankets and I sat on the back seat next to her. For the longest time, she lay there staring at me so I finally picked her up. For the next seven hours, she slept in my lap. We stopped several times and every time she got out of the car, Casey would look back at me. It was as if she was checking to make sure I was coming too. We bonded immediately and she was the love of my life.

Our neighbors back in Wichita were excited to meet her, and when we got home they were all outside waiting for us. Casey quickly became not only a part of our family but a part of the neighborhood. We lived on a golf course and she and I played catch for hours on the course as our neighbors watched and cheered for her. Everyone just loved her.

When Casey was about two years old, I had surgery. George brought me home from the hospital and as he helped me lie down in bed, Casey immediately jumped on the bed and sniffed around to see what was going on. I held my incision and George told Casey to be careful but she knew. She lay down next to me and put her paw on my shoulder and the two of us went to sleep. George had to coax her to go outside because she didn't want to leave my side.

Even in our daily routine, Casey really never left my side. I worked from home as a seamstress and Casey sat next to me or under my sewing machine as I sewed. When clients came over, she sat on the steps and visited with us. Sometimes I would swear Casey was a girl in a dog body because she was like one of the girls. Anytime my girlfriends and I got together, Casey would sit with her backside on the hearth and her front legs on the floor and listen.

Every Halloween, I dressed her up and we'd answer the door together. One year I dressed her up as bicyclist. I put my helmet and goggles on her and sat her next to my bike. I know she thought it was silly, but like so many other things, she did it because it made me happy. She was just a great companion and very tolerant of my sense of humor.

When Casey was five, we decided to get another golden from the same breeder. Our hope was to get a puppy with the same mom as Casey since Casey was such a sweet dog. We called the breeder and she said Lilly (Casey's mom) was due to give birth to another litter in the next few weeks. After the puppies were born, we again picked our next

Golden Girl through videotapes the breeder sent us. This time, we picked "Ms. Purple."

When the puppies were eight weeks old, George was away on business so my friend Donna and I headed to Missouri. We didn't know until we arrived at the breeder's home that Lilly had birthed nine puppies but the tenth puppy was stillborn and had to be removed. Lilly was sick and unable to care for her pups like she had done with Casey's litter.

The breeder had three different litters being kept in three whelping pools in her barn. A small fence around each one kept the litters separated. Not seeing our puppy, I asked the breeder, "Where is Ms. Purple? I don't see her here."

We looked around and finally found her in the back of the barn in a box with a barn cat. The cat had adopted and was taking care of the puppy. As a result, the puppy had begun to take on the qualities and behaviors of a cat, something that was obvious that day when, on the drive home, she crawled up my arm and wrapped herself around my neck just like a cat. That same behavior would play out for the rest of the puppy's life.

I named the puppy Samantha Lilly (Lilly being a tribute to her mother) but called her Sammie for short. Casey wasn't impressed or happy when Sammie and I arrived in Wichita and for the next three weeks sat with her back to me. Every once in a while, Casey would turn her head, sigh, then turn her head back as if saying, "I have nothing to say to you. I am so mad at you." She just didn't understand why we had to bring another dog into the house.

Despite her disapproval of me and the entire situation, Casey cared for Sammie as if she were her mother. When Sammie was in her crate, Casey would lay right next to the crate to be close to Sammie and watch over her. She coddled her and taught her the things she needed to know and they got along really well. Casey was very loving towards Sammie and just wanted to snuggle.

Sammie, on the other hand, was very independent and a little bit on the nutty side. I believe this was due to the different experiences they each had early in life. Casey had spent her early weeks with her siblings and mother. Sammie never got so spend time with her dog mom. Instead, she had a cat mom and in many ways acted like a cat her entire life.

She would slink like a cat and stalk Casey before pouncing on her. It was like a circus living with the two of them.

About three years after bringing Sammie home, Casey started vomiting several times a week and was generally not feeling well. The vet in Wichita was unable to find the problem and suggested we take her to the College of Veterinary Medicine at Kansas State University. They, too, couldn't find anything, and since she looked pretty healthy, they told us to keep an eye on her.

Casey seemed to bounce back, so when my husband got an opportunity in Washington State, we packed up the car and headed West. While Casey wasn't vomiting, she still didn't seem to enjoy the three-day ride.

We settled into our rental home in Washington State and four months later, when Casey still wasn't feeling or acting like her old self, we took her to a vet in our new hometown. Casey was dehydrated so they kept her overnight to try and hydrate her. The next night, I brought Casey home and her spleen burst. My friend Mary from St. Louis was visiting us and she drove to the emergency clinic while I lay in the back seat with Casey. We were in the room with the vet, petting and holding Casey, when all of a sudden her tail started wagging and she lifted her head. I told Mary, "I bet George just got here," and two minutes later, George walked into the room. Mary was there when we picked Casey up as a puppy and she was there when we had to put her down. All three of us stayed with Casey while they injected her and I am so glad we were there. She was no longer in pain and just peacefully slipped away from us.

After Casey passed, I was a wreck. I would lie down on the bed and Sammie would curl around me. I literally couldn't move and Sammie never left my side. She would lie next to me and pat my shoulder just like Casey had done after my surgery. For the next two weeks, Sammie whimpered and looked for Casey. She continued to mope around until she finally figured out she was now top dog. After that, she was fine and became very loving. She actually took on Casey's role in our home of being affectionate and loving after Casey passed.

For the next four years, it was just Sammie, George, and me. Back in Wichita, George had taught Sammie to pick up our neighbor's newspaper and deliver it to their front door. Sammie took her job very seriously and the neighbors appreciated her hard work—especially on snowy or rainy days—and left treats for her.

In Seattle, the landscape was very different from Wichita. There were only five houses on our cul-de-sac and every one had a big steep driveway, and most of our neighbors only got the newspaper on Sunday. Still, Sammie made sure everybody's Sunday paper was at their front door waiting for them, and just like in Wichita, our Seattle neighbors left treats on their front porch to thank her.

Our third year in Washington, we purchased and moved into our own home. A year later, Sammie wasn't acting right. The vet noticed a growth under her chin that turned out to be thyroid cancer. We started her on chemo and for a while she did just fine. On Thanksgiving that year, she bounced back and ran around and we did all kinds of things together. It was a wonderful day.

The next morning, the growth had grown almost four times in size overnight. I had never seen anything grow so big so fast. George and I looked at one another and we knew.

We went to the same emergency clinic we had gone to with Casey and they said the cancer had spread through her entire body. When it was time to put her down, she didn't lay down like Casey. Sammie was walking around the clinic, her tail wagging. After we spent a little more time with her and said our goodbyes, the vet took us into a separate room, gave her the shot, and Sammie went to sleep with George and me both holding her.

We had Sammie cremated and I kept her ashes under my desk, which is where I had kept Casey's ashes. One morning, about a month later, I drove to the park where we used to go to and spread their ashes near a small pond. I knew in my heart it was perfect because it was a place we had spent so many happy times together.

That was 2011 and we had lost three golden retrievers to cancer. Goldie passed when she was nine, Casey was ten, and Sammie was almost twelve. Even though we felt like our record was getting better, it was still so hard because we kept thinking that we just couldn't keep our Golden Girls alive.

A year after Sammie passed, we started looking for a new breeder, but for over a year, we would call breeders and they wouldn't call us back.

Casey, Mary, and Sammie

We started to think that maybe it wasn't meant to be until one night, I decided to try one more time. I found a breeder online who was about two hours south of where we live and hesitantly picked up the phone. She answered, and after telling her about us, she said she had a litter that had been born on May 14, which is George's birthday. When I learned the breeder's name was Alice, which is my mother's name, I felt we had been given the signs that we had found our breeder.

The puppies were only two weeks old but she said we could come see them. Since I was already scheduled to go out of town, George drove down to see them. He called me, very excited, and said he thought I was going to love "Ms. Orange." A few weeks later, we drove down together to see them and meet the puppies' mother and father. The father was a show dog who had won numerous competitions. He had perfect lines and was the most beautiful golden retriever I had ever seen in my life. But even more amazing was that the puppies' mother looked exactly like Sammie!

I picked up Ms. Orange. She seemed to like me but I put her down and sat in the whelping pool with her littermates to watch all of the nine puppies. After a few minutes, another puppy crawled into my lap, let out a sigh, and went to sleep.

I looked at George and said, "Ummm, I think we have a problem."

He looked at me and said, "Why, what's she doing?"

"Well," I said, "this isn't Ms. Orange. This is a different dog. This is Ms. Purple."

"So you want to switch?"

"No," I told him. "I'm thinking we should take both of them."

Since the puppies were only six weeks old, we decided to think about it over the weekend. We drove home in silence. Over the weekend, we

Maggie and Ellie

talked about what it would mean to have two puppies and weighed the pros and cons. Since there were more pros, we called Alice on Monday and said we would take them both.

We named them Maggie Mae and Eleanor Rigby and, as soon as they were eight weeks old, we went down and picked up our girls.

We took them to puppy manners class, obedience class, and agility. At every class, they weren't interested and learned nothing. In the puppy class, we were told to bring in a spray bottle filled with water. Every time the puppies barked, everyone would spray the water and all the dogs would stop barking, except for Maggie and Ellie. When we sprayed the water, they would start licking the water and get even more excited.

Maggie and Ellie are now two years old and have settled down quite a bit. When we open the door, they no longer jump on people. Our motto is "A tired dog is a happy dog" so we go on three walks a day. They are very sweet and I am glad we have them. It's nice to have two dogs who love me and they are very in tune with me. If I am upset, they know it and will come and sit next to me.

We don't know how the cancer happened in our last three girls. With Goldie, Casey, and Sammie we weren't as aware as we are now so we are trying to keep Maggie and Ellie healthy and give them the best care we can. We are conscious and deliberate with everything we do with Maggie and Ellie. We make sure we don't walk across pesticide-treated lawns. We avoid dairy and people food. We feed them special organic dog food to which we add organic pumpkin. We don't take them to dog parks because we are not sure what germs or problems we might encounter.

I'm glad I had other dogs before getting Maggie and Ellie because if they had been my first, I don't think it would have gone as well. Each one of my dogs prepared me for Maggie and Ellie and each of my dogs has taught me something.

With Goldie, I learned how to take care of a dog and what it meant to have a dog. After Goldie passed, I thought I couldn't do it again because I couldn't stand to bear that kind of pain ever again, but she taught me that having a dog was important—and helpful. Through Goldie, I learned how much love a dog has to give and that it is an unconditional love like no other.

Casey was a lovely, wonderful dog and so in tune with me. She taught me what real love feels like, and in many ways, I still haven't gotten over the loss of Casey. Casey was my girl.

With Samantha, I learned patience. She would see a rabbit in the backyard and stalk it like a cat. I think if we looked inside Sammie's brain, she would have been saying, "I'm a dog but I'm a cat . . . I'm a cat but I'm a dog." She was funny and full of life.

Maggie Mae is laid back and sweet, much like Casey, and Ellie is a little nutty like Sammie.

I now take Maggie and Ellie down to the park where I spread Casey's and Sammie's ashes. For a long time, it was a sad place for me but now it is a place where I can remember all the happy times with all my Golden Girls.

✦ UNDERSTANDING ✦
CANCER IN GOLDENS

Wanting to understand cancer (particularly as it impacts golden retrievers), I reached out to several experts. The first was Rhonda Hovan, who has been a breeder and owner/handler of golden retrievers for over forty years. She is the Research Facilitator for the Golden Retriever Club of America,[1] founded the Starlight Fund at the AKC Canine Health Foundation[2] (CHF) to support golden retriever health research, and serves on the board of directors of CHF. I spoke with Rhonda to get her thoughts about cancer in golden retrievers.

APPROXIMATELY 60 PERCENT OF ALL GOLDENS WILL DIE FROM cancer. By gender, that is broken down to 57 percent of females and 66 percent of males. (Human cancer is slightly skewed towards males so it's not surprising that the same holds true for dogs.) By way of comparison, 50 percent of all dogs over the age of ten die from cancer.

The two most common cancers in the breed, representing about half of all the cancers in goldens, are hemangiosarcoma, which affects one in five goldens, and lymphoma, which affects one in eight goldens.

I regularly encounter prospective buyers wanting to know how they can avoid cancer risks when they purchase a dog and seeking advice about where to get their next dog and what to look for from a breeder. For the most part, that is an ineffective approach.

There is currently no way for even the most conscientious, deliberate, well-intentioned breeder to breed away from cancer. We don't yet have any tools to let us know which dogs carry more or less heritable risk of getting cancer. People often think if a dog didn't have a close relative with cancer they're safer and, conversely, if they did have a relative with cancer, they're at risk. In reality, neither of those is true. For any given dog with cancer, there is no way to know whether its cancer risk was increased by inheritable genes or whether its cancer was sporadic (caused by random mutations that occurred over its lifetime).

Since investigation and research are ongoing, we're left with lifestyle choices, which are very powerful in humans and we think can be just as powerful in dogs. It's estimated that about three-fourths of cancer in humans is related to lifestyle choices. It may not be quite so high in goldens because there is a larger inherited component, but lifestyle modification is still a powerful tool that can be used to manage risk in dogs. The following lifestyle choices are not fully proven but there is good evidence leading in their direction.

The first lifestyle choice is to raise a puppy to grow very slowly. It is called The Slow Growth Plan wherein puppies are kept very lean. This is partly the responsibility of the breeder and partly the responsibility of the owner.

The first critical slow growth period is the first two months of the puppy's life, which are typically spent with the breeder. Most puppies go home at eight weeks, at which point, each should weigh approximately nine and a half pounds. We have all seen the images of chunky, roly-poly puppies, and while they are admittedly cute, they are much larger than they should be and it is unhealthy for them.

The next critical period is from two to four months and, since most puppies are adopted by this point, it now becomes the owner's responsibility to ensure the puppy stays lean. A good guideline is that the puppy should be lean enough to feel and count every one of their ribs. For specific exercise and weight recommendations, the slow growth plan is available by searching the internet.

The next lifestyle choice that we believe can reduce cancer risk is to keep the dog well-exercised. This advice, staying lean and exercising, is the same advice given to humans because the origins of cancer follow the same cellular processes in dogs as in humans. To a significant extent, cancer results from long-term, subclinical inflammation. Therefore, factors that increase inflammation also increase cancer risk, while factors that decrease inflammation help to decrease cancer risk. In dogs and in humans, body fat drives inflammation higher while exercise is one of the few factors known to reduce inflammation. So maintaining low body fat and getting abundant exercise can work together to reduce inflammation and thus reduce cancer risk.

Another proactive lifestyle choice is reducing exposure to fleas and ticks. Goldens that have been exposed to fleas and ticks appear to have a higher incidence of lymphoma and possibly hemangiosarcoma, too. Conversely, goldens treated with flea and tick preventatives appear to have a lower incidence of these two cancers.

Although there is a great deal of discussion and concern among dog owners and breeders regarding a possible relationship between vaccinations or diet and risk of cancer, there isn't any scientific evidence that either can impact the development of cancer. Owners should discuss vaccinations with a veterinarian they trust.

There is ongoing research looking for inherited genes that increase cancer risk in goldens and early findings are promising; however, we need to be careful how this information will eventually be used and interpreted. It is important to proceed very carefully when the first DNA tests for cancer risk genes become available. In our zeal to eliminate these genes, we could end up with additional, unforeseen problems caused by a shrinking gene pool.

Finally, average lifespan in dogs is closely tied genetically to height and body mass, and the eleven-year average in goldens (10.7 in males and 11.3 in females) is within the range predicted by its height and body mass. Further, within the breed, on average, shorter goldens live longer than taller goldens, and this difference can be significant. In females, the shortest goldens live 1.1 years longer than the tallest, and the shortest males live an average of 2.2 years longer than the tallest males. While these are just statistical averages and do not apply to every individual, it is a factor that some buyers may wish to consider when selecting a litter. The height of the parents is a reasonable predictor of the height the puppy will attain, while the size of the puppy compared to its littermates is not usually predictive of adult height.

Because of the genetic limitations that link longevity to height and body mass, even if most of the common cancers in golden retrievers could be eliminated, it is likely to add less than a year to average breed lifespan. While those extra months would certainly be precious, it's important to also be realistic in expectations because it is not currently foreseeable that breed longevity could be greatly extended. Nonetheless, cancer research is among the highest priorities for many owners, breeders, and researchers, and organizations such as the Golden Retriever Club of America and the Golden Retriever Foundation will be able to provide you with the latest developments in golden health and research.

Offering additional hope on the horizon is the Morris Animal Foundation's[3] Golden Retriever Lifetime Study, which will follow and collect data on 3,000 golden retrievers over the course of their lifetime. With the help of experts in veterinary health and epidemiology, the Foundation will use the study in part to more accurately estimate the incidence of the four most common (and fatal) cancers in golden retrievers.

"We estimated we could accurately determine the incidence of the four most common and fatal cancers in golden retrievers after ten years of monitoring, providing we could successfully follow 1,800 to 2,000 dogs for that entire timespan," said Dr. David Haworth, president/CEO of the Foundation. "Enrolling 3,000 golden retrievers under the age of two years would give us a number that would provide the statistical power to help answer questions about cancer incidence and give us clues about other factors that are critical to creating a healthy, long life for golden retrievers and all dogs."

Knowing the importance of early life exposures on lifetime wellness and longevity, the Foundation wanted to enroll dogs as young as possible to capture the complete health story of each dog. In 2012, they began enrolling golden retrievers under the age of two years. In March 2015, the 3,000[th] golden retriever was enrolled in the study.

"My admiration for our participants—dog owners, veterinarians, and, of course, the golden retrievers themselves, continues to grow," said Erin Searfoss, study director of the Canine Lifetime Health Project[4] of which the Golden Retriever Lifetime Study is a part. "Their dedication, the hard-working study team staff, and the support of our partners will make a lasting impact on veterinary medicine and the health of all dogs for many years to come."

Finally, I reached out to Dr. Demian Dressler,[5] who trained at Cornell University and practiced conventional veterinary medicine for many years. After researching dog cancer and discovering treatments and mindsets from other cultures and medical systems that can help dogs, he now considers himself a "full spectrum veterinarian." He is also the chief medical officer of Functional Nutriments, the maker of Apocaps and EverPup. Dr. Dressler's advice combines the best of conventional medicine along with nutraceuticals, supplements, diet, and mind-body medicine. Along with Dr. Susan Ettinger, a veterinary oncologist, he coauthored The Dog Cancer Survival Guide. *The following information is compiled from Dr. Dressler's book and appears here with the express permission of Dr. Dressler and his publisher, Maui Media, LLC.*

Cancer is now the number-one killer of dogs, and goldens are certainly no exception: it is estimated that two-thirds to three-fourths of all deaths in goldens are due to cancer. While lymphosarcoma (a white cell cancer), osteosarcoma (bone cancer), and hemangiosarcoma (usually in the spleen) are the most common cancers among goldens, there is a strong possibility of other aggressive cancers as well.

It sounds hopeless, I know—especially when you consider that at this time there is no "one cure" for systemic cancer. It's not like a broken bone; we can't just set it correctly and have it heal.

But here's a silver lining: if there isn't "one cure," that means there is also no "one absolute right way" to treat cancer. And we're learning more every day about what helps—it's possible we will soon see cancer as a manageable, chronic illness, like diabetes or heart disease. In fact, that's how I think you should view cancer right now.

If your dog has cancer, there are many factors you should consider, including your dog's overall health, the type and progression of the cancer, and your own resources in terms of both finances and time.

When there is so much to consider, it is helpful to break things down into smaller parts and look at each individually. That's why I outline a systematic approach to addressing your dog's cancer in my book, which includes: 1) conventional treatments (including how to manage the side effects); 2) nutraceuticals; 3) immune system boosters and anti-metastatics; 4) dog cancer diet; and 5) brain chemistry modification.

Keeping as calm as possible is critical, because we've seen evidence that emotional calm can both help the body to heal *and help us to make good decisions.* Our dogs tend to pick up on our emotions, so when we are upset, they are upset. Using the exercises in the book to manage your emotions *first* is an important part of full spectrum cancer care. Looking back, you want to know that you did everything you could, the best you could; by approaching your dog's cancer in a systematic manner, you can make confident (if difficult) decisions and minimize later regrets.

But what if you have a dog who is healthy, and you want to *prevent* cancer? Well, just as there is no "one way" to treat cancer, there is no "one way" to prevent it. Cancer arises in the body when a multitude of factors are present and the body is overcome—and it's one of our oldest diseases. So, rather than assuming you can prevent it from ever happening, I recommend *deciding to reduce risk.*

We know that certain lifestyle choices make a dog's body more hostile to cancer initiation and progression, so here are some common-sense steps you can take today to help your dog.

- Give your dog a dark—pitch black—sleeping environment to ensure that they're generating enough of the anti-cancer hormone melatonin every day.

- Avoid obesity, because it leads to a deficiency in the anti-cancer chemical adiponectin. Ask your vet to help determine your dog's ideal body condition and weight, and then take steps to get him there.

- Isolation and depression are strongly linked to cancer in humans; spend time with your dog and increase her joy any way you can. That smile is helping her stay healthy.

- Increase healthy and joyful exercise.

- Add brightly colored, low-starch veggies like red and orange bell peppers and broccoli to his diet.

- Favor leaner meats like white meats and fish over red meats in her diet to reduce the risk of mammary cancer.

- Limit high-carbohydrate foods like corn, wheat, and sugar.

- Choose dog foods that haven't been processed at high temperatures (kibble). Better-quality commercial dog food brands include The Honest Kitchen, Orijen, Blue Buffalo, Halo, Taste of the Wild, and Solid Gold.

- Avoid carcinogen exposure of all kinds when you can. Use glass and ceramic instead of plastic, and avoid pesticides, lawn chemicals, tobacco smoke, and car exhaust. Filter your water and your air—you'll all feel better.

When getting a new puppy, please consider the following:

- If you are set on a high-risk bloodline, like a golden retriever or a boxer, remember that it is probably impossible to know for sure whether your puppy has inherited a genetic problem or not. Choosing one of our favorite breeds is, in a way, choosing a dog with a much higher risk of cancer. In that case, taking steps to reduce risk are all the more important!

- Very early vaccinations may encourage the developing immune system to be hypervigilant to pathogens and *less vigilant about killing tumors*. This is a complicated subject, so please read this section of my book for more insight and the nuances of this discussion—but generally, I advise holding off on starting puppy vaccinations until the eighth or even tenth week of life. A booster shot can be given at one year, and then again three years later at four, and then at seven. Starting at age eight, instead of routine vaccinations, run titers on an annual basis, and only give vaccines *if your dog needs them*. Also, do not vaccinate for diseases that aren't present in your area.

- Weigh the pros and cons of surgical sterilization very carefully with your veterinarian. There are definite benefits to spaying/neutering, such as population control, calmer behavior, and a reduction in mammary cancer risk. There are, however, also risks. Sterilization, especially *early* sterilization, may both cause orthopedic issues and eliminate the cancer protection that sex hormones provide. This is another complicated and touchy subject, and there are many things to consider, so please take a look at the research Dr. Ettinger and I have on our blog and in our book for details about what shifted our thinking on this subject. In general, if you decide to sterilize, I recommend waiting until the dog is between the third and fourth heat for females, and between eighteen months and twenty-four months for males.

- Add dietary adaptogens to your dog's diet to support his health and well-being and keep his normal, vigorous body in top shape.

There is nothing better than the love of a dog, and I share these ideas and information with you in an attempt to help you keep your pups healthy and happy for as long as possible.

Chapter Sixteen
BECKY

Becky was the raven-haired beauty with a ready smile, sweet spirit, and brilliant mind who worked at the local natural foods market. Whenever I had a question about a supplement or product, I trusted and valued her knowledge and opinion. After getting a job at the market and becoming her coworker, despite our age difference, we grew extremely close. She calls me her Earth Mama and she is the daughter I always dreamed of having. On a beautiful spring day, we sat in my backyard with Fache and Sadie prancing and playing nearby as we talked about her journey with these two magical dogs.

WE HAD CATS UNTIL I WAS TWELVE AND OUR NEIGHBOR'S DOG Alf impregnated another neighbor's dog. Soon there was a slew of puppies in the neighborhood and we adopted a female puppy we named Lizzy. Lizzy was an amazing dog—sweet, kind, and gentle.

Years later, Lizzy got cancer and the vet came to our house to put her down so she could pass with all of us around her. She broke our hearts when she left us. We all loved Lizzy but my brother had slept with Lizzy every night and was exceptionally close to her. I will never forget the impact her passing had on him. Years after she

Sadie, Becky, and Fache

passed, I asked my brother if he had three wishes what they would be. He immediately said, "First, that Lizzy would live forever. Second, that Lizzy would live forever. And third, that Lizzy would live forever."

Lizzy left an incredible imprint on my life as well because she was the first one to teach me about unconditional love and the connection between a dog and their owner. I still feel her spirit around me.

It was fifteen years before my family started talking about getting another dog. My sister-in-law Colleen worked for St. Hubert's Animal Welfare Center and found us a Yorkshire terrier-Chihuahua mix.

The day she came into our lives, I had just taken (and failed) for the fifth time the certification exam to become a musical therapist. I was living with my parents and really feeling defeated. As I got out of my car, my father came out onto the porch, took one look at me, and said, "I have something I think will cheer you up." He opened the back door and out came this tiny little dog. She ran right over to me and I picked her up and immediately fell in love.

She was so tiny that we couldn't find a collar to fit her so my father ended up making one with a rubber band and some string. Even though she was tiny, she thought she was a big tough dog so I named her Harley. She was happy, full of energy, and loved life and people. She went everywhere with me and every night she slept in my bed or at my mom's feet in my parents' bed.

When Harley was a year old, I came home from work one day to a blood-curdling scream. My mother was standing over Harley who was having a seizure on the floor. I scooped her up and ran out to my car and drove to the vet.

The vet was unable to save Harley and said she may have had a brain aneurysm. We couldn't understand why she had to be taken so soon. To this day, I can remember every moment of that day and how it felt holding her in my arms driving to the vet.

My dad was devastated and retreated to his workshop at the house. His friend John came over and spent countless hours in the workshop with my dad helping him through the loss of Harley.

Six or seven months later, a coworker of mine headed to North Carolina to rescue dogs about to be euthanized. I wasn't sure if my parents were ready for another dog but I knew the only dog they would consider was a dog just like Harley, a Yorkshire terrier-Chihuahua mix. When my coworker returned, he said every dog they brought back was a Yorkshire terrier-Chihuahua mix.

My dad and I decided to go look at them. The entire way, we kept telling one another not to get too excited because we were just going to look. We walked in and two of the puppies, a little black one and a little white brindly one, ran over to us. We picked them up and fell in love.

As we walked towards the front door, my dad turned and saw a wood carving of a heron sitting on a wooden base. He smiled and said, "I know who made that because I made the base for it." My friend's wife smiled and said, "My dad made that." Her dad was John, my dad's friend who had comforted him after Harley passed.

Somehow we convinced my mom to get not just one but two puppies and when we went back to pick them up, my dad's friend, John, was standing there holding them. They each had a big red bow on and John smiled at my dad and said, "It's come full circle, my friend."

We named the puppies Iggy and Bella, and having the love, companionship, and joy of puppies back in the house vastly improved our quality of life. Now that my parents are retired, I'm thrilled they have Iggy and Bella for company.

A few years after Iggy and Bella came into our lives, my mom was driving downtown when she stopped at an intersection and a dog jumped into her car. She looked like a miniature Rottweiler and was a mess: dirty, matted, and scraped up with her skin growing around her flea and tick collar. My parents took her to the vet, and after getting a clean bill of health, she was put into a shelter to see if her owner would come forward. When no one ever came for her, my parents adopted her and named her Gracie because she literally fell from grace into our lives.

In my early thirties, I went through some difficult times. In July 2009, I decided a fresh start was in order and got a job as a music therapist in New Mexico and moved onto an eighty-four-acre ranch with an old college friend. Surrounded by the beauty and nature of the Gallinas Canyon, it was the perfect place to heal but it was a desolate area and there weren't a lot of opportunities to meet people or make friends.

After a few months, my job wasn't working out as promised, I was missing my family and friends more and more, and I was sad and lonely.

Even though my roommate had two dogs, I began praying for something of my own to love and nurture.

One morning, while getting ready for work, I heard a dog barking. My roommate was dog-sitting three dogs but they and his two dogs were all pretty quiet so the barking startled me. I was concerned because it was September and bears were beginning to scavenge for food in preparation for winter hibernation.

My roommate had shown me how to shoot a 9 mm into the air to scare bears away. I grabbed it and ran across the fast-flowing creek near our house and towards the barn where the barking was coming from. Getting closer, I could see mud had slid down the switchback trail and was piled up against the barn.

I walked into the barn and looked around. Our landlord was storing all kinds of things in the barn—cars, trucks, and furniture—but in the midst of it all I saw a beagle named Rachel. Rachel was head-butting a little ball of fur completely matted with mud, blood, and prickers. Thinking it was a baby bear, my first concern was where the bear's mother might be. Before I could figure that out, this little furry mess opened its mouth and let out a scream. Afraid the scream would draw the attention of the cub's mother, I grabbed all five dogs and took them back to the house before heading back to the barn.

Walking back into the barn, I picked up the tiny bear cub, held it next to my heart, and continued looking around. On the other side of the barn, I saw a little face pop up from inside a dresser drawer and look at me. It looked exactly like the little bundle I was holding except it had white on its nose—and I realized they were puppies!

I scooped up the second puppy, ran back to the house, and put them in the sink to begin cleaning them off. Blood and mud came streaming off of them and their fur was still thick with stickers. They both had cuts and bruises everywhere and the nose on one of the puppies had been ripped open. Their bellies were bloated, they were clearly exhausted, and they just sat in the sink crying.

I put some wet dog food and cottage cheese in a bowl but they looked at it not knowing what to do. I knew since they were so young they were probably still nursing but it was obvious they were starving. Eventually they gobbled up the food.

Not knowing where the puppies had come from, I ran back to the barn and up and down the trails to see if there were anymore puppies but I never found any.

I called my job, told them what had happened, and drove the puppies to a nearby vet. The vet said they were about two weeks old, weighed about one pound each, and advised me to get some bottles and formula. Along with a feeding schedule, she gave me some dewormer.

Assuming they were brother and sister, I called them Little Boy and Little Girl. Since my job situation wasn't working out, I had been seriously considering moving back to New Jersey. Knowing how difficult it was to find a rental that allowed pets, much less two dogs, I was afraid to name them because I was unsure if or how long they would be with me.

Little Girl wasn't walking and all the other dogs began to lick her neck. The vet checked her and found a hole the size of a pencil eraser on her neck completely filled with maggots. The vet said if I hadn't brought her in it would have killed her. He cleaned the wound with tweezers and showed me how to take care of the gaping wound. Every night for weeks, I held her and cleaned the wound out as we both cried.

I became a nurse to the puppies. Taking care of them took my mind off my loneliness and also gave me a reason to get up in the morning and come home after work. My prayers had been answered. I had been blessed with something of my own to love and nurture and those puppies were the most beautiful gift the Universe could have given me.

My roommate's dogs and the puppies got along really well. The puppies learned from the older dogs how to be and what to do. They were all always off-leash and we all spent a lot of time hiking together.

One morning, I woke up, looked at Little Girl, and said, "Her name is Sadie." My roommate looked at Little Boy and, because he always said the puppy had a dapper handsome face, said, "And his name is Fache." Fache is Italian for "face."

I had already begun to make plans to move back to New Jersey so my roommate offered to keep Sadie and Fache with him until I found a dog-friendly place to live. The day I left, it felt like I was leaving a piece of myself behind, but I came back to Jersey determined to find a place for the three of us. My prayer was always the same: a house with a fenced-in yard, a fireplace, and a washer and dryer.

I kept looking but couldn't find anyone who allowed pets until a friend of a friend said she knew of a place. The owner was newly married and moving but wanted to keep her house for sentimental reasons. She was looking for someone to watch over and care for the house in exchange for reasonable rent.

The house had a fenced-in yard, a fireplace, and a washer and dryer—and she allowed dogs! I immediately called my roommate who told me he was moving back to Pennsylvania and would drive all of my stuff and my dogs back East for me. The Universe had gifted me once again!

I moved in and got the house ready for Sadie and Fache: new dog beds, treats, and chew toys. When my roommate phoned to say he was dropping them off, I was still at work and that afternoon as I drove home from work, I was both excited and scared. It had been six months since they had seen me. How would they react? Would they recognize me? Would they be scared?

I opened the door and immediately sat down. Fache and Sadie were so excited. Fache crawled up and sat in my lap just like he did when he was a puppy—only now he was seventy pounds! Sadie came over and snuggled up under my arm and we all started crying. I kept hugging them and telling them, "We're together again. My babies are back. And you're so big! I love you, I love you!"

We had a wonderful time reconnecting and reestablishing our life together. We jogged together every day after work. I brought them around people to socialize them. Wherever I went, they went. They were my gypsy dogs.

A month after joining me in New Jersey, Sadie was still withdrawn. As a puppy, she had slept with me but now she wouldn't even sit next to me on the bed. I began to realize she had a tougher time than Fache with our separation and that I needed to earn her trust. One day, I sat next to her on the steps and told her, "We're in this together, Sadie. I don't think you know how much I love you. It's infinite. Don't you remember? I'm the one who rescued you and took care of you. I'm always going to care for you."

As I sat there talking to her, Sadie listened then slowly leaned her entire body into mine and put her head on my shoulder. I put my arm around her and we quietly sat there. Ever since, we have been inseparable.

A year or so later, I had an opportunity to move to Oklahoma, and shortly after the move, Fache began throwing up a lot. He had always been a strong, happy dog and would jog with me for miles but he just wasn't his old self and then one night he started convulsing. We went to Animerge and they kept him overnight for tests and X-rays. I wanted to stay in the crate with him because this was the first night since we'd been reunited that we were going to be apart.

The next morning, Animerge forwarded the X-rays to Dr. Roberts, a vet just down the road from where I was living. Dr. Roberts is a great doctor and an amazing human being. His son was in the hospital at the time yet he would leave the hospital to come talk to me about my dog. He was an absolute godsend.

Since Fache hadn't been able to sit still for the X-rays, they were a bit blurry but Dr. Roberts said it appeared Fache had a blockage. Since he had also been throwing up his dinner without digesting it, Dr. Roberts wanted to keep Fache, do a barium flush in the hope that it would push the blockage through, and repeat the X-rays.

After repeating the tests, it was determined that Fache had a blockage in his cecum (a small pouch where the small intestine and large intestine meet). The next step was exploratory surgery. Dr. Roberts explained they would open Fache up from his neck to his navel and attempt to squeeze the entire length of his intestines to see if they could push anything through.

I went home and prayed. All I kept thinking was that Fache had never done anything wrong to anybody. Why him? Lonely without Fache, Sadie and I headed out for a hike. Dr. Roberts called while we were hiking and said, "I have Fache open on the table and I have bad news." I fell to my knees on the trail as Sadie sidled up next to me.

Dr. Roberts said Fache's spleen was four times the normal size and there was a tumor the size of a tangerine growing off of his aorta. As if that weren't enough, he also said Fache's liver looked diseased.

Dr. Roberts explained that while a dog's spleen isn't necessary, it has a large number of veins, tissues, and vessels leading up to and surrounding it. His concern was that if he tried to remove it, Fache would bleed out and he could lose him on the table. Instead, he proposed sending pieces of Fache's spleen and the tumor to a pathologist. He also said that even though he had been performing surgeries for over thirty-two years, if it was determined that Fache needed surgery he wanted to try and find someone with more experience to do the surgery. I agreed. I hung up the phone and sat there feeling like I'd been turned upside down and had all the stuffing shaken out of me.

Sadie and I slowly walked back home and later that day drove over to bring Fache home. He was on a morphine patch for a few days so he mainly slept and Sadie and I slept on the floor next to him. I was thankful he was home, and very slowly, he started eating again.

When the pathology report came back we learned that Fache had stage 4/advanced sarcoma hematoma, a form of cancer. He also had an aortic tumor that was pressing on his liver. The prognosis was that Fache could die tomorrow or in a few months. Overall, it didn't look good.

I asked Dr. Roberts, "If this was your dog, would you put him through chemotherapy and radiation?" He said in his experience those treatments seemed to make the dog sicker and that it would mean a lot of time at the vet, including overnight on many occasions. "But," he added, "you know your dog. You know what is best. Only you can make these decisions." I thanked him for his honesty, compassion, and time with my baby boy.

It was almost Christmas and while we all desperately missed family and friends, I phoned everyone to tell them what was happening and that I wasn't sure we would make it home for the holidays.

I told Dr. Roberts we were going to stay in Oklahoma for the holidays to be near him. He listened then said, "I think it would be good for you to go back to New Jersey. Fache needs to be around family and friends and just be happy. Chart out emergency vets along the way but I think you should definitely go."

I took his advice and Dr. Roberts was right. Fache was happy being home with our family and friends, and so was I—and something happened while we were in New Jersey that would change things for all of us, but especially for Fache.

While back in New Jersey, I visited with longtime family friends Nancy and Bill. Many years before, they had gotten a kitten they named Baby Cat. At one point, Baby Cat got sick and they were told she wouldn't live more than two weeks. They enlisted the help of a homeopathic and integrative veterinarian, Dr. Michael Dym, and Baby Cat lived over twenty more years.

Fache and Sadie shortly after Becky found them

I phoned Dr. Dym to discuss Fache and together we designed a holistic approach for Fache's care that included homeopathy. I put together a protocol of natural anti-cancer herbs and supplements based on my years of working in that field combined with extensive research I had done.

Every day, I put my hands on Fache, prayed, and told his body, "This cancer isn't allowed here. Fache deserves to be here. He's noble, he's humble, he loves people, he loves kids. You need to take up residence elsewhere."

My father reminded me of the importance of true acceptance, especially acceptance of the situation. I continued to treat Fache like I always did. We walked and went for hikes. We played and cuddled. I continued to put my hands on him and pray. I told my roommate there was to be no arguing in front of Fache, no news or violence on the TV, nothing negative.

It has been almost two and a half years since Fache's initial diagnosis and he is healthy, exuberant, and loves life. Honestly, Fache is on a slew of supplements. Every day I put so much stuff in his food that it can't taste good but Fache trusts me and must know it is helping him.

Sadie and Fache will be six in September and it has been the most amazing journey. Our hearts are connected. I would give up anything to be with them—and I know it's mutual. I cannot put into words how they make me feel but it is inconceivable how much you can cherish an animal. They know you and love you unconditionally. Even in my most difficult times, Sadie and Fache sit like statues on either side of me and just love and protect me.

I don't know how much time we will have together and realize that

Sadie and Fache today
(Photo: Photography by Sharyn)

one day they are going to break my heart, so I simply treasure every day with them. I also know they never really leave. I see things they do that Lizzy did and I know she's still around. I will always have two dogs in my lifetime as a way to honor the legacies of all the furry loves that have been in my life.

There is an understanding among the three of us. In the folds of the connected silence when we are together, there is a bond I never imagined experiencing. They give me a reason every day to be a better person. They remind me of the importance of patience, of being in the moment and truly loving those we are with, and squeezing that love into every sweet moment together. Their story, our story, is my life; I can't remember my days before them. The truth is that all those years ago, in the mountains of New Mexico when I was feeling so lost and alone, I didn't rescue them. They rescued me.

✦ INDIVIDUALIZED APPROACH TO HOLISTIC VETERINARY CARE

Dr. Michael Dym, VMD,[1] was a Presidential Scholar graduate in animal science from Cornell University in 1986 and received his veterinary degree from Penn in 1991. In 1997, he began studying classical homeopathy, and today his practice includes a combination of traditional and integrative medicine as well as homeopathy. He is also the veterinarian Becky worked with. The following is from our discussion.

I HAVE BEEN A TRADITIONAL VET SINCE 1991. THE FIRST FEW years, dogs would come in with a problem and I would do what I had been taught. I would look at the symptoms, diagnose the problem, then dish out drugs or schedule surgery. But many of the dogs kept coming back with the same problem. I was also seeing an increased incidence of chronic illness, autoimmune disease, and cancer.

Then two cats came into my life. The first was a Persian cat who was diagnosed with hyperthyroidism. I gave the cat methimazole, which alleviates the symptoms but is a very strong drug. My cat, like me, is very sensitive to drugs and, after only a few doses, went into liver failure and had to be rushed to the Veterinary Hospital at the University of Pennsylvania—and this was from a drug I prescribed for animals every day. Imagine the guilt and shame I felt.

My other cat, a Himalayan, coughed every now and then. Being a traditional vet, I knew most coughing was caused by an allergy or autoimmune problem. It could be asthma or dust or dirt in their environment. The normal treatment is a round of cortisone or prednisone.

My cat's coughing was getting progressively worse and then her chest filled with fluid—all symptoms of chylothorax. Chylothorax is a relatively rare disorder in cats where lymph fluid accumulates in the space between their lungs and the inner lining of the chest wall. Unfortunately, I didn't know of a treatment for it.

Here I was with a cat who had a disease for which traditional veterinary medicine had no cure. I finally connected with Dr. Theresa Fossum, a veterinary expert on this frustrating disease, who suggested I try Rutin. Rutin is a bioflavinoid with strong antioxidant properties. In this case, it absorbed the fluids.

Based on my own experience and my growing frustration over the efficacy of what I had been taught in veterinary school, in 1997 I began studying homeopathy.

In traditional medicine, we do tests and come up with a drug protocol or surgery. Dogs with the same disease are usually all given the same drug. The drugs make the symptoms go away so the animal feels better but it doesn't address the underlying cause of the disease. Take, for instance, a dog with a thyroid problem. That dog will be placed on a thyroid medicine to address the symptoms, but since the underlying cause of the problem still remains, the dog will likely stay on the thyroid medication for the rest of his or her life.

With homeopathy, we understand that all disease begins with an imbalance. We recognize that symptoms are a reflection that the body is out of balance. Homeopathy treats all levels of the dog's being (spiritual, emotional, mental, and physical) to work with the dog's own healing power to bring about complete health, well-being, and homeostasis (balance). Every dog is treated on an individual basis with remedies that are gentle, subtle, powerful, and non-addictive.

There is almost an epidemic of cancer in younger and younger dogs like Fache. Food is an integral part of a dog's overall health. Thankfully, Becky was already feeding Fache a clean, organic diet so we only had to make some minor dietary changes. We made some changes to the supplements Fache was receiving including the addition of gemmotherapy.[2] We also gave Fache one specific homeopathic remedy on two separate occasions.

Gemmotherapy, supplements, and dietary changes all help support a dog's health but it is the homeopathic remedy that cures disease on an energetic level. With homeopathy, we allow dogs to achieve a higher level of health and reduce susceptibility to future disease flare-ups, rather than palliating or suppressing symptoms with drugs or surgery. That should be the ultimate goal for any doctor.

I work with clients all over the country and I'm not an extremist or fanatic. I have been a traditional vet for many years and I realize every case is individual. The route we follow depends on many factors. Some people want a quick fix and don't have the patience for homeopathy, or the owner may be unwilling to change the dog's diet. Perhaps the pathology is so bad that I need to use traditional medicine to relieve suffering. Each case and set of circumstances is different and it is important to look at the whole picture.

The bottom line is this: People love their animals. They are starting to ask questions and seek out other options. They are starting to educate themselves about complimentary therapies. As a licensed veterinarian, I understand the conventional medical model and use it when appropriate. Depending upon the client's goals for their pet, I will offer either an integrative approach utilizing both traditional and complementary medicine or a classic homeopathic approach. I have seen an owner begin homeopathy with their dog and ultimately begin paying more attention to their own health.

Dogs are pure, egoless beings who give us unconditional love. I believe dogs come into our lives and are drawn to us for a reason. I have seen it over and over in my practice where a dog comes into someone's life and teaches that person a lesson or opens them up to another way of being.

Chapter Seventeen
BONNIE

Bonnie and I met in fifth grade at Summer Music School. In our fifties, our friendship began to truly blossom when we both worked part-time at our local natural food market. During those years, Bonnie suffered a tragic loss, and witnessing her handle the loss with incredible dignity and grace allowed me to see the depth of her spirit and character. Bonnie is one of the strongest, bravest, and sweetest women I know. While sitting in my kitchen over a cup of tea, Bonnie shared her story and her memories of the dogs in her life.

MY FIRST DOG, A SCHNOODLE (SCHNAUZER/POODLE MIX) NAMED Cinnamon, came into my life at the perfect time. I was eight years old and going through a tough time.

Love

My parents' marriage was falling apart, and since there were so many years between my older brother and I, many times I felt like an only child. Cinnamon became my best friend and really helped me through everything.

After high school, I went away to college. Every time, I took out my suitcases to begin packing, Cinnamon knew I was leaving and would get upset. It was upsetting for me, too, since we had grown so close over the years.

When Cinnamon was seventeen, he began having some health problems and my family began having the difficult discussion about whether it was time. We all dreaded knowing one day we would have to make that decision, but Cinnamon made it easy for us when he passed in his sleep while I was away at college.

Ten years later, after getting married and moving into a house, I got another dog. It was a Samoyed named Nanook that someone was giving away.

Shortly after Nanook came into our lives, we got another dog, a Brittany spaniel mix we named Toni. Nanook and Toni got along so well that we ended up with a litter of nine puppies! The puppies were adorable. They had the fluffy hair of a Samoyed and the markings of a Brittany spaniel and looked like St. Bernard puppies.

As cute as the puppies were, we got Toni fixed and shortly thereafter Nanook got heartworm and went downhill fairly quickly. A local dairy farm had adopted one of Toni and Nanook's puppies, and several years later that puppy had a litter and we got one of the puppies. We had Toni and one of Toni's grandchildren living under our roof at the same time.

One day, I went across the road to mow my neighbor's lawn. Toni ran across the road to see me. The puppy followed Toni and was hit by a car. I was devastated.

I adopted a male Australian shepherd mix named Butchie and he and Toni bonded quickly. I was grateful they had one another because my marriage had begun to unravel and there was great deal of tension in the house. The dogs sensed it and it was the first time I realized how much impact the stress between humans had on our canine "kids."

Butchie and Toni loved being outside. During the day they stayed outside but they came inside at night to enjoy the luxury of a warm house and soft bed. On occasion, they would wake me up to go outside, but as a rule, they quickly returned.

Over time, as the tension in our home increased, their time spent outside at night had gradually gotten longer and they would often wander together at night. One night, I let them out to do their business and after a time tried to call them back. Knowing they always came back, I wasn't overly concerned when they didn't return and went back to bed.

In the morning, Butchie had returned but there was no sign of Toni.

My husband found her lifeless body on the side of the road and quickly went to task burying her in our backyard.

I was devastated by the loss of Toni, constantly expecting her to run into the house with Butchie. Butchie too was grieving and was never the same dog. My son, Ryan, was an infant and anytime he cried, Butchie would howl as if in mourning. I always suspected he was reliving the moment when Toni had been hit by the car.

After the divorce, Ryan and I moved into an apartment where we weren't permitted to have a dog. Several years later, after buying a town-house, I began thinking about getting another dog. Ryan was six, and while I wanted him to grow up with a dog, I was working two jobs and didn't have the time for one.

It was one of the loneliest points in my life. One of my constant prayers was, "God, could you please send me some love?"

After deciding to quit my part-time job, Ryan and I began visiting shelters where he fell in love with the first dog he saw: a Rottweiler mix.

Concerned how a Rottweiler would do in a townhouse, we kept look-ing, but it was the only dog Ryan would consider. Despite visiting a lot of different shelters and seeing a lot of dogs, he wouldn't look at any other dog so we finally went back to fill out adoption papers. The shelter told us the dog's name was Love and I realized God had answered my prayers and sent me some Love.

When we got Love home, I began to see what Ryan saw in her. She was probably about a year old but, from the moment we brought her home, she settled in without any real issues and was one of the most even-tempered dogs I ever had.

Love had no concept of play. She didn't know how to chase a ball or how to just play like a dog. A dog trainer suspected Love had been tied up all day without any real interaction with humans or other dogs. One day, my nephew came over with his dog Rocco. Love had such a good time playing with Rocco that Ryan and I decided it might be a good idea to consider getting another dog.

At the time, Ryan was a sophomore in high school, and despite being extremely bright, he was having a really tough time in school. I always suspected he was afraid he somehow wouldn't measure up and therefore decided not to even try. He was also dealing with some anger issues.

There were two things that always helped Ryan through difficult times: his dog and playing the guitar. No matter how mad he was at the world, the love of his dog always helped him feel better. Thinking another dog would be good for both Love and Ryan, we went back to the shelter.

Ryan picked out an Australian cattle dog, but, from the day we brought her home, she and Love fought. She was a sweet dog, but since neither she nor Love were willing to back down, in the month we had her I was bitten three times. I was in tears when I brought her back to the shelter but made sure they understood she definitely shouldn't be in a multi-dog household.

We decided to let Love relax after that episode and didn't get another dog until after Ryan graduated high school.

During that time, Ryan had met a young woman, Katie. I could see how much they cared about one another and knew Ryan had met the love of his life. When Katie and Ryan told me they wanted to get a dog, I said it was fine as long as the dog got along with Love. I did not want any of us to have to go through an experience like that again.

A few weeks later, Ryan and Katie saw an ad in the paper for a four-month-old English mastiff. The dog's owner had to travel extensively for his job, so out of fairness to the dog, he gave her to their veterinarian for adoption. When they walked into the vet's office to meet her, Sativa came over and put her head in Ryan's lap and that was that.

That night, Ryan and Katie walked in with a 125-pound dog, smiled, introduced me to Sativa, and said, "Okay, see you later. We have to go to work."

Sativa slept with Ryan and Love slept with me, and thankfully Love and Sativa got along. Love was almost nine and had begun to slow down but after Sativa arrived, Love turned into a puppy again. She couldn't move very fast but she would stand her ground and bark and play. Having Sativa gave Love a new lease on life.

We never found out the exact date Sativa was born but knew her birthday was in April. Even though I often said I was the April fool because I ended up with a 125-pound dog living under my roof, Sativa turned out to be 125 pounds of pure love and companionship, especially for Ryan. He was an only child, so Sativa became a sibling he could talk to, hang out with, and wrestle with. Anytime he was stressed or upset, Sativa was there to cheer him up.

The first summer we had Sativa it was extremely warm so I bought her a kiddie pool. Love wasn't overly fond of water but Sativa loved splashing around in the water and loved being in the pool. Every time I checked the pool, it was empty. I assumed it was because of her long legs but then I saw the plug in the pool was out and assumed her nails got caught on it and pulled it out—until I saw Sativa diving under the water and pulling the plug out with her teeth.

When Love was almost fourteen, she developed a massive tumor on her hind quarters and gradually began to decline. I always said as long as she had life in her eyes, I wouldn't do anything, but she let me know when it was time.

I made certain Ryan had a chance to say goodbye to Love before I took her to the vet's office. Love had helped Ryan through many difficult times in his life—from being bullied to dealing with depression—and always had an unlimited supply of love waiting for him. Love was the first dog Ryan knew and saying goodbye to her was a very emotional experience for him.

It was difficult for me as well. I spent time quietly holding Love and stroking her velvety ears. I whispered how much I loved her and thanked her for how much she had enriched my life.

At the vet's office, they asked if I wanted to stay with her until the end and I opted not to do so. My thought at the time was that I wanted to remember her as she was: healthy, loving, and full of life. Not being there with her was a decision I have always regretted.

Several days later, I took Sativa for her grooming appointment. The groomer said Sativa smelled funky and together we finally figured out the smell was from Sativa lying next to Love during those final days. It is my belief that Sativa never reacted in any way to Love's passing because she had been with Love, knew what was happening, and therefore wasn't surprised when I came home without Love.

As the only dog in the house, we all bonded even more. Sativa lavished love and support on all of us, but especially on Ryan. She could sense when he needed extra attention or love and was always willing to supply it to him.

I wanted to keep Sativa socialized with other dogs so I began taking her to a dog park. There were several dogs there and they all got along wonderfully. The only problem was when new dogs came to the park. Sativa and her friends had developed somewhat of a pack mentality but the bigger problem was the dog owners who allowed their dogs do absolutely anything. I realized it was probably time to stop bringing Sativa to the dog park and, since some of the other people in our group were having the same issues, they stopped going as well. We missed the park and our friends, so we continued to visit them on a regular basis.

I began making dog biscuits for Sativa and her friends and, in the process, saved thousands of dollars, plus I knew Sativa was getting fresh, organic ingredients that were good for her. However, the treats had an additional, unforeseen benefit on a visit with Sativa's best friend, a Boxer named Sophia.

Sophia's mom, Nancy, had a fenced-in yard and one afternoon, while Sativa and Sophia were running around the yard playing, Sophia spotted a hole in the fence and took off. Everyone was running around trying to catch her. Unsure what Sativa would do if I left her, I remained in the yard and said, "Sativa, come." She came and sat at my feet and, before we knew it, Sophia ran back through the hole in the fence and sat at my feet waiting for her biscuit. Never underestimate the power of a biscuit.

During Ryan's first year of college, he commuted to school. Evenings he often spent with his girlfriend but I usually waited for him to come home and we would talk about his classes, his friends, and his life. Listening to my son's dreams for the future far outweighed the sleep deprivation I sometimes experienced.

Shortly before the start of his second year of college, Ryan decided to rent an apartment closer to school. His lease wouldn't allow him to take Sativa, which was fine with me since I didn't really want to let her go.

Sativa and I settled nicely into our own routine and got extremely close. The only drawback was that most of the time Sativa slept on my bed. When a little dog twitches in bed, it's not a big deal but when a 125-pound dog twitches, it's a major disruption of your sleep.

Sativa and I looked forward to phone calls and visits with Ryan. Occasionally, I cooked one of his favorite meals and went to the local gym where he worked to surprise him with a quick visit and some home cooking. Ryan had become so focused and was working so hard towards his goals and dreams. I was incredibly proud of the young man he had become.

One morning at 5:00, Sativa and I were woken by a knock at our door. Opening my door, I saw two police officers standing on my front porch. They asked if I was Ryan Alley's mom.

"Yes," I said.

"He's been in an accident," they said. They told me which hospital Ryan had been taken to but provided no additional details.

My heart was pounding. I called Ryan's dad and Katie to meet me at the hospital, and after somehow managing to take care of Sativa, I hopped in my car to head to the hospital. The forty-minute drive there was surreal, as if I were part of a bad movie. I refused to let my mind drift to the myriad of possibilities that lay waiting at the hospital. About five minutes away from the hospital, the song "I'll Always Love My Momma" came on the radio. I knew it was either a really good sign—or a really bad one.

What I saw walking into Ryan's room was gut wrenching. My strapping six-foot-seven-inch son was pale, limp, and connected to every conceivable life-saving machine. I barely left Ryan's bedside during the day and neighbors took care of Sativa.

At night, the hospital staff encouraged me to go home and get some rest for the road ahead. Each night at home, Sativa offered quiet comfort, always instinctively providing exactly what I needed.

The other source of my strength was Ryan's girlfriend, Katie. A compassionate, loving young woman, I had the utmost respect for her. We developed a bond I knew would endure no matter where this journey or life took us. Regardless of the outcome, we would face it together.

One week after the accident, Katie and I were in Ryan's room when the alarms on the machines attached to Ryan sounded. Katie and I were immediately whisked out of the room. We waited anxiously outside his room, huddled together holding one another's hands. A short while later, they came out to tell us that Ryan had passed. Just as with Love, I had once again missed a loved one's final breath.

I didn't know how Sativa was going to react but, just like with Love, she didn't mourn and didn't look for him. Even when I drove Ryan's car, she never seemed to look for him. About a year later, I found out why.

I never have any digestive issues but on this particular day, while at work, I got horribly nauseated and ended up leaving work and going home. As I walked through my front door and tossed my keys on the nearby table, something told me to check my email. Wanting to crawl into bed, I decided to trust my instincts and turned on my computer. The first email was from a pet store advertising an upcoming event with an animal communicator. Space was limited for the event so I picked up the phone to register. The line remained busy for the next half hour. When I finally got through, I got the second to last spot for the event. If I had stayed at work that day, I never would have been able to go.

The day of the event, I brought pictures of Sativa. After handing them to the woman, she looked at them and said, "She keeps telling me to ask you about kids."

I explained I had a son who had passed. Shaking her head, she said, "That's why she wanted me to ask you. She wants you to know that when your son died, he stopped by to tell Sativa why he wouldn't be around anymore." That explained why Sativa had never mourned or looked for Ryan.

Sativa also told the woman to ask me why we no longer went on long walks. We had always loved going for long walks but had stopped since her legs were getting weaker. After that, Sativa and I started going for walks again and I allowed her to tell me how long and how far she wanted to walk.

Sativa also had arthritis in her back legs. One leg was more impacted than the other and when she could no longer make it up and down the stairs, I had a decision to make. We're a pack and have always slept together in my bed. Not wanting her to be alone at night, I went to the local furniture store and told the saleswoman I needed a couch big enough for me and a 125-pound dog. She laughed and said, "You would be surprised how many times I hear that."

Sativa is such a huge part of my life. I am retired now so we spend a lot more time together these days. When I am home alone, I am never alone. Half the time, when I am watching TV, Sativa's head is on my lap. She has the most soulful eyes I have ever seen.

Usually when you think back on a part of your life with a certain dog, it feels like such a short time, like a drop in the bucket. With Sativa, there have been so many monumental changes in my life since we have been together that it feels like I've spent an entire lifetime with her. Together, we went from Ryan graduating high school and trying to find his way in life to him going through a series of jobs. After working for a mortgage company and then a financial investment company, he realized that wasn't what he wanted to do for the rest of his life. Realizing he wanted to make something of himself and his life, he decided to go to college.

Ryan went from being a student who hated school and almost not graduating high school to someone who was incredibly focused and excited about his future. An international business major, his long-range goal was to work for the CIA.

Over the years, he had always been drawn to Russia and Russian culture. I remember the first day of his Russian class in college he called and said, "Mom, it's so cool to be able to speak another language!" I laughed because for the past thirty-seven years, I had been a German teacher. Ryan had received a scholarship to study abroad in Russia for a year, but we didn't find out he had been selected for the scholarship until after he passed.

Sativa is eleven, which is old for a mastiff; they typically, only live to about seven or eight. At her most recent vet visit, all her bloodwork came back great. I have her on many herbs and other natural things. Sometimes I feel like a witch doctor making all these creations but apparently they are working.

I believe Sativa's intelligence and sensitivity enabled her to be in tune with whatever Ryan and I have needed over the years. She came into our life because of Ryan. She helped him heal and got him through so many rough patches in his life. Then, after Ryan died, Sativa was the one who helped me heal.

I often ask myself why I don't sob every single day since Ryan died. We had such a close relationship and I will miss him every day of my life, but several things help me get through the tough times.

First, Ryan and I never ended a conversation—whether in person or on the phone—without saying "I love you" to one another. Ryan knew,

Sativa

without a doubt, how much he was loved. And I know, without a doubt, he loved me too.

I have received so much support from my friends, and even to this day, from several of Ryan's friends. I also know Ryan would want me to continue to follow my own dreams in life.

Finally, there is the unconditional love I get every day from a crazy, 125-pound mastiff. In spite of the fact that over the years she has eaten two and a half couches, she gives me a reason to laugh, someone to cry with, and a multitude of memories of the bond that she and Ryan shared.

It is going to be a mixed blessing when Sativa passes. On one hand, I am going to lose a connection to Ryan, but on the flip side, I know they will be running around Heaven together.

There's a quote that sums up my situation quite well: "You never know how strong you are until being strong is your only choice."[1]

Bonnie's Peanut Butter Coconut Dog Treats
(one of Sativa's favorites)

1 cup oat flour
1 cup brown rice flour
1 cup unsweetened shredded coconut
1 egg
½ cup unsweetened, unsalted peanut butter
1 teaspoon vanilla (optional)
¾ cup filtered water

Note: You may use other varieties of flour. Adjust the amount of water if necessary.

Preheat oven to 350 degrees. Add all ingredients to large bowl and mix completely. Depending on the desired size of the treats, place either a ½ teaspoon or 1 teaspoon of dough on an ungreased cookie sheet (or, even better, one covered with parchment paper). Flatten each treat with a fork.

Bake treats for 17 to 22 minutes (adjust cooking time depending on the size of the treats). Treats are done when the edges are a golden brown. Cool completely. Treats may be refrigerated for up to 5 days or frozen for 3 months.

Bone Appetit!

The power of a treat

DOGS DURING DIFFICULT TIMES

THE BENEFITS OF SIMPLY PETTING OR BEING IN THE PRESENCE of a dog are well documented and include:

- Decreasing depression, anxiety, and levels of stress hormones
- Reducing blood pressure and heart rate
- Improving anger management and frustration tolerance
- Elevating and stabilizing mood
- Decreasing feelings of tension or stress
- Regulating breathing

Many people also believe their dog picks up on their emotions and can sense when they are upset or sad and respond accordingly.

This was examined in a study led by Dr. Deborah Custance and Jennifer Mayer, both from the Psychology Department of Goldsmiths College, University of London.[1] Using eighteen pet dogs of various breeds and ages, they attempted to determine if a dog was able to demonstrate empathy when confronted with humans in distress by exposing the dogs to four separate twenty-second experimental conditions. In each, either the dog's owner or an unfamiliar person pretended to cry, hum in an odd manner, or carry out a casual conversation.

"The response was extraordinary," Custance said. "The dogs paid little attention to the people who were talking or humming but nearly all of the dogs came over to nuzzle or lick the crying person, regardless of whether it was their owner or a stranger.

"More dogs looked at, approached, or touched the human as they were crying as opposed to humming, and no dogs responded during talking.

"We're not saying this is definitive evidence that dogs have empathy but they are social creatures who respond to us, and our emotions, quite sensitively," Custance said. "When humans show us affection, it can sometimes be quite complicated. There may be expectations or judgments, but with a dog, it's very uncomplicated and non-challenging. If you're going through a hard time, it's lovely to have that."

In a study led by Sara Staats, Professor Emeritus of Psychology at Ohio State's Newark Campus, college students (the majority who still lived at home) were surveyed to see how their pets helped them through difficult times.[2] Students who lived with a cat, a dog, or a combination of the two were less likely to feel lonely or depressed, which was directly attributed to their pet.

According to Staats, "We may not think college students are lonely but college can be a very stressful environment for them and sometimes students can feel isolated or overwhelmed with the change." Many college students are away from home and on their own for the first time in their life. They are in a new environment and experiencing a new way of life while also building a new network of friends. All of this may leave them feeling isolated or they may withdraw from their environment.

"While pets aren't a substitute for human social interaction and support, they do provide interaction for those who might feel isolated from their current environment and that is extremely important," Staats said. "College students and adults alike said their pet was important in helping them cope during difficult times. Many studies have focused on the impact of pet ownership on adults or older generations who have health problems or special needs. There hasn't been much recognition of the fact that young, healthy college students also derive benefits from pet ownership to ward off loneliness and improve their ability to cope."

One of the most difficult times in a person's life is following the death of a loved one. Just as Sativa supported Bonnie after her son passed, a dog can help ease the pain and provide comfort. An increasing number of funeral directors understand this and are now allowing certified therapy dogs (or a well-behaved family dog) to be present at the funeral home.

"We have an area in the funeral home dedicated to our therapy dog program," said Daniel J. Wright, owner and executive director of Wright & Ford Family Funeral Home in Flemington, New Jersey. "There are therapy dogs at hospitals and nursing homes. Why not funeral homes? Dogs love us unconditionally and can often sense exactly who needs comfort and what kind of comfort to provide."

We all have times when life, circumstances, or our emotions overwhelm us. The presence of a dog, as well the wordless love and total acceptance they offer, can provide us with a place to feel safe and loved, and ultimately, to heal.

Chapter Eighteen
MICHELE AND DAN

At the wedding reception for my best friend's son, I was seated with two of my favorite people: her sister and brother-in-law, Michele and Dan. They are two of the most upbeat, positive individuals to walk this Earth and it is always sheer joy being around them. During the course of our conversation that night we began talking about dogs, and they shared their story and memories of a dog named Tom.

MICHELE: AS KIDS, WE BEGGED MY MOM FOR A DOG BUT IT wasn't until we were in high school that she finally relented. Since then, I have never been without a dog in my life for any significant amount of time.

Tommy

Dan: I got my first dog at the age of four. He was a huge, gentle St. Bernard named Kelly. Kelly came into my life when I was still too young to go to school and lived until I was a sophomore in high school. He was a true companion for a very long time and when he passed it was probably the first time I really felt loss in my life.

Michele: When our son Josh was fourteen, we went to the Humane Society to look for a dog. There were two dogs in the same pen and they brought them both out for us to meet. Josh kept playing with one dog and I kept looking at the other dog. There was something about him. He was behaving himself and was just so darn cute. He was a six-month-old "Heinz 57" dog, a little bit of this and a little bit of that: Rhodesian ridgeback, German shepherd, hound, and probably a few other things thrown in for good luck. His name was Tom.

We didn't know a lot about him, but based on his behavior with food, we suspected he came from a house with too many dogs. When we put his food out, he would go to the bowl, get a mouthful of food, and then go to the other side of the room. He would do that three or four times before finally just staying at his bowl and eating. He never gobbled his food and there were days he would eat and days he wouldn't eat. It was almost as if Tom felt that if he didn't eat today, he would just eat tomorrow.

Dan: I worked from home and was usually always busy very early in the morning. One morning was particularly quiet with work, so I decided to go in the backyard and relax with a cup of coffee. I got out there and Tom was nowhere to be found. We had a fenced-in yard so I immediately ran to the gates. They were both locked so I started to panic. I start calling for him and a few seconds later, I saw Tom crawling under the fence. I asked him what he was doing and my neighbor Mike popped up from his chair and walked over. "He comes over every morning to have coffee with me," Mike said.

"Really? How long has this been going on?"

"Ever since you moved in," Mike said.

I was shocked. Although it clearly didn't bother Mike—who said his day wasn't complete unless Tom came over to visit—we never knew about Tom's daily visits and we had been living there for nine months!

We had another episode with a fence, this time with our next-door neighbor Kelly. He had a fence around his property and in the part of his fence that bordered our yard, there was a hole big enough for a dog's head to fit through—and that's exactly what was happening. Kelly had two German shepherds, Calleb and Hobbs, and they and Tom would sit by that hole and look at each other and talk all day long.

Kelly and his father-in-law decided to rebuild the fence, and on the day the fence was finished, the three dogs went nuts when they discovered there was no longer a hole. They howled and barked to each other all evening long. Finally Kelly came out, grabbed his electric saw, and cut a hole in the fence so the dogs could see each other again. Needless to say, his father-in-law was none too happy about a hole in his new fence but he understood—and the dogs were happy.

Michele: We had heard that dogs don't like oranges or any kind of citrus. One day, I called Dan over and said, "Watch this." There was Tom pulling the low-hanging oranges off the tree in our backyard. He lay in the grass, put the orange between his two front paws, and bit the top off, then stuck his nose into the hole and ate the entire contents. We had a bunch of half-moon orange skins under that tree. Apparently Tom didn't know he wasn't supposed to like oranges because any time he wanted an orange he simply picked one off our tree.

The other thing Tom loved was to get vacuumed. He shed like a beast but it was never a problem because whenever we took out the vacuum, Tom would follow us around until you got the brush out and vacuumed him.

Tom was, hands down, the best dog we ever had, and perhaps the greatest thing about Tom was his connection with humans. If there were dogs and humans in a room, Tom would gravitate towards the humans. He was all about the humans.

Dan: Michele's Aunt Wee and Uncle Tiv used to come and stay with us every winter. Their bedroom was at the top of the stairs but their bathroom was at the foot of the stairs. Tom would sleep outside their door all night. If either of them got up during the night to use the bathroom, Tom would escort them downstairs, go into the loo with them, and escort them back upstairs. Normally he would sleep outside our door but he knew Aunt Wee and Uncle Tiv were aging and felt they needed him more.

Michele: My aunt said it felt like Tom was there protecting her. I know what she meant because there was a period in my life when I was extremely depressed and my favorite place was in a hammock on a covered porch by our pool. Tom would sit by me for hours, and he always wanted me to be touching him. I didn't have to pet him, I just had to be touching him, even if it was just with my toes. Tom loved physical connection—and that connection helped me through a difficult period in my life.

Dan and Michele's son, Josh, with Tommy

Dan: Tom was Michele's protector. After we moved into a new house, Tom became an indoor pooch and would position himself in the living room where Michele had to have at least her foot in contact with him. He would face the front door at all times to make sure he knew if someone was coming in. He always placed himself between Michele and the rest of the world.

Michele: One time when my uncle was visiting, his hip started hurting him. As soon as my uncle started limping, Tom started limping, too. I always believed Tom, on some level, tried to take everybody's pain away, whether it was emotional or physical pain. It was almost as if that was his mission on this planet.

Dan: I saw what Michele is talking about when Uncle Tiv hurt his hip and Tom started limping. I had never witnessed anything like that in a dog before and it was somehow eerie and comforting at the same time.

Michele: When Tom was eight, we had to put our cat Alley down. The following year, Tom had severe hip dysplasia. On the day we put Tom down, I was holding him as the vet gave the injection. Afterwards, the vet left quietly so I could be alone with him. I continued to hold Tom, and after about five minutes or so, I felt his soul leave his body. I could actually feel his soul leave and go right through me. I then saw him run down the alleyway with our cat and imagined they ran away together to pet heaven. That moment was one of the best gifts anyone has ever given me.

Dan: The day Tom died was possibly the closest I have ever been to a nervous breakdown. I absolutely could not go with Michele and it was one of my real days of weakness. Instead, I stayed at home and dug his grave. I placed him outside my office in the cool shade of an oak tree and tended his grave weekly until we moved away. I told the new owners where he was buried and asked Tom to watch over them just as he always watched over us.

The day Tom died, Michele's Uncle Gregg wrote us a poem.

As I told Dan I'd love to see the poem, a young woman came and sat down at our table. Without hesitation, Michele pointed at the young woman and said, "You really need to talk to her." Dan nodded his head in agreement. I did, and her story follows.

And, as promised, Dan sent me the poem Uncle Gregg had written for them on the day that Tom died.

Tommy

They give us hope
They keep us calm
They keep us in this moment, now.
No sins to be ashamed of.
No expectations to let down.
We follow in their footsteps,
on a leash or through the snow.
They smell so deep, hear so far,
how can we ever let them go.
Because they must be what God meant,
when he designed how love should be.
Uncompromising and unconditional,
full of patience and simple dignity.
Because with them, life is a banquet,
one strong aroma, one big open, kitchen door.
And with just a word
just a touch
one glimpse of you . . .
Joy!
Joy.
Such joy.
If we could only feel joy that way!
So lucky Tom,
to live in beauty, and be with you
every moment, for all his days.

Gregg Loughridge
Seattle, May 2005

Chapter Nineteen
JILLENE

The young woman Michele and Dan told me about was named Jillene. I had been watching her, completely captivated by how much fun she was having on the dance floor, constantly laughing and completely free and uninhibited. I wanted to talk to her, but rather than attempting to pull her off the dance floor, we instead spoke a few days later. As she told me her story, I gained a whole different level of understanding and admiration for Jillene, her journey, and her love for her dogs.

WE GOT MOLLY, A BLACK AUSTRALIAN SHEPHERD, AROUND TEN years ago. Until then, I had been a cat person.

My family hadn't had a dog for four years. We had begun talking about getting one but then one day, my mom called and said, "Come over. I got an early Mother's Day gift and I want you to see it." I walked into the house and there, lying down, was Molly. She hopped up and came right over to me, her little butt shaking sideways the way Aussies do, and it was love at first sight. For me, Molly is "that dog"— the dog you connect with on a completely different level.

My sister Autumn had

Jillene, Buddy, Flint, and Molly on the farm
(Photo: Photography by Sharyn)

gotten Molly at eight weeks old from a woman she worked with, and it was obvious from day one that she was extremely smart. When she was around six months old, we enrolled her in puppy class. Molly was the biggest one and as she walked past the other puppies all she had to do was swat at them and they would fall over. She wasn't being mean, she was just so much bigger than the rest of the puppies in the class.

After we completed puppy class, we began Molly in agility class. Her sisters and brother were in that class so we got to see them and she was really good at and loved agility. She would go into the tunnel and when she came out the other end, she was going so fast that it looked like she was in midair flying.

I had been going through some changes and shifts in my own life, and when we first got Molly, I didn't realize how important she would ultimately be in my life.

When I was nine, I started having episodes where it felt like I was having trouble breathing or like my throat was closing up. The doctors didn't believe it was asthma since I wasn't wheezing but, not knowing exactly what it was, they gave me an inhaler in the hopes it would help. It didn't.

The episodes went on undiagnosed for years. When I was eighteen, I was driving and felt faint. The doctor said it was a panic attack. The attacks continued through college, and in my last year of school, depression set in. Two different doctors examined me and I was diagnosed as having a form of bipolar disorder called bipolar II.

Before my diagnosis, I could be driving down the road when for no apparent reason, I would suddenly feel incredibly sad. When I found out I had bipolar, everything began to make sense.

There are different forms of bipolar disorder and it impacts each person differently. For me, bipolar II means having ups and downs and taking medication every day. A lot depends on what is going on in my life. My symptoms don't occur while something is happening, they occur after the fact. For instance, I recently attended two weddings and my cousin's funeral, which I spoke at, within one week. I was fine that week, but after everything was over, my symptoms started flaring up and I had a full-blown panic attack in the car with my mom. It was my first panic attack in five years—for the most part, I am able to control them. I was lucky Molly was with us when it happened, because having her with me helps immensely.

I was twenty-five when Molly came into my life. Knowing that my attacks mainly happened in the car, I would always take Molly with me. As soon as I begin to feel anxious, I pet her and think about something else and that usually works to calm me down and keep a panic or anxiety attack at bay.

I know when I'm going to get an attack because I go into a deep stare and feel a tingling in my spine. The tingling then moves throughout my body, including my face, and I begin to feel numb all over. I also begin to hyperventilate. Because I can sense when they're happening, if I'm in the car, I pull over and grab a paper bag from my glove compartment. I breathe into the bag until the attack is over. Having Molly by my side has always been key in helping me deal with the attacks. I don't know if Molly knows exactly what is going on but I know she can tell something is wrong because she just stays by me and is quiet.

I had always been really outgoing and worked in the theatre for years. In that forum, having bipolar was a gift. Since I feel things more intensely it makes it easier for me to convey a variety of emotions onstage. Offstage was a different story.

When people started finding out about my diagnosis, many felt it was appropriate to say something about it to me even though they didn't really understand it. They would say, "You don't act like you're bipolar," and I would try to explain that was because of the medication. Or if they were having a bad day, that was fine but if I was having a bad day, they automatically asked if I had taken my medication. Or they would make rude remarks. I found myself getting blamed for things I had nothing to do with. People with mental illness are often easy scapegoats.

Since I was living alone at my grandparents' farm house, I kept bringing Molly to stay with me. I was lonely and loved having her with me for company and protection, and Molly loves the farm. She loved running around in the fields and sitting outside all day. We would end each day with her doing a lap around the farm to check on things before coming and lying back down next to me on the porch. If we go out fishing, Molly loves to be out on the boat with the wind blowing through her hair or helping us reel in the fish.

Molly feels like home to me. I don't have to explain anything to her—and she knows all my secrets. However, I began to feel bad that Molly was spending so much time with me rather than at my parents' house, so I finally suggested to my dad that we consider getting a farm dog.

While he was considering it, my cousin Kevin asked me to pick up his puppy from our uncle who breeds and trains English setters. Walking into Uncle Irvie's house, I saw this white puppy with black eyes and ears and freckles all over. It was the prettiest dog I had ever seen. I looked at my uncle and he immediately knew what I was thinking and said, "If your father will let you have him . . ." I picked up the phone, dialed my dad, and handed the phone to Uncle Irvie. When my uncle hung up the phone, he turned to me and said, "He's yours, but if he and Molly don't get along, you can return him."

When we got home, the puppy walked into the house and lay down on his dog bed. The next night, he fell asleep on the back of the couch and I kept looking over at him thinking, "This dog is all mine!" I had never had my own dog and every day I fell in love with him more and more.

Initially, I was concerned how Molly and the puppy would get along since Molly was older. It turned out the puppy was really good for Molly because he kept her alert and helped keep her energy up.

His registered name is Locking Down Flintlock but I call him Flint. English setters are supposed to be bird dogs so I put Flint in a trial once to see how he would do. He could not have been less interested in hunting birds that day. He just wanted to play with the other dogs, and at one point was running so fast that he actually ran over top of another dog. Flint came in last place but he was still first place in my heart.

He's only two and has a lot of energy but everybody loves Flint. He is an absolute goofball and is so happy all the time that it brings me joy.

Like Molly, Flint loves living on the farm because English setters love to run and play. He loves the wide open spaces where he can run to his heart's content. Most days, he runs over to visit our new neighbor who is the nicest person you will ever meet. When she first moved here, she built a barn for her three horses and I took Flint over to meet them. I wanted to make sure he would be comfortable with and wouldn't bother the horses. He met them and everything went really well.

A few weeks later, my neighbor called and said, "If you're looking for

Buddy and Molly
(Photo: Photography by Sharyn)

Flint, he's over here lying on the deck watching the sunset with me." Flint goes over on his own to keep her company and runs around with the horses. The other day she called and said, "I see Flint trying to come over across the field. It's okay if he wants to come visit." She even has a water bowl for him, so in some ways, Flint is leading a double life these days—but I'm glad he is so happy living here.

About a year ago, a friend was going to study abroad and asked me to watch his long-haired dachshund, Buddy, while he was gone. When he returned, he said he couldn't take Buddy back. That was fine with me because I didn't want to give him back. I had known Buddy since he was a puppy and had seen him get passed from house to house and didn't want him to go through that anymore. When I first got him, he had been an inside dog who only went outside to go to the bathroom and was very overweight.

In the past year, Buddy has completely changed. He has lost weight, has a lot more energy, and loves being outside. When I first got him, we would walk down this path to the valley. There is a little pond and stream on the walk, and when Buddy saw them, he would turn around and start walking back to the house. Now he walks in the stream and when I call him, he ignores me. Buddy is now a complete farm dog.

I once read that if you looked up the word "spunky" there would be a picture of a dachshund next to it, and I believe it. Buddy is full of energy and curiosity and is a tiny dog with a big personality. He has no idea he's less than half the size of the other dogs. He runs through the fields with them and does everything Flint and Molly do.

Buddy is our first little dog. My dad calls him Red because of his color and takes him for rides on the four-wheeler. He is obsessed with Buddy.

Flint
(Photo: Photography by Sharyn)

Until Buddy came here, he didn't know what it was like to be a dog. I always remind him that he has a forever home here, and as time goes by, I think he is beginning to know that. Buddy recently turned seven and I had a party for him with cake and my entire family came to help us celebrate.

All the dogs get along and sleep with me every night. Even though I live alone in the farmhouse, I never feel alone or lonely because they are around. They are my kids. At Christmas, I love shopping for them.

I am forever grateful my dogs are in my life because they love and protect me and also provide me with emotional support. I used to be afraid to get in my car to drive because of my panic attacks, but I'm not anymore thanks to Molly's calming presence. Now if I am having a bad day or start to get nervous or anxious, having one (or all) of them with me immediately calms me down. Buddy is the easiest to take since he is so tiny so I call him my "travel dog."

If I had to describe my dogs in a word, I would say Molly is the queen, Flint is the prince, and Buddy is my little knight. They are all precious (and spoiled) and they bring me so much joy and comfort. I constantly tell them, "I'm so in love with all of you and can't believe you belong to me." I would do anything for my dogs and believe, in my heart of hearts, they know that.

Chapter Twenty
DOT

Dot and I met in the 1960s at Summer Music School where we both shared a love for baton twirling. In high school, Dot was one of two oboe players and I was the only E-flat clarinet player so we sat side by side in band class for four years. I am grateful we kept in touch over the years. She is a creative, unique, and beautiful soul. One fine morning, we sat in my kitchen having tea and talking about dogs. And for the record, we both still love baton twirling.

OUR FAMILY MOVED FROM BROOKLYN, NEW YORK, TO NEW JERsey in 1957. My father began working as a doctor at the local hospital and Dr. Reynolds, another doctor at the hospital, gave us a tri-colored collie puppy as a welcome gift. We named him Chief, and at some

Mattie on the plane getting ready to land

point, we bred Chief and kept one of his puppies who we named Brave. We also had a schnauzer named Schnapps.

Along with all the dogs, we had other animals, including two monkeys—Chico, a squirrel monkey, and George, a woolly monkey. My brothers Dick and David collected lizards and snakes and my parents had also gotten goats and sheep for the farm.

Once in New Jersey,

dogs kept finding their way into our home and family. After Chief passed, we got a two-year-old Newfoundland named Little Bear, who had belonged to a family who worked at the hospital with my Dad. They were relocating to the Middle East so they gave him to us. He was a big bear of a dog and absolutely gorgeous. He had a big white chest with a star on it and was extremely sweet. Looking back, I think out of all of our dogs, Little Bear was my favorite. After my brother Dick moved to Vermont, he rescued a Newfoundland so I guess Little Bear wasn't just my favorite.

When my father's aunt passed, we took in her long-haired dachshund, Hansie. When Hansie came to our farm, he was an eight-year-old city dog, a lap dog, who now found himself in the rough and tumble countryside. In the beginning, he was very depressed and I believe he missed his life in the city. Whenever my mother took him into town and he saw a fire hydrant, he would get excited. I actually felt kind of sorry for him. I'll never forget when Hansie was outside running with the other dogs. The grass was so high on the farm and Hansie's hair was so long that when he ran it looked like he was gliding across the grass.

The dogs were all dogs in the true 1950s sense of the word: they stayed outside, barked when someone came into the driveway, and chased the sheep and goats if they came too close to Dad's garden.

After I moved out on my own, I put off getting an animal for a long time since I was commuting for work and didn't have the time to devote to a dog. I was also a single parent at the time and had my hands full with raising two boys. There was also a neighborhood cat who would come and hang out with me and then go back home at night. At the time, it was the perfect solution of having a pet companion without any of the responsibility.

When I met my second husband, Harry, he had several large Borzoi dogs. Harry is a real dog person and always said he wanted another dog but I kept telling him no. We were travelling a lot, all of our children were finally grown and out of the house, and I knew a dog was a big responsibility and required a lot of attention.

It wasn't until a close friend, Kim, said he wanted to coparent a dog with us that I started to seriously consider getting a dog. Knowing I wouldn't be totally responsible for the dog made me feel more secure.

Then something happened to help me finally decide to get a dog. My husband's daughter, who lived in California, was critically ill. We were living in upstate New York so I began flying back and forth to monitor her and her care. We were in a tèrrible situation emotionally with Harry's daughter being so sick. We knew we were losing her and there was so much sadness.

Kim, who in addition to being our friend is also our physician, continued to encourage us to get a dog. Knowing how much Harry wanted a dog, I finally decided a dog would cheer him up.

In March 2013, we welcomed Mattie, a tiny little multi-generational Labradoodle puppy, into our home, lives, and hearts. Even though one of the reasons I initially got Mattie was because of the whole coparenting arrangement, Mattie has never slept at Kim's house. Once Mattie arrived he became totally our dog.

Mattie brought light and laughter back into our lives and lessened the severe depression brought on by the stress and anxiety of our situation. Getting Mattie was the best medicine anyone could have given us. Within a year, we lost Harry's daughter and my mom, so having Mattie was a huge blessing.

We found a wonderful dog trainer who helped us get Mattie to do all the things you want your dog to do. She also told us to never let him sleep on the bed because, "He won't respect you. You have to be the alpha dog." We considered her advice but the reality is I like Mattie on the bed so it came down to a little less respect but a lot more love and I can live with that. Mattie is crate trained but still spends his early morning sleeping hours in bed with us.

Mattie has become the ultimate City Dog and Country Dog since we live in two places on two different continents: we live in both upstate New York and Paris. Mattie is also somewhat bilingual and responds appropriately to commands in either French or English.

Mattie is a registered Emotional Support Animal (ESA). As an ESA, Mattie can ride in the cabin of the plane alongside us on our flights between Paris and New York.

The airlines and passengers we have met have all been very supportive about Mattie traveling with us on the plane. He is very well behaved and goes through the confusion of security checkpoints and passport

Mattie and Harry on an
early morning walk in Paris

control like a champ. We usually try to get bulkhead seats so there is extra space for him to sleep and we bring snacks and toys to keep him happy. Most people don't even realize Mattie is on the plane until they see him with us at baggage pick-up.

On our first trip to Paris, Mattie made some friends, and when we returned the second year, he knew exactly what doors to check to see if his friends were home. One of the wonderful things about Paris is you can go almost anywhere with your dog. You can't take them to the movies or museums, but other than that, it is a very dog-friendly city. We love that we can go out to eat at a restaurant and Mattie can come along and relax next to our table.

Paris also has one of the most beautiful dog parks in the world: the Jardin du Palais Royal. It was created in 1633 for the Cardinal de Richelieu, but after his death in 1642 the palace became the property of the King and acquired a new name: Palais Royal. It is within walking distance of the Louvre and housed royal families for generations until the Palace of Versailles was built. Dogs are permitted in designated areas of the garden and we love to just go and watch all the different people and dogs.

There is a man I have seen twice now in Paris. I believe he is a dog walker. He has eight or nine dogs with him and one of his dogs, possibly a black Lab, actually holds the leashes of three of the dogs in his mouth and walks them down a very busy street to play in the Palais Royal.

Mattie walking in Paris

Back home in upstate New York, Mattie enjoys the freedom and wide open spaces of the forty-two acres that surround our home. He loves riding in our Gator utility vehicle—as soon as we start up the engine, he is ready for a ride.

Last winter, Harry let Mattie out to pee and went back into the studio to grab his leash. When he turned around, Mattie was gone. There was three feet of snow on the ground and the temperature was below zero. Since Mattie loves the Gator, we started it up thinking he would come running but he didn't. We started trudging through the snow thinking maybe he had chased a deer and gone into the woods. We were out there for about an hour but couldn't find him.

We came back to the studio and started crying hysterically thinking we had lost our dog. We called Kim and he suggested we call our neighbors.

I picked up the phone and called our neighbor Stephanie, who owns a horse farm down the road. "Steph," I said, "we think we lost Mattie."

"No," she said, "he's here in the barn. I called you about an hour ago to tell you."

We went over to get Mattie and the three of us figured out that just as Harry let Mattie out, they had started their Gator and Mattie took off across the paddock to go for a ride.

Since then, and with our growing concern over the increased presence of coyotes in our backyard, Mattie is no longer allowed off-leash. Instead, we installed a dog fence around our home that gives Mattie an acre to play, run, catch Frisbees and balls, and have some independence. Mattie is also a good swimmer and enjoys our pond. Every night, she sits with us on the deck overlooking the pond and together we watch the sun go down. For us, it's the perfect way to end each day.

At twenty-nine pounds, Mattie is a medium-size dog with a big dog personality. When he wants attention, he simply stands up on two feet and looks around until someone pays attention to him. He can also dance and walk on two feet.

We go to a hardware store in Rhinebeck, Williams Hardware, that keeps doggy biscuits at the counter. Mattie gets excited as soon as we pull into the parking lot because he so enjoys being given the biscuit. If they forget to give him one, Mattie will stand there and stare at them as a reminder.

A few months ago, we were at Williams when Mattie suddenly grabbed a stuffed rabbit off the shelf and wouldn't let it go. Obviously, we bought it for him. I get to spoil Mattie in a way I never would my own children.

Unlike the dogs I grew up with, Mattie really is a member of our family. I never bonded with an animal before like I have with Mattie. Our childhood dogs were family dogs but it always felt like they were animals instead of members of the family.

I thought I was getting Mattie for Harry. I didn't realize he was going to become my dog too and how he would change me.

I always considered myself to be a recovering mother. While I loved being a mom, after my sons were grown, I no longer wanted to be that responsible for anything. I didn't realize how distant I had become from the people and things in my life. Mattie managed to break through the wall I had built and has taken me outside of myself through his gift of unconditional love.

EMOTIONAL SUPPORT ANIMALS, SERVICE/ASSISTANCE DOGS, AND THERAPY DOGS: WHAT'S THE DIFFERENCE?

Stephanie Colman[1] is a writer and professional dog trainer in Los Angeles, California. A sucker for dark red retrievers, she currently shares her life with Saber, a career-change search and rescue dog. She recently dove into the complex world of service dog issues in a comprehensive article for Whole Dog Journal. *As a long-time subscriber, I read Stephanie's article in the July 2015 issue and contacted her about sharing some of her insight and wisdom.*

AS DOG LOVERS, WE HAVE A DEEP UNDERSTANDING OF THE many ways sharing our lives with dogs can bring great happiness, enrichment, and joy. For an individual with a physical or emotional disability, a dog can be an integral part of allowing them to live a full, independent life.

Beyond basic pet ownership, there are three main ways in which dogs (and in some cases, other species) work in partnership with humans to improve their quality of life: service/assistance dogs, therapy dogs, and emotional support animals.

Service dogs have been specifically trained to perform tasks that mitigate the handler's disability. The key words here are *trained* and *disability*—meaning that to qualify for a service dog, one must meet the definition of "disabled" under the American with Disabilities Act (ADA), and the dog must be specifically trained to perform tasks related to the disability.

The most obvious example is a dog trained to perform guide work for a visually impaired handler. However, service dogs can match a wide variety of job descriptions, such as alerting to impending seizures and other medical emergencies, detecting potentially deadly allergens, retrieving dropped items, stabilizing someone with mobility issues, recognizing a medical crisis and summoning help, or easing the symptoms of psychiatric disorders by interrupting self-mutilating behaviors.

Service dog and handler teams are guaranteed access to most public places under the ADA. There are some exceptions. For example, service dogs are not allowed in sterile areas such as hospital operating rooms and food-prep areas, and handlers must be given permission to bring their service dog into religious buildings, federal courthouses, jails and prisons, and private clubs.

Under federal law, service dogs are not required to be certified or wear any type of identifying gear, although many handlers choose to use identifying vests in an effort to keep the public from distracting the dog while it is working. There is no legally recognized national service dog registry, despite the online presence of official-sounding organizations that offer to "register" a dog for a fee. (Such companies, considered scams by experts in the disability community, play on the ignorance of the public, and partly explain why we sometimes see ill-behaved "service dogs" in non-pet-friendly places, with inconsiderate owners looking to bend or break the rules.)

Service dogs are required to be well behaved and under control at all times. Business owners have the right to ask the handler to remove the dog if it is misbehaving. (If the handler is asked to remove the dog, the business must attempt to provide alternate accommodations.) If a business doubts the authenticity of a service dog, under the ADA, only two questions can be asked:

1. Is the service dog required because of a disability?
2. What work or task has the dog been trained to perform?

Staff may not ask for specifics as to the handler's disability, nor can they ask that the dog demonstrate its ability to perform a task. The handler's answer must be credible. For example, "He provides emotional support" is not a valid answer, as emotional support is not a trained task.

But in some cases, emotional support is just what the doctor ordered! While emotional support does not qualify as a task for a public access, the medical community does recognize that in many cases, the presence of an animal can be physically or psychologically beneficial to a disabled individual. Again, the key word is *disabled*. To qualify for an emotional support animal, one must meet a clearly defined standard of disability. A treating medical provider must diagnose the person with a disability and state that having access to the animal, which does *not* need to be trained to perform tasks specific to the owner's disability, will be of physical or psychological benefit.

Many people mistakenly believe that emotional support animals, which can include other species besides dogs, qualify as service animals, but this is incorrect. In fact, the ADA specifically states that "dogs whose sole function is to provide comfort or emotional support do not qualify as service animals under the ADA." Handlers with emotional support animals do not have the right to bring those animals into non-animal-friendly places of public accommodation.

They are, however, allowed to rent in most "no pets" housing under the Fair Housing Act (FHA), and can have the animal (with some species exceptions) accompany them in the cabin of a plane under the Air Carrier Access Act (ACAA), provided they can show proper medical documentation supporting the handler's need for the emotional support animal.

Here again, the Internet is rife with sites offering "prescription" letters for a fee. This has allowed many people to take advantage of the FHA and ACAA by buying their pet's way into "no pets" housing or keeping a pet out of the cargo hold of a plane. Disability experts say it's highly unlikely that anyone would ever need to legitimately rely on a paid service to provide a prescription letter for an emotional support animal. To legally qualify one, you must be disabled and therefore are most likely under the ongoing care of a medical professional who can write the letter. Buying a prescription when you don't legally qualify for one is no different from parking in a handicapped spot when you don't legally qualify for the special parking. It's dishonest, illegal, and potentially further complicates life for those who live with various disabilities.

Therapy dogs (and in some cases, other species) are personal pets owned and loved by people who volunteer their time to visit others in partnership with their animals with the goal of providing comfort. Teams often visit patients in hospitals and assisted living facilities. Therapy team assignments can also include R.E.A.D. programs, where children practice reading to the dogs; visits to family court to support children before and during difficult proceedings; and even therapy animals in airports to help calm the nerves of frazzled travelers.

Therapy dogs must be relaxed and confident in public, extremely well behaved, and skilled in advanced obedience behaviors, which often includes the willing acceptance of "clumsy" petting (as might be received when participating in a patient's physical rehab) and other encounters not commonly experienced by pet dogs. There are no federal or state regulations regarding therapy dogs, but they must pass a test, often administered by a representative of Pet Partners (formerly Delta Society) or Therapy Dogs International in order to become a certified therapy dog.

Certified therapy dogs provide a wonderful and extraordinarily beneficial service to the community, but they are not legally service dogs. Therapy dog handler teams do not enjoy public access rights (they visit "no pets" establishments by special invitation), they are not allowed to live in "no pets" housing, and they have no special right to accompany their handler in the cabin of a plane.

Chapter Twenty-One
MARY-
ANTOINETTE

I met Mary-Antoinette many moons ago at a women's writing retreat in Taos, New Mexico. She was beautiful, brilliant, and moved with a grace, confidence, and ease that displayed a knowledge of herself and the world around her. She spoke and wrote of her love for dogs, and their significance in her life, and when I asked if she would like to write something for this book, she immediately agreed. As you will see, her story is rich with literary significance as well as her love for dogs.

AS A LITERATURE PROFESSOR, I AM ALWAYS ATTUNED TO POSSIble literary references behind a dog's name. I wonder if Ophelia is a reference to Shakespeare's *Hamlet* or perhaps Stella was named after the character in *Streetcar Named Desire*. This fascination has led to engaging conversations with fellow dog lovers and also explains why my own dogs have been saddled with names full of literary, historical, or religious significance.

For almost sixty years, my life has been enriched by the

Mary-Antoinette and Victor

presence of amazing dogs, beginning with Cisco, a hyperactive, yappy Chihuahua who joined our family when I was seven years old. He was a gift from my paternal grandmother who heard an old Southern wives' tale that Chihuahuas were good for asthmatics. While Cisco never proved to be a curative for my younger brother's asthma, he did prove to be a problem for me since I was terrified of dogs.

Every encounter with Cisco resulted in my trembling, screaming, and crying until someone came and whisked him away. Over time, my fear began to disrupt the harmony of our household and it all came to a head one Sunday afternoon.

For my father, Sundays were reserved for rest, beer, and televised major league baseball. On this particular Sunday, as I was tiptoeing into the hallway, I crossed paths with Cisco. Instantly falling into my normal hysterics, my father, angry and agitated at the interruption, came in and took Cisco in one arm, me in the other, and carried us both into the kitchen. Pulling out a chair, he sat me down, plopped Cisco in my lap and said, "Stay there until I say you can get up!" and returned to his game.

As every imaginable fear began to go through my mind, I opted instead to look at Cisco, and for the first time began to stroke him ever so gently. By the time my father returned, about an hour later, Cisco and I were best friends.

From that day on, I was never afraid of Cisco, or any dog, again. I also learned an important life lesson: By facing my fears, I realize there is usually no real basis for my fear in the first place.

We then welcomed Princess, a furry terrier mix, into our family. Cisco sired two of her litters and we kept one of their puppies, who we named Biggie because of the size of his head: big.

One day, a small, short-haired tan mutt "followed" my younger brother home from school. Daddy, laughing, said, "So, he 'followed' you home with your belt around his neck like a leash?" He let us keep him and we named him Dijon. I now had four precious canines to love and who loved me in return.

Eventually Cisco, Princess, and Biggie passed on; while I was in college and on a study abroad year in England, Dijon died. The lessons I learned from each of these dogs still impact my life and the choices I make to this day.

After college, I moved into my own apartment and decided to get a dog of my own. Whimpey, my parents' tan German shepherd mix, had a litter of puppies sired by Prince, the randy old shepherd next door, and I claimed a beautiful little tan-colored pup. I named her Victoria after the Queen of England since I was earning a master's degree in Victorian literature.

In our thirteen years together, Victoria and I grew incredibly close and we did everything together. She was there when I was awarded my master's degree, during my time as a public relations/advertising professional, and during the first years of my doctoral program. Victoria also became my support and anchor during some very trying times.

I was in my twenties and early thirties and establishing my career and life. Although I had always wanted to be an English professor, I succumbed to parental and societal pressure and instead established myself as a business professional. My eight-year stint in public relations and advertising wasn't a good fit for me at all, which led to my being very unhappy and an extremely secretive and self-destructive period of drinking. I drank behind closed doors, always presenting a very polished public persona, so no one knew.

I was a blackout drinker so while I never saw or remembered the unsightliness of my behavior, Victoria did. She was amazingly smart, and if ever a dog knew her owner, Victoria knew me. She knew me to the core of my soul, and as my best friend, she took care of me when I was at my soul-sickest.

Having Victoria gave me the responsibility for another being—a being who loved me unconditionally. She gave me a reason and the courage to finally sober up and get physically, psychically, spiritually, and emotionally healthy. After taking the first AA step of admitting my powerlessness over alcohol, I began pursuing my doctorate so I could realize my dream of becoming a literature professor.

In my final year of school, I began applying for professorial jobs. My first interview was at Massachusetts Institute of Technology (MIT). Victoria stayed with my parents, and as I prepared to say goodbye to her and head to the airport, I saw how weathered she looked. At thirteen, her health was noticeably declining and I made a mental note to take her to the vet upon my return.

The interview went well and that night I celebrated by ordering room-service at my hotel and watching the film *All Dogs Go to Heaven*. The next day on the plane ride home, I looked out the window and saw something miraculous: a completely round rainbow! Not only did I see it, but it remained there throughout the duration of the flight. To this day, there has never been a rational explanation for its presence. I believe it was Victoria's visual soul mark, for I learned, upon returning to my parents' home, that she had passed.

I believe Victoria chose to pass while I was in Boston for several reasons. First, knowing her advanced age and declining health might prove difficult in the new future that now lay before me, she chose to clear the way for me to go forth unencumbered. Second, she knew witnessing her death would have devastated me so she chose to pass on before I returned home. Next, she had manifested her spirit as a mystical round rainbow to provide me with confirmation that she had passed on to that realm where "all dogs go to heaven." And, finally, Victoria timed her death so I could find her successor who would accompany me through the final year of my doctorate and the coming changes in my life. While I was incredibly sad, having a fuller understanding that her death was another example of her love and loyalty to me made it easier for me to move forward.

As I began searching the local animal shelters for Victoria's successor, I had a specific goal in mind: a female tan-colored German shepherd mix. The reason behind my quest was plain, simple, and pragmatic.

Eleven years prior, Victoria and I had moved into a one-bedroom apartment with a spacious yard. Our landlord allowed me to have a dog but he had passed and his wife, who had taken over maintenance of the property, was much less dog friendly. Not wanting her to discover that Victoria had died, my hope was to find and sneak Victoria the Second onto the property.

My choices at the shelter were limited so I adopted the closest thing I could: a tan, male, sort-of-German-shepherdy-looking dog. He was seven months old and extremely sweet tempered. I named him Victor because phonetically it was the closest thing to Victoria and also because he had been a victor over his own death. He had been scheduled to be euthanized two days prior, but thankfully there had been a delay. He was truly a rescued dog in every sense of the word, and during my years with him, I suspected he understood and was grateful I adopted him.

The landlady came by once a week and, after about three months, she asked if he was "the same dog." I told her Victoria had died and, thankfully, it was never an issue that Victor had come to live with me.

The job at MIT never came to fruition but I ultimately got a job at Seattle University. From the day I began working there, Victor and I were embraced by my new campus community and the head of my department even designated the chair outside my office "Victor's Endowed Chair." For over a decade, Victor and I shared many good years and memories together, both on- and off-campus. He accompanied me through several major changes and trials in my life, including moving with me when I was hired as a professor and purchasing my first home. He was there during my courtship by the man who would become my husband—and was there when the marriage ended in divorce and I fell into untold depths of despair. Had it not been for Victor, I likely would not have survived the devastating impact of the divorce.

Consumed by my own grief, it never occurred to me that Victor would be affected by the divorce until he began to succumb to his own depression. He became lethargic and almost reclusive, no longer wanting to go outdoors. When I let him out to do his business, he would pee and come right back into the house, only to find out later that he had pooped on the carpet. My students and colleagues were incredibly supportive of us during this difficult time. When I realized that my sadness and depression were impacting Victor, I decided it was time to pull myself together so he could get better, too. I began eating better and exercising rather than sulking, and we both got better.

When Victor turned thirteen I noticed that, in addition to slowing down, he had an odd drainage from one of his eyes. Our vet examined him and said the drainage was due to a retrobulbar tumor fingering its way through his head. The ongoing growth and intrusion of the tumor began to render Victor deaf and blind.

After telling me Victor's death was eminent, the vet reassured me that Victor would choose a time to depart that was good for both of us. No longer able to bring my now bedridden Victor to campus with me each day, I grew increasingly lonely. My students and colleagues once again rallied behind us and began writing notes to Victor. Every night, I brought the notes home, curled up on the couch with Victor, and read each of the notes to him. It provided much-needed solace and became a daily comforting ritual for us.

Victor's health continued to decline until one morning when I looked at him and realized he was refusing to go because he didn't want to leave me alone. I knew it was time, and mustering all the courage I had, I put Victor in the car. Knowing this would be our last ride together, we went on a memorial drive around town and reminisced about our years and adventures together. Victor sat stoic and quiet on the seat next to me, and witnessing his heroic courage made it easier for me to let him go.

Our vet was waiting for us. I opted not to stay, and instead whispered a final message in his ear, tearfully kissed him goodbye, and left, entrusting Victor—body and soul—to our vet's care.

After saying goodbye to Victor, I immediately went to the animal shelter in search of a girl-dog to name Vesta, after the Roman goddess of home and hearth. Walking around the kennel, I was stunned to see a puppy who was the mirror image of Victor when I first adopted him! The shelter informed me the puppy, just six months old, had been put out for adoption just fifteen minutes prior to my arrival, coinciding with the precise moment that Victor was put to sleep. Ever since witnessing the miraculous appearance of Victoria's rainbow, I had become a firm believer in the mystical made manifest, especially when it came to dogs.

Gazing at the little puppy, I noticed his kennel-assigned name was Barney. He was a boy-dog, but I had my heart set on a girl-dog. The shelter ranger, seeing me turn to walk away, said, "He's awfully cute. Maybe you should take him out into the meet-and-greet area outside."

"Why not?" I thought, so out into the yard Barney and I went. He raced twice around the perimeter of the yard, came towards me like a torpedo, and jumped into my arms. He began to lick my face profusely as I protested. "No, no, no! You're lovely, but I need a girl-dog!" The licking continued as I continued to protest. "No, no, no! I already have her name! Vesta!" Again, the licking. "Well, maybe . . ." which became "Well,

I guess I could add an 'r' to the end . . ." and thus Barney became Vestar and assumed his role as the "god" of my home, hearth, and heart.

As we drove away from the shelter, the Savage Garden song "I Knew I Loved You" began to play on the radio. The significance of the song—which talks about believing you knew someone before you ever met—was eerie, beautiful, and incredibly appropriate for Vestar and me.

The immediate connection and joy between us let me know that Vestar's adoption had been sanctioned by Victor. It was further confirmed when I took Vestar for his first vet appointment and the vet gasped, "He looks like Victor's little brother!"

Although Vestar and I became fast friends, almost as if we had always known each other, I still felt the void left by Victor. After Vestar and I picked up Victor's ashes, we placed the container in the meditation room in our home. Little did I know that Vestar's ashes would join Victor's sooner than I could have imagined.

Vestar's vibrant personality and exuberant approach to life hid the illness that was lurking within him. When he was a little over four years old, I noticed lesions on his chest. Thinking they were scrapes or scratches from the blackberry brambles in my yard, I didn't do anything about them. However, when they didn't go away after several months, I took him to the vet and it was diagnosed as a mast cell tumor: cancer. After getting over my initial shock, I invested in cancer surgery, which seemed to revive and relieve Vestar. I thought he was cured, but after about three months, Vestar went into a rapid decline and died within three weeks.

Vestar and I had only been together for four and half years. Assuming we would be together for many years, I was hurt and angry at the thought of losing him so soon. Just as with Victor, Vestar chose a time to depart that was good for both of us. As we began our final ride together, a Savage Garden song came on the radio. The lyrics of the song "Truly, Madly, Deeply," once again, proved to be incredibly significant. As the song played and I listened to the words—about being strong and faithful, about counting on a new beginning, a reason for living, and a deeper meaning—I knew that, although Vestar was departing, he would be with me always. He would always lend me hope and love and his soul would guide me forward to a reason for living with a deeper meaning.

As Vestar was prepped for his passage, he remained placid and assured. This time I made the decision to remain in the room. I am glad I did, for I was able to witness his miraculously noble departure—with amazing composure, Vestar gently lifted his paw to receive the lethal injection.

As I grieved the loss of Vestar, I came to a richer understanding of his life and death as well as the bounty of lessons learned from him. When he came into my life, I was still holding onto residual gunk from my marriage, divorce, and a collection of other lifelong challenges. Knowing this, and knowing his days were numbered, I believe Vestar (by osmosis) had taken my residual gunk into his ailing body. Wanting me to journey forth whole and healthy, my "god" of home, hearth, and heart took it all with him and it is the most generous gesture I have ever experienced.

Vestar knew I would go straight to the animal shelter to meet the dog his soul had selected as his successor. Once again, I walked into the shelter looking to adopt a girl-dog who I would name Virginia Woof. Believing our dogs choose us, I kept an open mind regarding her breed, but the dog's color was not an option. I wanted a solid white, black, or brown dog.

As we began walking around, my friend Sonora immediately started cooing over a four-month-old black and white border collie mix puppy. "Oh, Mary, look!"

I looked and immediately said, "Oh, no. I don't 'do' spotted dogs!"

"But, oooh, Maaarrry . . ." she said.

"Absolutely not. And besides, it's a boy. I'm looking for a girl."

Fidget (as the dog was known) had just been picked up as a stray that morning. Since there was a five-day waiting period to allow his owner time to find him, he wasn't available for adoption. At Sonora's insistence, I left my name and number, and five days later, the shelter called. I decided to stop by, do a meet-and-greet with Fidget, and also look around at other available dogs.

That same day, I adopted Fidget and renamed him Dominic after St. Dominic. His colors (black and white) are the colors of St. Dominic's religious order and his birthday is November 1, which is All Saints' Day. His full name became Dominic Ignatius DePorres.

Mary-Antoinette and
Dominic Ignatius DePorres

As a puppy, Dominic never responded to any stern attempts to correct him. My dog sitter said Dominic didn't seem to understand the concept of "no," so over time, we discovered ways to communicate commands to him without using the word "no." Dominic matured into a well-adjusted, well-behaved pooch, who lives a life that is utterly and completely all "YES!" In Dominic's world, "no" doesn't exist, only "YES!"

Dominic is now almost six years old. In addition to his own unique traits, I can see within him the most endearing qualities of all of his canine predecessors: Cisco, Princess, Biggie, Dijon, Whimpey, Victoria, Victor, and Vestar. Dominic has been such a blessing, for he embodies, and constantly mirrors back to me, the best qualities of all of my dogs. That is a most precious gift, for it provides me with the opportunity to celebrate all of the lessons I have learned thus far in my life. Dominic is also teaching me how to live according to his ever-affirming approach to life. And to that, I say a resounding YES!

Chapter Twenty-Two
CHRISSY

Chrissy and I worked together at a local natural foods market. She was shy, quiet, and hard-working, and I was immediately drawn to her smile and kind nature. In the ensuing years, Chrissy began to share more of her personal story with me, and when I learned all she had been through it made me respect her and her journey even more. She is brave, strong, and compassionate with a heart and soul of gold driven by her love for animals and one very special dog named Buddy.

I'M THE YOUNGEST OF FOUR and the only girl. My brothers, who range from nine to seventeen years older than me, all had dogs growing up. Since the responsibility for the dogs ended up falling on my parents, by the time I came along, they didn't want any more dogs.

I had a cat named Dusty but was always envious of my friends who had dogs and loved when my oldest brother, Barry, came to visit with his dog Socrates. He was a beagle mix and, despite his name, was probably the dumbest dog ever. My father always joked that if you threw a scrap of food and it

Chrissy and Tres, her three-legged
rescue cat
(Photo: Photography by Sharyn)

landed between Socrates's legs, he wouldn't be able to find it. Socrates loved to run and, since we didn't have a fenced-in yard, every time he escaped we would spend hours chasing him or going door to door asking our neighbors to keep an eye out for him.

When I was in my late twenties, my first dog found me.

I was working for Honeywell and left the office one afternoon to drop a package in the FedEx box at the end of our cul-de-sac. As I walked up to the box there was nothing and no one around. I put the envelope in the box, turned, and a dog was lying there staring up at me. I smiled and said, "Well, hello puppy," but the dog just lay there. I knelt down to pet him and check for a collar or ID tags but there weren't any. Next, I tried to encourage him to come with me but he wouldn't (or couldn't) get up.

Unsure what to do, I ran back to work to get my friend Ellen, who was a real dog person. When Ellen couldn't figure out what was wrong with the dog, we decided to take him to the vet. He was unable to get up or walk but did allow us to pick him up and put him in the back seat of my car.

After checking him over, the vet said the dog had shattered and disintegrating vertebrae in his upper back and neck, his paws were raw and bleeding, he was covered in fleas and ticks, and he was severely dehydrated. He was also very depressed. In short, the dog was a mess.

Over the next few days, I called constantly to check on the dog. The vet explained that, over time, arthritis would probably settle into the dog's spine and he would no longer be able to walk. He felt the dog would never have a normal life and probably wouldn't live more than a year.

The dog remained at the vet's office so they could administer fluids, medication, and try to get him to walk again. In the meantime, I posted fliers around the neighborhood and ran ads to see if anyone would claim him or lead me to his owner but no one ever came forward. Even though it was obvious from the dog's condition that he had been on the road a long time, I couldn't understand how someone could have abandoned him or not wanted him back.

I also wondered what his life was like before I found him. The vet believed he was a Lab-border collie mix and probably five or six years old. How many of those years had he spent on the road? Were his paws bleeding from walking? The vet said sometimes when a dog gets hit by a car, they slide and it tears up their paws. Is that what happened? Was his back damaged because he had been hit by a car or did somebody intentionally hurt him? What I struggled with the most was trying to understand how anyone could abandon this wonderful dog.

Sometimes I wished he could talk and tell me what his life was like before and what had happened to him. For me, the toughest thing was not knowing but maybe it was better I didn't know. I made what seemed to be the most logical and compassionate decision: I brought him home to live with me so I could care for him and keep him comfortable during whatever time he had left on this earth.

I named him Buddy because one of my best friends, Curt, and I called each other Buddy and to me, Buddy meant best friend.

When I brought Buddy home, his legs had gotten a little stronger. While he was able to stand up for short periods, he was still unable to walk. Since I was living in a third-floor apartment, I carried him up and down the stairs. Unsure if his inability to walk was because of his feet or his back, I put little socks and soothing ointment on his feet. I bathed him to keep the fleas and ticks out of his beautiful shiny black coat. He got all the food and fresh water he needed, as well as a few extra snacks, and before long Buddy became very full figured. He loved to eat and was probably so grateful he no longer had to scrounge for food.

Buddy followed me around the apartment, and in doing so, his legs got stronger and he began walking again. From the day I found him, Buddy never needed a leash. Not once. He was the mellowest dog I had ever met and was never anxious or upset—until the first time I left him to go to work.

I remember that day vividly. Before leaving for work, I put Buddy in his crate, which was in my bedroom. I closed the bedroom door and went off to work, confident he would be fine until I got home. When I got home that afternoon, Buddy met me at the front door. He had somehow squeezed through the bars of the crate, chewed his way through my bedroom door, and by the time I got home, he had begun chewing a hole in the front door.

After that, rather than locking him in his crate, I put something against the front door so he couldn't chew his way out. Eventually, he accepted and understood that even though I left, I always came back.

Buddy also had five cats to keep him company. While I believed the cats secretly loved Buddy, they teased him unmercifully. But Buddy was nice to everyone, including the cats, and went along with whatever the cats did to him. He didn't like disagreements so the only time he put his foot down was when the cats got into a fight. Then he would get right in the middle of the fight to try and stop them.

When Buddy came to live with me, I was in a relationship with a man who was really good to all of us. After that relationship ended, I moved back into my parents' house with Buddy and all my cats.

Buddy developed a special relationship with both of my parents and even though my dad acted like he didn't care about Buddy, I could tell he loved him. He picked meat off of bones for Buddy to make sure there wasn't anything Buddy would choke on. Dad took Buddy to the golf course, where Buddy patrolled the woods and fields for squirrels and birds while Dad played. He was good company for my dad and loved going anywhere in the car with me or my dad.

As he got older, the injuries he had sustained in his younger years reared their head and it became increasingly difficult for Buddy to get into the car without assistance. At first, Buddy developed a method where he would do a lap or two around the car and build up enough speed to jump into the car. But eventually he had to be hoisted into the car. I remember how sad my dad was when he realized Buddy could no longer jump into the car by himself.

Buddy was also a blessing to my mother who had begun to show signs of Alzheimer's or some form of dementia. Over time, while we were all doing the best we could in dealing with my mom and the progression of the disease, my mother was spending quite a bit of time alone. She spent most of her day watching old movies from the '40s and '50s with Buddy sleeping at her side. My mom's favorite snack was mini muffins that she always shared with Buddy: two bites for my mom, and the last bite for Buddy. When the muffins were gone, Mom would say, "No more, Buddy," and he would lie down next to her and go to back to sleep. I am so grateful my mom had Buddy because my dad was busy, my brothers all lived far away, and I wasn't able to be there for her.

For several years, I had been dealing with a drug problem and things were starting to get a little crazy. Since I wasn't home, sometimes for days, my parents began caring for Buddy and my cats. They fed Buddy, took him out, and gave him the love he deserved because I was nowhere to be found. I wasn't there for Buddy physically, mentally, or spiritually. I wasn't there for anybody.

My parents were elderly, and since my behavior was starting to negatively impact them and their health, my brothers banded together and told me I needed to move out of my parents' house along with Buddy and my five cats. I don't blame them. I would have kicked me out too.

A friend allowed Buddy, the cats, and me to move in with him, but after a few months, I began to steal in addition to doing drugs. I was constantly disappearing and people who cared about me were always worried I had died. Again, my friend made the right decision and kicked me out.

I landed a good job and an apartment in a beautiful suburb near Paterson, New Jersey. It was a huge break for me, but again, it didn't last.

My father had passed, my mother had officially been diagnosed with Alzheimer's and placed in a nursing home, and I hit the proverbial rock bottom. I was getting high every day because nothing seemed to matter anymore. I was going into Paterson every day for drugs and wouldn't come home for days. A friend told me many years later that he knew my soul was completely gone when I started to neglect my animals.

I thank God for my landlord who lived upstairs. Seeing what was happening, she let herself into my apartment to feed Buddy and the cats and take Buddy for walks.

Buddy, who had always been able to get up, move around, and go outside to pee or walk around, was in pretty bad shape at this point. The last time I saw him, the arthritis in his spine was so bad he could no longer get up and walk. I had to carry him outside and hold up his back end so he could pee and poop. I knew Buddy was in pain, but being in such bad shape myself, I was unable to do anything for him.

The next time I disappeared, my landlord had the SPCA come into my apartment and remove all my animals. When I finally returned home, my apartment was empty and there was a notice on the door for me to appear in court for abandonment of animals. I learned Buddy had been taken and put to sleep.

I understand when a dog reaches a point where they are no longer able to move and in a lot of pain the compassionate thing to do is have the dog put to sleep, but I was incredibly sad that day and still am—not that Buddy died because I don't think he was enjoying himself or his life anymore, but because Buddy died without me being there. I had promised Buddy I would always be there for him, and at the moment he needed me the most, I wasn't there. It still haunts me to this day.

Coming home that day to absolute and utter emptiness, I turned around and, leaving my few possessions behind, walked out of my apartment and never went back. For the next few months, I lived on the street until thankfully I got arrested.

It was April 17, 2004: the day I decided to give life a chance for the first time in almost twenty-five years. After a brief incarceration and a yearlong stay in a rehab and halfway house, I began a new life and adopted two cats: Stinky and Squish. Things were going fine for a while, but I relapsed and ended up back in jail. Despite all I had been through (and put my loved ones through) there were still lessons for me to learn. There was still something missing. Even though I was clean and sober, I hadn't changed. Inside, I was still the same person.

I went back to rehab and treatment while a friend gave Stinky and Squish a home. Once out and back on my feet, I brought Stinky and Squish to live with me again. They are still with me today and I am so grateful.

Finally, with a clear head and another chance at life, I began to face my past, including what had happened with Buddy. Probably one of the hardest things I have ever had to face was that Buddy was alone at the end of his life. I had put drugs in front of my family, my friends, and my pets.

That moment of clarity is the driving force behind who I am and what I do today. Not only do I want to live my life but I want to be of service to animals. During treatment, there was a counselor who guided me in the right direction and I started taking classes at the local community college, where I realized I loved learning and getting good grades.

I also met a woman who introduced me to a rescue group and I have been involved in rescue work ever since. After my first time in treatment, I realized two things that were missing from my life: gratitude and service. Both are now a big part of my life. For me, there is no better feeling than being of service and taking an animal off the street. I believe it is my purpose; by doing this work, I am able to honor the pets who saved my life. There were many mornings when Buddy and the cats were my only reason for getting up. Many times, I lived another day for them.

Chrissy with Mouser, one of the many cats she has rescued
(Photo: Photography by Sharyn)

I think Buddy understood I was in pain and desperately needed him. He let me hold him and cry and sob into his fur for as long as I needed. He was always by my side, protecting me, watching my face and looking into my eyes. He and the cats all knew I was in pain and were afraid one day I wasn't going to walk back in the door. In spite of everything we went through, they all showed me unconditional love because that is what animals do.

When I first found Buddy, it was like he came looking for me. He was a pretty good-sized black dog and it isn't like he could have been hiding somewhere. So where was he when I was walking up to that mailbox? He wasn't there. I didn't see a thing but then I turned around and there he was.

When I first found him, the vet told me Buddy wouldn't live another year. Luckily, the vet was wrong because Buddy lived another six years and I am so thankful he did. He was a gift that saved my life. More than anything, I hope if Buddy can see me now, he is proud of what I am doing.

DOGS AND ADDICTION TREATMENT

Given the well-documented evidence of the positive impact dogs have on our mental, physical, and emotional well-being, it came as no surprise when I learned dogs were being used to assist with addiction treatment and recovery. While a dog can't cure an addiction, they can be an integral component in an addict's journey towards wholeness. This was further substantiated in a study that had been conducted in Troy, New York, as well as in an innovative program at an alcohol and drug treatment center in southern Florida.

TERRI MILLER, AN ADDICTIONS COUNSELOR WITH SETON Addictions Services in Troy, New York, conducted a twelve-week study to determine the impact (if any) therapy animals would have on inpatient substance abuse clients. [1]

Three rescue dogs were used for the project: Silk, a greyhound rescued from the racetrack; Rose, an orphaned greyhound/pit bull mix; and Alexis, a full-blooded pit bull who had carried many scars when rescued from a crack raid. All three dogs were now certified therapy dogs.

Every week, for approximately one hour, the dogs were brought in to interact with the clients. In addition to being an enjoyable activity, the study hoped to determine if the use of animal-assisted therapy would help the substance abusers identify and intervene with self-defeating patterns in thought, actions, and feelings, especially those that might relate or contribute to a relapse.

A total of fifty-six clients participated in the project. What the study found was that when the dogs were present, over half of the participating clients interacted spontaneously with the dogs and ultimately revealed significant portions of their histories, especially as they related to violence, loss, self-esteem, family dynamics, and consequences of drug and alcohol use. This seemed significant in light of the difficulties some substance abuse clients experience with trust.

The study went on to report that:

- Clients tended to withdraw if the dogs did not initially interact or respond when approached or if the dog didn't like them.
- Intervention was provided by helping clients change body or vocal signals.
- In most cases, clients admitted that their reactions with the dogs mirrored their expectations, behaviors, and communications with people. This is extremely important since clients are recommended to attend twelve-step meetings and obtain new support networks in sobriety. Physical or emotional distancing can severely hamper the client's ability in this area.

When Alexis the pit bull was present, there seemed to be a higher degree of disclosure about violence among the participants of the study. This may be attributed to the fact that pit bulls are a breed commonly abused and tortured in the drug community for either dog fighting or for guard dog purposes. These disclosures provided important information on the client's thought processes regarding anger management, the need for power and control, self-image, and peer relations.

Although only a pilot project, the preliminary results of this study indicated the benefit of using animal-assisted therapy with adult substance abuse clients. It specifically allowed for increased opportunities to gain insight and information about a client's background and history as well as their thought and behavioral patterns. It also provided opportunities to identify unhealthy coping mechanisms in order to educate and guide the clients towards new behaviors and choices. All of these are critical in assisting someone build a new life and support system geared towards abstinence from alcohol and drugs.

"Animal ownership can provide immeasurable therapeutic value to addiction recovery patients," says Tammy Malloy, chief clinical officer of Behavioral Health of the Palm Beaches,[2] which operates several alcohol and drug treatment centers located in Florida. Seaside Palm Beach, one of the Behavioral Health of the Palm Beaches facilities located in south Florida, developed a one-of-a kind innovative program allowing their clients to bring their own pets with them to their luxury rehab facility.

"Animal lovers can lean on their own non-human friends for strength and support and are overwhelmed with joy at the prospect of being able to have their animals with them during this challenging process," Malloy explained. "By the very nature of their presence during treatment, the dog becomes a part of the treatment. The dog also provides a benign and comforting reminder of their life before rehab."

Scientific research has shown that a dog can reduce stress, lower blood pressure, and provide us with a sense of calm and peace. These health benefits, along with the unwavering loyalty, trust, and companionship a dog provides, can be powerful allies to those struggling with addiction, helping them remain calm and resist the urge to relapse.

Those dealing with addiction are also more inclined to spend time with and open up to a pet than to a family member. "The dog is a completely non-judgmental sounding board for their fears, complaints, reservations, and troubles," said Malloy.

The task of simply caring for their dogs also allows the patients to reacquaint themselves with the concept of selflessness and nurturing. "It makes them responsible for a life other than their own," said Malloy, explaining that, "Having another living thing to care for and love may be one of the best reasons for someone to have a dog beside them during recovery. Knowing the dog depends on you for its care and survival means stepping up to the plate. The dog may motivate the individual to be worthy of that love, trust, and loyalty and, in short, become the person your dog already believes you are."

Chapter Twenty-Three
JEAN

I was introduced to Jean many moons ago by a mutual friend and was immediately drawn in by her eyes and her laugh. Her unique laugh was heartfelt and contagious. Following the death of our mothers, sharing that common experience and the journey of healing from that loss connected us on a whole different level. As we spent more time together, I learned more about this remarkable woman named Jean, including her life with and love of dogs.

MY SISTER AND I WERE RAISED WITH ALL KINDS OF ANIMALS: ducks, cats, iguanas, and, of course, dogs. Looking back, I'm glad we had that experience and wish all children could have pets because it teaches you a lot about compassion, life, loss, and responsibility.

We were also blessed to have a mother who allowed us to have pets while also instilling important values in us. My sister and I will never forget the night our mom didn't give us dinner because we forgot to feed the animals and she wanted us to see what it was like to go without a meal.

Dogs have always been my best friends and, as an adult, I have always had a dog. There have been a lot of different dogs in my life, including several pit bulls, and each one has been wonderful, unique, and my best friend.

Peabody

I got my first pit bull puppy, White Hog, while visiting California. He was a really sweet dog, protective of me, and great with kids.

After getting White Hog, we found out about a litter of pit bull puppies and went to see them. The situation was terrible. The puppies were in a chicken wire cage and there were kids going into the cage, grabbing for the puppies. I adopted a female puppy and named her Fauna. When I got her, she had a distended belly but not long after coming home with me, she was healthy and happy.

Because of Fauna's early experience around children, I decided to keep her in a separate room if there were children around, not because she had ever done anything wrong or misbehaved in any way, but because I always wanted to make sure she felt safe and secure.

Fauna and White Hog got along really well. In fact, they got along so well that they ended up with puppies of their own! We named one of the puppies Dozer because he would literally bulldoze through all the other puppies to get at his food. My sister took one of the puppies and all of the rest were adopted into good homes.

When I moved back into my mother's house, Fauna came with me. One day, my sister's puppy and Fauna disappeared and never came back. We put up posters and asked everywhere but we never found them. My main concern was that someone had picked them up and was either using them as bait dogs or fighting them. They were sweet dogs and I hope and pray that isn't what happened to them.

The next dog I got was a mix-breed puppy (possibly a shepherd-Lab mix) I named Peabody. Peabody was a birthday gift from my sister. I remember what she said when she gave him to me. "Happy birthday, Jean. I thought you could use some responsibility in your life." While I knew exactly what she meant—and that she was right—I wasn't ready to admit that I needed a change of any kind in my life.

At the time Peabody came into my life, my addiction to drinking was progressing. Since I took Peabody with me almost everywhere I went, he also came with me to my favorite watering holes. When we were there, I could see the discomfort in his kind eyes but my drinking took precedence.

No matter what I did or didn't do, Peabody forgave me and loved me anyway. I never physically abused Peabody in any way but some of the situations I put us in were certainly mentally abusive to him. He was a really sweet dog and despite everything he went through he was my best friend. Today it brings tears to my eyes and pain in my heart to think of the abuse this innocent, loving dog endured because of my addiction at that time.

I was caught in a vicious cycle of blackouts, remorse, self-loathing, and empty promises to myself—only to be back out two days later doing it all over again. This behavior went on for several years and had it not been for Peabody, I may have gone out one day (or night) and never come back. But I knew I needed to make sure Peabs was fed, loved, let out, and all the things we do for those we love who love us. He was probably one of the biggest factors in saving my life.

I finally quit drinking and Peabs and I had lots of good years together. I am immensely grateful I was clean and sober when Peabody needed me.

When he was around thirteen, Peabody began having difficulty controlling his bowels. My mom watched him while we were on vacation, and when we returned, she said, "You're going to have to start thinking about it." I knew what she was talking about but Peabody was still eating and happy.

I took Peabody to the vet and asked him what to do. He said, "It's your decision but I'm not going to euthanize him if you're going to feel guilty." I left, deciding when Peabody could no longer get up I would think about it. And then Peabody started having trouble getting up.

Then I decided if he lost his appetite, I would think about it. Before long, the brain-body connection was impacted and he began urinating in the house. I cut a big sheet of plastic and put that under a pile of blankets for him to lie on.

One night, we were going to a Christmas party. I put a diaper on Peabody because we were going to be gone for a while. He wasn't used to that and when I looked down at him, he was just lying in the corner of the laundry room. It broke my heart.

One morning, I woke up and realized it wasn't Peabody anymore. I made the vet's appointment for the next day. That night I made Peabody a big steak dinner and we just stayed together.

The next day everyone at the vet's office was so kind. They didn't fault me and said I had made the right decision at the right time. After the vet gave Peabody the shot, she left me with him on a blanket on the floor and I just held him. I felt guilty then, and even now, I still feel guilty thinking maybe I should have quit my job and taken care of Peabody a little longer. Peabody had been such a huge factor in saving my life that letting him go was very difficult. Probably the hardest thing I have ever gone through, besides my mother's death, was having Peabody euthanized.

Knowing I was stuck in feelings of guilt about Peabody, my chiropractor gave me the name of an animal communicator and suggested I contact her.

The first time I called the communicator she said Peabody was really tired and resting. "Give him time to rest and call me back in a month or so." Several months later, I called her back and this time she said, "It is as if Peabody is sitting up and looking around to tell everyone how proud he is of you." When I told her I was still having a hard time living with myself and my guilt, she said, "Peabody wants to remind you that you *did* take care of him. You took care of him when he needed you." While it was a help to hear, even now I feel there was more I could have done for Peabody.

After Peabody, I decided not to get another dog because his passing just hurt too much. My sister and her kids kept talking about my getting a dog but I remained steadfast. I didn't want another dog. When my niece Savannah asked, "Aunt Bean, what do you think about a puppy?" I explained we weren't going to get a dog.

"Savannah, we're travelling too much. We don't have anyone to watch the puppy when we were gone."

Without missing a beat, Savannah said, "We'll watch it."

A few days later, Savannah said, "So, Aunt Bean, if you were to get a dog, what kind of dog wouldn't you want?"

I immediately said, "A pit bull." Not because I didn't like them. I loved pit bulls. They were always some of the best dogs I ever had and are humorous, loving, and wonderful dogs. I didn't want one because of the way people view and judge them.

A few months later, on Christmas Eve, my sister and her kids came over with a basket and put it under my tree. The basket was moving and when I looked inside, there was Toby, a four-week-old pit bull mix puppy.

My first comment was, "He's awfully tiny." My niece explained that she had seen an ad at a pizza place for a litter of puppies and the young woman on the phone said they could come see them. When they arrived, the couple went down into the cellar and brought the puppies up. The more they saw, the more concerned my sister and her kids were for the puppies. My sister's overall impression was that the young couple wasn't taking very good care of the puppies and was simply hoping to get rid of them as Christmas presents.

Knowing people did weird and sometimes hurtful things with animals, especially pit bulls, my sister and her kids decided it was better for the puppy to be with someone who would nurture him rather than him getting into the wrong hands—even though he was so young.

To this day, Toby doesn't like to go down into the cellar. We have to coerce him if we want him to go down there and I can't help but wonder if that is because of an early memory of something that happened to him down in that cellar.

My husband grew up on a farm and all their animals, including their dogs, were always kept outside. The thought of another dog in the house didn't exactly thrill him.

Five months later, my husband's father passed, and after that, Toby was constantly at my husband's side. My husband had never really been affectionate with other people's dogs but he has now become a dog person. Toby brought out a side of my husband that was always there but never had a chance to come out before.

I believe Peabody was here for me. He came to help me through so many challenges and changes in my life. We went through a lot in our fifteen years together but we got through it all. I don't have the same kind of connection with Toby but that's because I believe Toby is here for my husband.

When Toby was a little puppy, my husband would put his forehead on Toby's belly. Toby would lay completely still and submissive, and in Toby's mind, I believe it made my husband the dominant one. I am low man on the totem pole, and although initially my feelings were hurt, I am now glad they have one another.

Toby relaxing at home
(Photo: Photography by Sharyn)

Toby always tried to play with my mother's and sister's dogs, but since those dogs were all older, they snubbed Toby. Also, since Toby was taken away from his mother and littermates when he was so young, he didn't learn "dog language" or get the early socialization from being around other dogs. Normally, a puppy learns bite inhibition while nursing and playing. When nursing pups bite too hard, their mother will stand up and walk away. When playing with other pups, if they bite too hard, the pup who has been bitten too hard will yelp, stop playing, or growl. All this helps teach a puppy to be conscious and aware of the force of their bite.

Without bite inhibition, a dog could seriously injure another dog or person. Since Toby was removed at such a young age from his mother and littermates, we had to teach him bite inhibition. We never had to punish Toby because he has always been a good dog.

We socialized Toby with a variety of situations and people, including the FedEx and UPS men. He loves cats, and if they run away from him, he thinks it's a game. Toby is just a really good dog. He has never been mean or destructive and is also very humorous. We have dressed him up in a pink tutu and he just takes it in stride. He loves kids. If I even mention my sister's kids, he starts getting really excited, so I have to be really careful about saying their names unless we're actually going to see them.

Toby doesn't get along well with other dogs and we just respect that is part of his personality. He has learned to play a lot by himself and with my husband. My sister recently got a new dog and her dog and Toby are beginning to warm up to one another but we still keep an eye on him.

Sometimes when I walk Toby around town, I get "the look" from people. I know they are judging him simply because he is a pit bull. He is a very sweet dog and it breaks my heart that people would judge him simply because of what they incorrectly believe is true about the breed. It isn't fair for anyone, animal or human, to be judged based on the way they look. Everyone deserves a chance to have people get to know who they are, not on the outside, but on the inside.

Chapter Twenty-Four
CYDNEY

Cydney was one of the people I met by accident (although since I don't really believe in accidents, I prefer to say I met her by "magic"). I was researching a study done with therapy dogs and was unable to locate the first person listed for the study so I went to the second person: Cydney. We talked about the study and when we discovered we were within an hour of one another at the time, she invited me to meet her at a coffee shop halfway between us. Outside of the study, I didn't know anything about Cydney but something instinctively told me I should meet her. I'm glad I trusted my instincts so I can now bring you the story of Cydney and her organization, Out of the Pits.[1]

Cydney and Stella

EVER SINCE I WAS YOUNG, ALL I ever wanted was a horse and a dog. My mom was busy raising four kids, building a business, and caring for a home and family and she absolutely didn't want to add animals to that list of responsibilities.

Then, one Christmas, we got a call from the train station in our hometown telling us to come down and pick up a package. My grandfather, who raised beagles in Iowa, had put a six-month-old un-housebroken beagle on the train and sent it to us. I can still remember my mom's face. At the time, I was five, one of my brothers was four, my sister was three, and my other brother had just been born. My poor mom, who didn't want any animals, suddenly had three toddlers, an infant, and a puppy that wasn't housebroken.

We named the dog Queenie. Since there wasn't as much understanding back then of the importance of spaying and neutering, a few years later, my neighbor's dog got Queenie pregnant. The local butcher adopted one of the puppies and named it Woodchuck. Woodchuck spent his entire life greeting customers at the butcher shop, as well as people passing by, and became somewhat of a figurehead in the town of Chatham, New York.

Queenie was a sweet, happy dog. She died of old age when she was eighteen, and it was really difficult for me when we lost her since she was my first dog.

When I was twenty-two, I was visiting one of my horses on a farm when a little puppy ran up to me. The man who owned the puppies wasn't doing anything to contain them or keep them safe, and I was concerned the puppy might run into the road and get hit by a car. I brought her home and named her Nikki.

Nikki was the first dog I could call my own. She was a border-standard collie mix and absolutely amazing. Every day, she came to school with me and stayed in my office while I taught. She was a really sweet dog and everyone loved her.

When Nikki was six, she got really sick. Thinking she had a ruptured esophagus, the vet performed surgery. During the operation, he discovered she had myasthenia gravis, a rare disorder that impacts the transmission of impulses from the nerves to the muscles. For many dogs, the esophagus is impacted, which is what happened with Nikki. She got inhalant pneumonia from the surgery and was incredibly sick. I wanted her to live but I didn't want her to suffer so I held her and prayed, "Please either save her or let her go."

When we went back to the vet, they were all shocked. "That dog is still alive?" they said. "You must know someone upstairs because there is no way that dog should still be with us." That was my first real experience of the connection between my faith and the work I do with dogs.

Nikki lived to be thirteen. Even though I had to give her daily injections, she took everything in stride and had a wonderful life.

I then began adopting dogs and had a German shepherd, a collie, a sheltie, and a fox terrier when I found out about a greyhound that was about to be euthanized. I drove to Massachusetts hoping she would be a black dog. I always loved black dogs and wanted a black greyhound but God puts things in our lives for a reason. It may not be what we want but it's what we need. And that was true of my fawn-colored greyhound, Jesse.

Jesse was extremely elegant and unique. I had researched greyhounds and read that they don't jump or dig, so when I got Jesse home I put her in the fenced yard and the first thing she did was take a flying leap over the fence.

Jesse did a lot of things that weren't greyhound-like but that is common. People think if they get a certain breed they are going to be or act a certain way, but dogs are still individuals despite their breed's characteristics. It is no different than assuming every person of a certain nationality will look or act exactly the same.

One of my best understandings of that happened while I was managing a municipal shelter. I wanted to know, in my heart of hearts, that every animal would have the most peaceful passing possible, so I had trained to be a euthanasia technician.

One day a man came into the shelter with an eleven-year-old black and white pit bull. He could barely speak English but was able to tell me that his wife had left him and he was having a problem finding a place to live that would allow the dog. He was hoping to place the dog in the shelter but it was extremely aggressive towards other dogs.

We sat and talked about the dog living safely and happily in the world. Keeping it in a shelter with other dogs barking and around it constantly would have been torture for the dog. For that and other reasons, we decided the kinder thing was to have the dog put down. I asked if he wanted to stay but he looked at me and said, "I don't think I can do it. I've lost everything in my life except for this dog. He has been the only constant in my life for ten years." I explained it would be better for the dog if he was there so he went and sat in his car for quite a while. When he came back in, he looked at me and asked, "Will he forgive me?"

I told him the beauty of dogs is that they are ever-forgiving and ever-loving. He stayed with the dog and it was very peaceful. We all stood around and cried with him. Here was this man who had spent time in prison, covered in tattoos with connotations to violent crimes he had committed, telling me, "That dog was the only thing that ever really loved me."

I often think about that man and dog. It was an amazing experience and a powerful reminder to never prejudge a person (or a dog). No matter who a person is, no matter what they look like or what they do or what they have done, if their heart belongs to a dog, we are all connected by that common bond.

Then a dog came into my life that completely changed me and the course of my life.

In 1993, I was contacted to take photographs of Tux, an eighty-pound pit bull and weight pull champion. It was my first close-up experience with a pit bull. My friend Mary Allen had gotten the dog from a police officer who brought it to the vet to be euthanized. Mary Allen was active in greyhound rescue, and as I took the photos we began talking. She told me about a litter of puppies in Indiana that were a greyhound-pit bull mix. Since the puppies had pit bull in them, nobody wanted them. When the puppies were brought East, Mary Allen took two and I ended up adopting one and naming her Rose.

Rose was a female and a combination of the best of both greyhound and pit bull. She was red and absolutely gorgeous and when she first looked at me, something happened: there was an immediate connection. There are dogs you love and then there are your heart dogs. Nikki had been my first heart dog and I never thought I would be blessed with another, but eleven years after Nikki passed, Rose became my second heart dog. If someone asked me, "If you could only have one thing in your life what would it be?" my answer would be Rose.

As I began researching pit bulls, Mary Allen called to tell me she was at the vet with a pit bull that had been thrown out of a car on the Taconic Parkway. When we both realized nobody was helping pit bulls we decided to start an organization to help them. We started Out of the Pits in 1994 and we are the oldest pit bull rescue in the United States. In twenty-one years, we have placed over 6,000 pit bulls.

I adopted another pit bull, Alexis, and began working with both of them on agility. While Alexis and Rose were fine working together, they didn't want to live together so I kept them apart at home.

We were once at an agility event when we walked past three women. Alexis walked right over to one of the women. She didn't have any hair and had an oxygen tank attached to her walker. The woman looked at Alexis then at me and said, "She came right to me! She chose me!" When I saw the positive impact Alexis had on this woman, I thought, "I have to do something with this. I'm going to train this dog to bring joy to people."

In 1997, Alexis became the first pit bull to become a registered therapy dog. Seeing how Alexis and Rose enriched the lives of people in nursing homes, jails, and the other places we visited got me to really begin focusing on therapy work.

One day, Alexis and I were at a nursing home when an administrator stopped me just as we were about to walk into a room. "The man in that room has been there for three months," she said, "but he hasn't spoken to anyone. You can go in and see if anything happens but don't be discouraged if he doesn't react or respond."

Alexis and I walked into the room. The man was laying back in his recliner and Alexis walked right over and put her paws on the foot of the man's recliner and looked at him. The man looked at her and said, "A pit bull!"

I put the foot down on the man's recliner so he could reach and pet Alexis. Alexis licked him as the man smiled and said, "I had a pit bull when I was a kid. She's so beautiful." I glanced out into the hall and the administrator was crying. It was amazing.

It's not uncommon to get that kind of reaction from an elderly person because many of them grew up with pit bulls. They used to be a well-respected breed, and in fact, they represented America on World War I posters because they were loyal and brave. It wasn't until the media got a hold of the fact that pit bulls were being used in dog fighting that public opinion towards them began to shift. The media planted and fed the belief that if pit bulls were fighting dogs then they must be dangerous for people and in neighborhoods.

I always use ex-fighting dogs as my therapy dogs. First of all, pit bulls make awesome therapy and service dogs because they love everyone. I also want people to see they are dogs of good character that needed a break in life.

One of our missions is to get people to understand the fighting is something that happened to them, rather than what they chose. People think when dogs are taken from a raid that they won't be good dogs. A few aren't suitable as pets, but the vast majority can live long, wonderful, and loving lives.

I am always grateful when they do a raid and bring in someone knowledgeable to evaluate the dogs to see if they can comfortably live in the world. If they can, we keep the dogs and train and manage them. I offer free training because it's important for people to understand their dog and how to manage it.

Alexis was a sole survivor of a dog-fighting ring. While she didn't want to share her life with other dogs, she was very polite around other dogs while working in public. In her lifetime she saw over 8,000 school children.

Another one of my dogs, Grace, was taken in a drug raid. There were also suspicions of fighting. Grace had lived her entire life on a chain. When I got her she was seven and had spent a year and a half in a shelter. Every day a woman visited her at the shelter and gave her treats because she was convinced Grace was going to be put down. As a result, this thirteen-inch dog weighed sixty-five pounds and could barely move. She had advanced heartworm, was overweight, and had lost one ear completely and the other was almost gone. She also had cancer. I took steps to get her healthy, including surgery to take care of the cancer, and within eight months of getting her healthy, Grace had her Therapy Dog certification, Canine Good Citizen certification, and her American Temperament Testing title.

In August 2010, one month shy of her sixteenth birthday, Rose passed. Rose was a giant blessing to me and a lot of other people in her life. After Rose, I never thought I would get another heart dog, but three years later, it happened.

In August 2013, there was a raid of three Southern states: Alabama, Mississippi, and Georgia. It and the dogs from it came to be known as

The 367 because in that one raid, 367 dogs were seized. It was the second-largest dog-fighting raid in United States history.

I was asked to go down and evaluate some of the dogs, which ranged in age from a few days to twelve years old. While I was down there I met Stella, my next heart dog.

Stella was nine years old and had lived her life on a chain. I knew instantly that she was my dog, but Grace wasn't feeling well and I didn't want to bring another dog into the house. Instead, I started paying to have Stella boarded until the spring of 2015, when Grace passed. Then I began working with Stella on some environmental challenges so I could bring her home and get her therapy certified.

My dogs participate in a variety of programs for children. In some, the children are heavily challenged and rely on the dogs for stimulation; in others, the children read to the dogs to improve their reading skills.

A little girl once started crying as soon as I walked into the room with the dogs. When I asked her what was wrong, she said she was afraid because they were pit bulls and pit bulls were mean dogs. I said, "But you haven't met them. How do you know that?"

She said, "Somebody told me."

"Would you like it if somebody thought you were mean because somebody else said it or because of how you looked?" I asked her. She looked at me and understood. We try to help the children understand, using the dogs as an example, that we are all different and shouldn't be judged by the way we look.

We also ask the children if they would like it if someone they didn't know came up and started hugging them. When they say no we explain that dogs don't like it either. The dogs allow us to educate the students about the proper way to meet, greet, and interact with a dog.

To do this, we tell the kids to stand sideways and offer the back of their hand flat, palm down, while they avert their eyes or only glance at the dog. We explain to never get their face close to a new dog, stare into their eyes, or lean over it. If—and only if—all is well do they pet the dog under the chin rather than the top of the head.

Probably 99 percent of people greet a dog the way they greet another human being—approaching it from the front, leaning over it, petting it on its head, or bending down to hug and kiss it. A dog has a split second to make a judgment whether it's a safe situation and if they haven't been exposed to that person, or if the person is wearing a hooded sweatshirt, sunglasses, or any other number of things, the dog may become fearful and react.

It is not uncommon for the dogs to provide a bridge, or opening, for discussions and conversations that might not otherwise happen. We are part of a program for girls between the ages of eleven and eighteen who are housed in a high-security prison after being tried for murder, assault, or another violent crime. About four years ago, we started going once a month to visit the girls. The dogs are one of the biggest incentives for the girls to behave appropriately—if they haven't had a good month, they are not permitted to see the dogs. The dogs also provide the girls with a sense of normalcy and help prepare them for life after incarceration.

Initially, the girls just sat on the floor with the dogs but slowly they started asking about the dogs, petting them, and laughing, and more importantly, they started talking to us.

One girl was especially drawn to Grace. When we first met her, she was acting really tough and said, "I'm not gonna f***ing sit down," but then Grace went over to her and she smiled. I said to her, "You have the most amazing smile." She looked at me and everything shattered. After that, all she wanted to do was talk. She wanted a picture of Grace, her, and me and she has it hanging in her room.

A girl once pointed to the dogs and said they were fighting dogs. I said, "That's true but the dog didn't make that choice, she was made to do that and it doesn't mean she wants to live her life like that."

The dogs are a great example for people in rehab, jail, or just going through a tough time that even when something bad happens, you can still make

Grace

something good out your life. We had a dog who had been adopted and it only had one leg. The dog didn't care, she just went on living her life. Another dog without any front legs was adopted and became a therapy dog. I tell people, "Look at this dog. It didn't have anything good happen to it for the first six years of its life and she is still going forth and living her life."

I want people to see the connection between dogs and us and to understand that dogs live each day like we were designed to live. We were designed to love every moment of every day. Instead, something happens and we obsess over it or feel sorry for ourselves or worry. We stop the process of moving forward with joy. These dogs have had everything bad happen to them and they still wake up the next day filled with joy and love.

I believe we are here to do all the good we can in the time we are here. For me and my dogs, our time will be spent helping people.

Chapter Twenty-Five
MEG

As we walked out of the coffee shop, Cydney turned to me and said, "You need to talk to Meg!" Just as I instinctively knew I should talk to Cydney, I trusted there was a reason I needed to talk to Meg. When I phoned Meg, she was sweet and generous with her time. I learned she was a musician and songwriter and had recently released a documentary.[1] Her story contained pieces of so many other people's stories, yet it was also uniquely and beautifully her own. I am over-the-moon honored and excited to share the story of Meg and her magical dog Austin.

ALL THROUGH MY CHILDHOOD, I LOBBIED FOR A DOG TO NO avail. As soon as I turned twenty-one and was independent, I found my first little rescue, Osa, in the basement of a nearby dairy farm. There were eleven Lab-shepherd puppies in the litter and Osa was the runt. I knew something wasn't right because they were all so itchy, but having never had a dog, I didn't know what it was. The first night, Osa scratched all night and neither of us slept a wink. The next morning I took her to the vet and found out she had mange.

It took about a month for Osa to regain her

Meg and Austin
(Photo taken by Austin's foster mother, Mary Allen)

271

health. During that time, we built a really strong bond because she realized I was helping her. That bond was integral because we went through some tough years together.

I had always been a happy, even-keeled kid. My mother had always called me her golden child because I was the cheerful, chipper middle child. My life appeared to be easy on the outside, but increasingly, I was having trouble living up to that role. In my teens, I began to have periods of being depressed and had difficulty being around people.

Music became a way for me to cope with this inner landscape I didn't understand and that was becoming incredibly challenging. My highs were getting higher and my lows were getting lower. My first major depression happened when I was nineteen but I continued to hide it from the people closest to me and chalked it up to having an "artistic temperament" and being a creative person.

Music, which had begun as my medicine, was slowly becoming my career, but the touring was tough on me. It was a lifestyle complete with a lot of travel, time-zone changes, and partying, all of which pushed me towards ultimately hitting rock bottom. In 2006, when I was twenty-eight, my brain reached a final breaking point after returning home from a tour in Europe. I spiraled into what is called a mixed state where I was manic and depressed at the same time and unable to sleep. I finally went to my family and said, "I need help. My brain isn't working."

I was hospitalized and the next six weeks were pure hell. It was a very frightening time for me. Osa was such a comfort and dear friend to me during those years. Spending hours every day hiking in the woods with Osa, who loved me unconditionally, was a natural mood stabilizer. That was nine years ago and it has been an amazing nine years of recovery and learning to not just get better but to find health in a deeper way in my life.

In 2008, Osa got cancer but she totally rocked it. The vets would gather in a room, look at her X-rays, and say, "If we saw these X-rays without seeing her we would think we had to put this dog down right now." But Osa was still this happy, frisky girl. She was absolutely heroic and everyone was amazed she did so well for years after her cancer surgery.

Just before Christmas 2012, I lost Osa. She was almost thirteen years old. Osa was my first dog and had seen me through so much. I thought I could never love another dog like I loved Osa.

I went a year without a dog and my life felt so empty without that friendship. Cydney, a woman who had been my first music manager when I was seventeen (and who was my first real supporter when I got involved in music), always reached out to me because she knew how much losing Osa had impacted me. Over time, she started delicately sending me pictures of various rescues from her organization, Out of the Pits (OOTP).[2]

Eight months after losing Osa, my sister was preparing to adopt a dog from OOTP and put me down as a reference. When the volunteer called me for a reference, she began to tell me about a dog named Austin they had just gotten custody of that week. The details were so fresh in the volunteer's mind, and his story went right to my heart.

Austin had been removed from an abusive home where he was the target of his owner's rage. Austin had been thrown down stairs, kicked with steel-toe boots, and beaten with a plunger and a baseball bat. From the X-rays taken of Austin, there was evidence that many of his ribs were broken along with some older breaks that had already healed. His skull was fractured, and both sides of his pelvis were broken. The heads of both femurs were broken off and every time he moved, they moved. The femurs were also broken. He had been rescued on June 4 and taken to a shelter where he lived with his injuries while the court case against his owner was tried. He was released in August to OOTP. By that point, there was so much atrophy in his hind legs that he was balancing himself on his front legs. Despite being in extreme pain all that time, Austin had never been grumpy from the moment he was rescued. He had double hip surgery from which he was slowly recovering. He had trouble walking in the beginning because he had to rebuild muscle.

I began following Austin's recovery on the OOTP Facebook page. So many people were coming together to help him including a big auction to help pay for the cost of his surgery and rehabilitation. While his story touched me, I wasn't ready for another dog. I had just released a record and was doing a lot of traveling. I was also still comparing every dog I met to Osa.

The day Austin became available for adoption, Cyd sent me a picture of him sitting next to Santa Claus. I couldn't believe what he had been through and how brave he was. Every time I looked at pictures of him, I cried. I felt a connection with him long before I ever thought about him being my next dog.

Then, on the exact anniversary of Osa's passing, I had a dream. In my dream, I was sitting in a lawn chair and Osa ran up to me with Austin behind her. I could see Austin so clearly in my dream and feel his presence. In my dream, Austin just stared at me and I could feel he was just this big-hearted dog. In the dream I also saw a scar on his side that looked like a cigarette burn.

In my prayers, I had always told Osa that if I was supposed to have another dog, she needed to give me a sign and make it very clear. I woke up and there was no denying this dream was the sign. I knew Austin was my dog so I sent Cyd a text and said I wanted to meet him.

Mary Allen, one of the founders of OOTP, had been fostering Austin so my sister and I drove to meet him. Austin was so excited to have company he was literally bouncing off the furniture. He was like a little wild horse. I saw his charisma and loved him right away but I also saw how excited, anxious, and mouthy he could be and thought, "This is going to be a handful."

Within ten minutes, I told Mary, "If he's game for me, I'm game for him." Mary had done an incredible job of building his body back up but Austin was very attached to her since she was the first person he had ever felt loved and safe with. I didn't want to take him away from her too abruptly so I spent the next five days going to Mary's house. We would spend hours just playing and being together. I wanted to ease him into getting to know and trust me.

What was interesting is that Mary lived fifteen minutes from my hometown. Her house was a half mile from the vet who had seen Osa all those years and where she'd been put down. I had let Osa go a half mile from where Austin came into my life.

The other interesting thing is that Austin had a scar on his face that looked exactly like the scar I'd seen in my dream. In all the pictures I had seen of Austin, I never noticed the scar.

When I got Austin to the city, everything was a new experience for him. Every loud noise or crash would frighten him. He was very insecure and followed me around the house. I could tell he thought at any minute all of this could change and he had no faith that life would stay good for him.

It was the middle of winter and I was dealing with snow, ice, and freezing cold as well as a dog that had an incredible amount of energy and anxiety. In the beginning, we had many adventures as I tried to figure out how to make Austin feel safe. Whenever he was anxious or insecure, it would quickly escalate and he would get even more insecure or wild. I realized in his past life he had probably been beaten for getting so wound up and wild.

Then I learned about Temple Grandin and her invention, the squeeze box.[3] She had invented the device because she had found the deep-pressure and contact helped calm hypersensitive people. They discovered that the same contact helped animals feel safe, too.

I realized all Austin wanted was to be held really tightly. I call it "squishing him." Whenever he would start to get anxious or wild, I would say, "On the couch." He would leap up on the couch and I would hold (or squish) him and talk to him. Initially, he would wrestle and try to get out of my arms but, within minutes, he'd let out this big sigh and calm down. Squishing him allowed him to reboot and he began to realize I wasn't going to hurt him if he got wild—I was only going to squish him and talk to him.

I lost so much weight because I was now squishing him around the clock and hiking in the snow for hours with him every day.

Leaving him alone presented another challenge. When I left him, he was beside himself. He wouldn't just bark, he would wail. He believed I was never going to come back. He had been through so much suffering before being rescued. Things had changed so often for him in the first year of his life that he had no faith in continuity. He was easily frightened by situations and I had to really ease him into being alone in short installments. It took a couple of months for him to have faith that when I left I would come back.

While easing him into being alone, I started bringing Austin with me to gigs. The first one I brought him to was a short one. I only had to play for thirty minutes so I left him in the car. He flew around inside that car like a little tornado and the entire time I was playing I could hear him outside honking the horn in the parking lot. When I got back to the car, everything in the car had been turned upside down.

The next gig was in a church and I was headlining. Knowing I couldn't leave him in the car, I brought a crate and set it up in the green room. Mary had told me Austin could get out of a crate but I didn't believe her and besides this was a full metal crate. I got him set up with toys and went onstage. Five minutes later, Austin was out of the crate and running down the aisle of the church. Luckily, there was an awesome woman in the audience who held onto Austin and let him sit and chew on her throughout the entire show.

When I went back to the green room, the crate was still there and the door was still latched. Austin had pried open one corner of the crate and squeezed through it. I looked at the crate and looked at him and thought, "Now what do I do for the next gig?"

I went out and bought a thirty-five-pound weight and a tie-out leash he couldn't chew through. When I went onstage, I brought out his big cushy orthopedic bed along with the weight and leash and put it next to me. By the second song, Austin was completely passed out and content. He didn't care that 100 people were staring at us, he was just happy to be with me and he was so psyched that I was singing. He was happy throughout the entire gig so that became our strategy.

Austin is an Emotional Support Animal (ESA) and has an ESA vest but I'm careful about when and how I use the vest. I think there are some people who are taking advantage of the term, but more importantly it's a term he and I are still growing into. But is Austin my Emotional Support Animal? Absolutely!

Our friendship has been so good for my mental health. It's stabilizing to have that companionship, along with hours of hiking every day. Unlike Osa, who always wanted to be in her own bed, Austin wants to snuggle all the time. He wants to be as close to me as possible.

Having to get up and care for a dog or go out and walk or hike with them every day helps with depression. For someone who has trouble with social interactions it can also be helpful to have a dog beside them. When someone is depressed, their self-esteem is low and they often turn inwards. A dog never asks, "What's up with you?" They just look at you as if you're the best thing in the entire world and are absolutely the best support.

Sometimes Austin can be a handful right up until the gig starts, but as soon as I begin, he just sleeps besides me. With him right next to me, I feel totally supported. Having him with me on stage is great. When I'm offstage, I can be very shy so Austin plays a huge role in supporting me with that as well. After the gig, people, especially those who are suffering or going through something, will immediately gravitate to Austin and rub his belly. Austin has no fear of crowds, which makes me think he understands that the majority of people are good. In a crowd, he feels safe and a lot of people come up to pet and snuggle with him. He actually thrives when people dote on him.

In June 2015, *Pack Up Your Sorrows: A Story of Illness, Hope & Transformation* was released.[4] It is a feature-length documentary about mental wellness told through the lens of my own journey. In it I go around the country interviewing a variety of people, like neuroscientists, psychiatrists, authors, and historians as well as some amazing people who have gone through some of the same experiences as I have. Some of these people are leading the way in understanding more about the brain, improving medications, and understanding how meditation can help. It's an educational and fun film to watch so we can reach more people than with a clinical film.

One thing I have been noticing in the recent press about my film is that people always say, "She's bipolar." One of the things I would like to educate people about is being mindful of our language and how we talk about things. When someone has cancer, you don't say, "She's cancer." I am not the disease. I am not bipolar. The truth is: I am living well with bipolar.

There is so much discrimination about both mental illness and pit bulls. I feel like one of Austin's and my tasks as buddies is to reset some of the misconceptions people have. While I am talking about mental illness, I can see the wheels turning in people's minds. Then they see this pit bull calmly sleeping next to me and welcoming them after the gig. You can see people readjusting their assumptions and understanding that mental illness isn't scary and pit bulls aren't scary.

There are stereotypes that create a lot of pain for dogs and humans. Look at how many pit bulls get put down just because of their breed. Look at how discrimination can fuel suicide or a tragedy. Austin and I

Austin

are working to change that. I think that is one of the reasons we found one another.

Watching Austin has been a lesson for me in resilience and in what a spirit is capable of. He has taught me so much about what I am capable of.

Austin is wiser than his years and has a knowledge and deep presence from what he went through. Every day, he wakes up with an attitude of "Wow! This is really great!" He has an understanding that life *is* really great now and he doesn't take it for granted. He is grateful—it is both visceral and visible.

To have your hips and femurs broken with a baseball bat and still have faith in humans, to me, is astonishing. What has floored me is how eager Austin is to overcome his fears. He so easily reframes a situation and is so resilient. He has grown far beyond what most humans would be able to overcome. People who have been through something often tell me, "If he can get through that, I know I can get through my own trauma." The agony of what he went through is hard to fathom but he never let it impact his heart. It made him a nervous, anxious boy but it's beautiful to see he has now become a teacher for others.

Austin is a miraculous creature, a big-hearted, goofy, joyful survivor. He is a blessing in my life and a truly magical dog.

Epilogue
MAGICAL LESSONS

THE DAY I SENT THE FIRST DRAFT OF THIS BOOK OFF TO MY EDItor, I got four emails. The first was from Bonnie.

The month before, I had received a text from Bonnie: *Hi Patti. I wanted to let you know that Sativa is now with Ryan. I know they're running around in Heaven.*

Later that day, Bonnie shared the story about Sativa's passing:

Sativa tried to jump on the couch where I was and fell. I knew she was in pain and my vet said I could bring her right in so I recruited my neighbor, Roy, to help me get her into the car.

The vet inspected Sativa's leg and then took her for an X-ray. Walking back into the room with tears in his eyes, he told me Sativa had cancer in her leg, which was why her femur had broken so easily. Ironically, the femur is the same bone Ryan had broken twice. The vet said there wasn't anything that could be done for Sativa other than to end her pain—a decision I had anticipated.

For several days, knowing I was on borrowed time with Sativa, I asked Ryan to be waiting for her. I also told Sativa, before the vet gave her the injection, to tell Ryan that I love him. I stayed with Sativa until the end and then the vet left the room, quietly closing the door behind him.

I was holding Sativa close to me when the door blew open. There was no wind and no one was there to open the door—except for Ryan—and I knew, without a doubt, Sativa and Ryan were in Heaven running around together.

I continued to check on Bonnie but then my emails and texts began going unanswered. I was getting concerned until I received an email from Bonnie that said: *Sorry I haven't been in touch lately. I've been a little distracted. Meet Barnabas.*

Barnabas

I phoned Bonnie and her first words were, "I couldn't stand the quiet." She said Barnabas was rescued from a high-kill shelter in Georgia and brought to New Jersey. Bonnie saw him at an adoption event and he came home with her the same day. "My vet confirmed he's a five-month-old 100 percent mutt," Bonnie said, laughing. "I forgot how much energy puppies have." I could hear the lightness and joy in her voice.

The second email, from Joan, said:

My former dog sitter, Kelli, called and asked if I could foster a dog. She explained her friend was at a shelter in Wichita and there were dogs that were going to be put down in the morning. Her friend wanted to take them but didn't have room for all of them.

I really didn't want to because I was having a terrible time letting go of Sabrina but since it was just a foster, I agreed. When I went to her house that night, I was greeted by a diverse group of dogs. Over in the corner was a frightened, little blonde mix—the one they wanted me to foster for a few days. I asked about her. "She was used for breeding. She has cigarette burns on her and was full of fleas. She has kennel cough and doesn't like men. And she is really scared."

Her name was Paris —a city I love —but at home, she didn't come when we called her. We kept trying different names but she didn't respond to any of them. I finally picked her up, and looking into her eyes, said, "You have to tell me your name."

I put her down and walked into our kitchen singing the song "Lilly" by Pink Martini. The lyrics are about how Lilly comes when you call her and how the singer wants Lilly to stay.

As I sang, she ran right over to me. I asked her, "Is your name Lily?" and she circled around me and that was it: Lily Rose Le Fleur (for the flower of France: the fleur de lis).

Lily immediately climbed up on my bed and knocked over a picture of Spirit and Sabrina and I realized she was telling me they had sent her.

Lily Rose Le Fleur

We'd been told about her fear of men, but aside from some initial fear and barking, within thirty minutes she was all over my husband, David, and followed him around like a little shadow.

As I watched her adjust and feel at home with us, we decided to bring her into our hearts and home permanently. Lily needed a home and I needed to open my heart again. So here we are, taking it a step, a breath, and a moment at a time.

Lily found us—as dogs do. She is rescuing my heart and showing me that love is love. There are miracles that unfold so perfectly when you least expect them.

The next two emails were from people sending me stories "for my next dog book." I was stunned. The thought of "my next dog book" hadn't crossed my mind.

I sat back and thought about these four emails. I thought about Bonnie and Joan and all the people and dogs I'd met and the stories I'd heard. Stories of dogs that had brought hope, second chances, new beginnings, and healing when they were least expected. Dogs that were living, breathing proof that it doesn't matter who you are, where you've been, or what you've been through— life keeps giving us choices, chances, and opportunities if we simply stay open to possibility, miracles, magic, and especially opportunities for love.

If I had to narrow down the message dogs bring into the world to one word it would be: love. In the end, this has been One Big Love Story.

As I reread the stories sent to me for "my next dog book," I pondered if perhaps my journey with magical dogs has only just begun. Perhaps there are other dogs and other stories to be told. If there are, just as with this book, I know we'll find one another and I'll begin writing again. After all, I've always been a sucker for a great love story.

While it's exciting to think my journey with magical dogs may not be over, I'm not going to try and figure that out right now. Right now, I'm going to put a period on the last sentence of this book and go make a cup of tea. After that, Ava and I are going out for a nice long walk.

Until we meet again, remember: Stay Open to Miracles, Possibility, and Magic. Stay Open to Love.

Notes

Chapter 1: Brooke
1. For more information about the use of ice packs for seizures, visit: http://www.canine-epilepsy-guardian-angels.com/icepack.htm.

Chapter 2: Ava
1. This quote is from the book *Peter Pan; or, the Boy Who Wouldn't Grow Up or Peter and Wendy* by J.M. Barrie. It is Barrie's most famous work. Published in the form of a play in 1904 and then as a novel in 1911, it tells the story of a young boy who can fly, Peter Pan, and his adventure with Wendy, Tinker Bell, the Lost Boys, and Captain Hook. The play and novel were inspired by Barrie's friendship with the Llewelyn Davies family.

Chapter 3: Heesun
1. For more information about the Association of Professional Dog Trainers, visit: https://apdt.com/.
2. To learn more about Dr. Ian Dunbar, his books, videos, or blog, visit: http://www.dogstardaily.com/.
3. To learn more about Pet Karma NJ and their rescue work, visit: www:petkarmanj.com.

Chapter 3: The Importance of Puppy Socialization
1. This is an excerpt from the article "Puppy Socialization: Stop Fear Before It Starts" from Dr. Yin's blog on her website and is also adapted from her book *Perfect Puppy in 7 Days: How to Start Your Puppy Off Right*. For more information or to read the article in its entirety, visit: www.drsophiayin.com.

Chapter 4: Laura and Great Dawg Rescue
1. To learn more about Great Dawg Rescue and the work they are doing, visit: http://www.greatdawgrescue.org. On Facebook: GreatDawgRescue.

Chapter 5: Labs4Rescue
1. For more information on Labs4Rescue, visit: www.Labs4Rescue.com. On Facebook: Labs4Rescue.

Chapter 6: Connie
1. For more information on National Greyhound Adoption Program, visit: www.ngap.org. On Facebook: National Greyhound Adoption Program.

2. For more information on Pet Partners, visit: www.petpartners.org. On Facebook: petsforhealth.
3. The information Connie found on how to train Stella to sit for her therapy dog certification test can be found at: http://neversaynevergreyhounds.blogspot.com.

Chapter 6: Greyhound Rescue and Grey2KUSA

1. To learn more about Grey2K USA Worldwide, visit their website at: www.Grey2kusa.org. On Facebook: GREY2KUSA.
2. To read the report in its entirety, visit: http://www.grey2kusa.org/pdf/USreportWeb.pdf.

Chapter 7: Sarah and Matt (FlyPups)

1. For more information on FlyPups and the work they are doing, visit: www.flypups.org. On Facebook: Flypups.

Chapter 7: Home for Good Dog Rescue

1. For more information about Home for Good Dog Rescue, visit: www.homeforgooddogs.org. On Facebook: HomeForGoodDogRescue.

Chapter 8: Reading Education Assistance Dogs Program

1. For more information about Intermountain Therapy Animals or the R.E.A.D. Program, visit: www.therapyanimals.org. On Facebook: Intermountain Therapy Animals.
2. For more information on Pet Partners, visit: www.petpartners.org. On Facebook: petsforhealth.

Chapter 9: Shari

1. For more information about type 1 diabetes, visit: www.jdrf.org. On Facebook: My JDRF.

Chapter 9: Diabetes Alert Dogs and Diabetes Alert Dog Alliance

1. For more information about diabetes alert dogs and Causey Labradors, visit: www.CauseyLabradorsandTraining.com. On Facebook: Causey Labradors.
2. For more information about DADs and the Diabetes Alert Dog Alliance, visit: www.diabetesalertdogalliance.org.

Chapter 10: Barbara

1. For more information about Barbara and her books, visit: www.joyfulpaws.com. On Facebook: Barbara Techel.
2. To learn more about National Walk 'N Roll Day and the Frankie Wheelchair Fund, visit: http://nationalwalknrolldogday.com. On Facebook: National Walk N Roll Dog Day.

Chapter 10: Eddie's Wheels and Dodgerslist
1. For learn more about Eddie's wheels and their custom wheelcarts, visit: www.eddieswheels.com. On Facebook: Eddie's Wheels for Pets.
2. For more information about Dodgerslist and IVDD, visit: www.dodgerslist.com. On Facebook: Dodgerslist.

Chapter 11: Joan
1. To learn more about Joan or The Pet Alchemist, including workshops, consultations and products, visit: www.joanclark.com.

Chapter 12: Corinne
1. To learn more about Corinne and Rudy, their books and paintings, or to see where they'll be appearing next, visit: www.corinnehumphrey.com. On Facebook: The Tao of Rudy.

Chapter 12: Animal Communication and Intuition
1. For more information about Marta Williams, including her workshops, consultations and books, visit: www.martawilliams.com. On Facebook: Marta Williams: Animal Communicator.

Chapter 13: Tracy
1. For more information about Woodlands Wildlife Refuge, visit: www.woodlandswildllife.org. On Facebook: Woodlands Wildlife Refuge.

Chapter 14: Animal Reiki
1. To learn more about Kathleen Prasad, her books and classes, or about Animal Reiki Source, visit: www.animalreikisource.com. On Facebook: Animal Reiki Source.
2. For more information on Shelter Animal Reiki Association, visit: www.shelteranimalreikiassociation.org. On Facebook: Shelter Animal Reiki Association.

Chapter 15: Understanding Cancer in Goldens
1. For more information about the Golden Retriever Club of America, visit: www.grca.org. Rhonda also recommends learning more about the Golden Retriever Foundation at: www.goldenretrieverfoundation.org.
2. For more information about the AKC Canine Health Foundation, visit: www.akcchf.org.
3. The Morris Animal Foundation is a nonprofit organization that invests in science to advance animal health. For more information, visit: www.morrisanimalfoundation.org.
4. To learn more about the Canine Lifetime Health Project and the Golden Retriever Lifetime Study, visit: www.caninelifetimehealth.org.
5. *The Dog Cancer Survival Guide* is available everywhere books are sold. To learn more about Dr. Demian Dressler, his books and videos, or to read his blog, visit: www.dogcancerblog.com.

Chapter 16: Individualized Approach to Holistic Veterinary Care
1. For more information about Dr. Michael Dym and his approach to veterinary care, visit: www.doctordym.com.
2. Gemmotherapy is a form of herbal medicine. Unlike herbal remedies that use parts of a mature plant, gemmotherapy extractions are made from the germinating parts of trees and shrubs (buds, shoots, seeds, rootlets, etc.) since it is believed these are more potent than whole herbs and plants and that these germinating embryonic parts contain plant growth hormones (similar to human stem cells).

Chapter 17: Bonnie
1. This is a quote from Bob Marley.

Chapter 17: Dogs During Difficult Times
1. Custance, Deborah M. and Mayer, Jennifer. 2012. "Empathic-like responding by domestic dogs (*Canis familiaris*) to distress in humans: An exploratory study." *Animal Cognition*, 15(5), pp. 851-859. ISSN 1435-9448. For more information, visit: http://research.gold.ac.uk/7074/.
2. Staats, S., Wallace, H. and Anderson, T. (2008). "Reasons for Companion Animal Guardianship (pet ownership) from Two Populations." *Society and Animals*, 16, 279–291. For more information, visit: https://animalsandsociety.org/assets/library/774_s5.pdf.

Chapter 20: Emotional Support Animals, Service/Assistance Dogs, and Therapy Dogs: What's the Difference?
1. For more information on Stephanie Colman, visit: www.StephanieColman.com and www.CaninesteinTraining.com. To read her article titled "Service Please" on the world of service dog issues as it appeared in its entirety in the *Whole Dog Journal*, visit: www.Whole-Dog-Journal.com.

Chapter 22: Dogs and Addiction Treatment
1. For more information about the study titled "The Use of Therapy Dogs With Adult Substance Abuse Clients: A Pilot Project," visit: http://www.tdi-dog.org/images/SubstanceAbuseStudy.pdf.
2. For more information on Behavioral Health of the Palm Beaches, visit: www.bhpalmbeach.com.

Chapter 24: Cydney
1. For more information about Out of the Pits, visit: www.outofthepits.org. On Facebook: Out of the Pits Inc.

Chapter 25: Meg
1. For more information about singer-songwriter Meg Hutchinson and her

music, visit: www.meghutchinson.com. On Facebook: Meg Hutchinson Musician/Band.
2. For information about Out of the Pits, see footnotes above for Chapter 24.
3. Mary Temple Grandin is an autism activist and consultant as well as a best-selling author. She is the inventor of the "hug machine" (also known as a hug box, squeeze machine, or squeeze box), a deep-pressure device designed to calm hypersensitive persons, usually those on the autism spectrum. For more information about Temple Grandin, her books, DVDs, and workshops, visit: http://www.templegrandin.com.
4. For more information about the documentary *Pack Up Your Sorrows: A Story of Illness, Hope & Transformation,* visit: www.packupyoursorrowsfilm.com. On Facebook: Pack up Your Sorrows—The Documentary.

About the Author

Patti Kerr is an author, speaker, Certified Alzheimer's Educator, and animal lover.

She previously authored *I Love You, Who Are You?: Loving and Caring for a Parent with Alzheimer's*, a guide for those caring for loved ones with Alzheimer's. Patti is a popular and much-sought-after speaker at conferences, care facilities, and caregiver support groups. For more information on her work with Alzheimer's and caregivers, visit her website: www.pattikerr.com.

Patti still lives in the same small rural New Jersey town where her family has lived for generations, on the same street where she grew up. She enjoys traveling, meeting, and writing about dogs and their humans and is currently working on more *Magical Dogs* books.

If you have, or know of, a Magical Dog or would like to reach Patti, all correspondence should be addressed to: PO Box 766, Flemington, NJ 08822. You can visit her on her website: www.magical-dogs.com or on Facebook: Magical Dogs Book.

Dear Reader:

Thank you for joining me on this journey with *Magical Dogs*. The fact that I—someone who spent a good portion of her early years petrified of dogs and never got a dog until I was almost fifty years old—was the one these dogs chose to write their story still mystifies me. I believe that, too, is part of the magic of dogs.

Long before I ever finished writing *Magical Dogs*, I decided a portion of the proceeds of the sale of this book would be donated to animals in need as a way for Brooke, Ava, and I to keep the magic flowing. Therefore, the simple act of purchasing this book—for yourself or someone else—will continue to help animals in need.

If you know of an organization, rescue, or shelter who would like me do a book signing or speak at an event or fundraiser on their behalf, please get in touch with me.

Finally, if you have (or know of) a Magical Dog, please send me your story at: PO Box 766, Flemington, NJ 08822. You can also reach me on my website: www.magical-dogs.com or on Facebook at: Magical Dogs Book.

I am honored to have shared the stories of these dogs—and their humans—with you and look forward to bringing you more Magical Dogs stories in the future. So until we meet again, stay open to love and possibilities—and, especially, stay open to magic.

Patti

81016160R00170

Made in the USA
Middletown, DE
19 July 2018